African Democracies and Africa

Human Security in the Global Economy
Series editor: Professor Caroline Thomas (University of Southampton)

Also available

The Politics of Human Rights
A Global Perspective
Tony Evans

Global Governance, Development and Human Security
The Challenge of Poverty and Inequality
Caroline Thomas

The Politics of Microcredit
Global Governance and Poverty Reduction
Heloise Weber

The Political Economy of Global Communication
An Introduction
Peter Wilkin

African Democracies and African Politics

M.A. Mohamed Salih

Pluto  Press

LONDON • STERLING, VIRGINIA

First published 2001 by Pluto Press
345 Archway Road, London N6 5AA
and 22883 Quicksilver Drive, Sterling, VA 20166–2012, USA

www.plutobooks.com

British Library Cataloguing in Publication Data
A catalogue record for this book is available from the British Library

ISBN   0 7453 1725 1 hardback
ISBN   0 7453 1724 3 paperback

Library of Congress Cataloging-in-Publication Data
Salih, Mohamed Abdel Rahmin M. (Mohamed Abdel Rahmin Mohamed)
   African democracies and african politics / M.A. Mohamed Salih.
       p. cm.
Includes bibliographical references and index.
   ISBN 0-7453-1725-1 (hardback) – ISBN 0-7453-1724-3 (paperback)
   1. Democratization–Africa. 2. Authoritarianism–Africa. 3.
   Africa–Politics and government–1960- I. Title.
   JQ1879.A15.S25 2001
   320.96–dc21
                                                                    00-012647

Designed and produced for Pluto Press by
Chase Publishing Services, Fortescue, Sidmouth EX10 9QG
Typeset from disk by Gawcott Typesetting Services
Printed in the European Union by TJ International, Padstow, England

Contents

List of Boxes and Tables

BOXES

TABLES

1
Introduction

Africa is experiencing an impressive transition from one-party states, military rule or civilian dictatorships to various forms of political pluralism. Africa's drive to democratise state and society has clearly not been without difficulties and the process has exerted immense pressures on both. In its attempts to comply with internal demands for democracy and the rule of law and the externally driven democratisation and good governance project, the African struggle for democracy is unique and absorbing. Its uniqueness stems from Africa's historical experiences and problems, which have meant that its struggle for democracy is complex, traversing social, economic and political structures. It is absorbing because large portions of the post-colonial period have, in some measure, been no more than extensions of the colonial experience, overwhelmed by economic dependence, underdevelopment, the debt burden, elite hegemony, civil strife, and social and political conflicts. These factors have, in different ways, been detrimental to the shift from democratic transition to consolidation. Retrospectively, the colonial experience that had initiated the first wave of democratisation and secured a semblance of peace between Africa's different ethnic groups was in fact neither democratic nor humane. The colonialists ruled the continent with an iron fist, exploited its resources and denied its people the right to govern themselves, with a sustained assault on traditional political institutions and cultures.

Unfortunately, after the departure of the colonialists, the African political elite who inherited the reins of power behaved much like their departing masters. With some exceptions, the African political elite continued to deny the African peoples their basic freedoms and human rights. Some societies had thus graduated from a non-democratic oppressive colonial rule to an equally non-democratic authoritarian national rule. In most African countries, the parallels between colonial and post-colonial political structures and the capacity of both for coercion are intriguing but bewildering. Because they both, in different ways, denied African people's human rights, the right to basic freedoms, and democratic rights, very few African states have really experienced democratic governance or have had a sufficiently long-term experience of democratic practice to facilitate a smooth transition to democracy, as many commentators would have wished.

During the second half of the twentieth century, most of Africa was governed by repressive post-colonial states, which in some cases kept intact the most destructive elements of the non-democratic and non-participatory colonial system of government. Yet somehow Africa is expected to develop instant democratic institutions, political parties and effective systems of checks and balances. Both colonial and post-colonial regimes have suppressed the voices and aspirations of the African people and curtailed the possibility of the emergence of a truly participatory system of government, restricting people's participation to periodic voting.

Within the transition to democracy, various forms of state authoritarianism persisted, thus compelling people to defy state-centred politics and opt for alternative political arrangements outside the state structures and institutions. Political disengagement and relocation of political activities beyond mainstream national politics became the norm, along with signs of political apathy and withdrawal. One consequence of this has been the emergence of social movements, opposition and pressure groups defiant and at times confrontational toward the state. Some sectors of civil society have adopted violence as a mode of expressing their disappointment with the state's handling of the national question. Some have resorted to 'internal liberation' wars led by national liberation fronts (Ethiopia, Sudan, Angola, Mozambique, Nigeria, Mauritania, Mali, Liberia, Sierra Leone and Djibouti, among others). A second generation of national liberation wars – internal wars against an exceedingly oppressive state, or what I have referred to as internal colonialism (Mohamed Salih 1993) – sprang up (for instance, Sudan, the Ethiopian–Eritrean war, the Western Sahara and so on), some of them continuing unabated for decades.

None the less, despite the many odds stacked against democracy (poverty, underdevelopment and conflicts), donor agencies and advocates of Western democracy expected Africa to be readily able to adopt Western-style democratic political institutions and the accompanying structures of government, and to deliver instant democratic results. Western commentators, aware of the colonial experience and the post-colonial excesses of the African states, nevertheless continue to blame Africans for having failed to emulate Western-style democracies since emerging from the ashes of the national authoritarian regimes that ruled the continent for decades. Most incredible is the ability to ignore the obvious underdevelopment, abject poverty and high levels of illiteracy in the African continent, factors that often hinder the transition to democracy. The emergence of responsible democratic governance requires more time than the majority of political analysts and democratic-rights activists seem to have thought necessary. Democracy is much more than political operators who pose as democrats, and hollow internally non-democratic political institutions. It is a process that can be encouraged and enhanced, but not engineered.

There can be no serious grounds for attempting to compare the political situation in Africa, and the struggles of the people for political rights, with what is taking place in the West. This is an unrealistic analogy. It is not that African societies are structurally non-democratic, but rather that their colonial and post-colonial histories have, by and large, been histories of non-democratic authoritarian rule. Democracy is not about the mechanical transfer of political experiences from one society to another. It is about political participation, the ability of people to express their preferences freely and without intimidation, and how this is guaranteed according to a given institutional framework and jurisdictional powers. To that extent, democracy constitutes the sum total of values and attitudes that people nurture over a long period of trial and error whilst improving on its quality. Democratic values are expressed differently by different societies and the process of developing democratic institutions often takes different routes in different societies.

The slow pace of democratic consolidation in Africa, oddly perceived as a structural failure to democratise state and civil society, should be judged against the sobering realisation that with all its shades and colours, democracy is more difficult to manage than dictatorship. To manage democracy requires the internalisation of the values and norms associated with those democratic governance institutions that integrate people's actual lives, their economic expectations, political aspirations and their struggle to improve their well-being. The far-reaching implication of this statement is that African democracies cannot and should not be treated as potential replicas of Western democracies. Because democracy is more than elections and political parties (although these are extremely important), it cannot be treated in isolation from the totality of the prevailing social, economic and political environment.

African civil society and state are both under pressure to take their responsibilities seriously in order to be able to create legitimate and accountable governance. These pressures originate from at least two sources: internal pressures exerted by civil society and the quest of human rights activists for democratic leadership and accountable political organisations in societies with little or no long-term experience with modern democratic institutions and practice; and external pressures exerted by a democratically inclined global civil society. Some global actors demand nothing short of the introduction (one might almost say imposition) of 'instant democracy', although they know that Africa's experience with liberal democracy is embryonic at best. In some cases, African civil society has found itself in confrontation with emerging political party operators as educated political elites have failed to develop accountable and democratic political institutions. Most political parties remain unaccountable at best, and authoritarian at worst, run by party operators acting like civil dictators, much to the fury of democracy's advocates within and outside the continent.

Admittedly, African politics of democratisation is practised in an anomalous context in which the prerequisites of Western-style democracies are absent. This context has at least five characteristics: 1) abject poverty and inequality, 2) elite hegemony, 3) weak governance institutions, 4) distorted and marginalised local governance institutions, and 5) external pressures to replicate Western-style democracies, resulting in undue political and economic conditionality. These factors may be found in different combinations and patterns in different contexts, and their magnitude and influence in hindering or advancing the transition to democracy also varies from one society to another.

DEMOCRATISATION AND THE RETURN
OF POLITICAL DEVELOPMENT

Although it is often argued that the democratisation and good governance 'industry' became possible only after the end of the Cold War, the project is not new and dates back to the late 1960s and 1970s. It grew out of the ideological orientation of the Western Alliance and its desire to extend the type of political and social systems prevalent in Western democracies. Ake (1996) reminds us that during the Cold War, the West adopted a posture of indifference to issues of human rights and democracy in Africa in order to avoid jeopardising its economic and strategic interests and to facilitate its obsessive search for allies against communism. Now that these concerns have diminished, the West finds itself free to bring its African policies into greater harmony with its democratic principles. The West now argues that democratic values are a prerequisite to peace, premised on an assumption that political systems that share these values also share common economic and political interests. Although this assumption may hold true for the industrially advanced Western democracies, it holds little credence for the 'democratic' or democratising developing countries.

By and large, the Western-style democratisation-cum-good governance project reflects three old tendencies, largely informed by modernisation theory and political development. The first of these is the belief in a positive trade-off between political development and economic development – the hallmark of modernisation theory's explanation of underdevelopment (see, for example, Almond and Coleman 1960; Apter 1965; Rostow 1960; Almond and Powell 1966; Huntington 1968, 1971;

and Heegar 1972). The second is the tendency to see underdevelopment as a result of cultural, behavioural and attitudinal lag, a point critiqued by dependency theorists for its insensitivity to the structural anomalies inherent in the colonial legacy, periphery–centre relations, and unequal exchange. The third view is that political development is a prerequisite to economic growth, emphasising the primacy of the relationship between political systems and socioeconomic and structural conditions (see Lipset et al. 1993). Here there is an explicit assumption that economic growth cannot be attained without securing the social conditions necessary for democratic consolidation.

The ideas of political development and modernisation theorists came under attack from various sources. In a rare show of scepticism, Huntington (1968: 391–2) observed that 'the gap between theory and reality is evident in the fact that the development of authoritarianism, instability, ethnic conflict, and institutional decay instead of democratisation, order, nation-building and institutional rationalisation and differentiation have spread in the modernising developing countries.' In the same vein, Randall and Theobald (1998) are equally critical, characterising political development as an ethnocentric embodiment of naïve optimism that failed to understand the drawback of economic dependence. They summarise their critique in four points:

1) Tradition and modernity are not necessarily opposite poles and can coexist peacefully. Not all traditions are anti-modern or hostile to progress, since modernity itself can reinforce traditional values and the resurgence of ethnic and religious movements.
2) The approach is Eurocentric in judging development merely with reference to Western institutions, thus denying the developing countries their own histories and socioeconomic and political specificity.
3) The approach encompasses two contradictory models: one privileges modernisation, while the other supports tradition. In other words, the approach argues that traditional values and practices do persist in modern societies, therefore tradition is not necessarily an impediment to political change.
4) The insistence on behavioural change as a prerequisite to political development is premised on psychological reductionism, which ignores the role of a prolonged colonial experience, the international division of labour, and their contribution to the making of the 'Third World'.

Modernisation revisionism has heralded the reincarnation of political development theory, albeit with two major changes in the context within which it is practised: the end of the Cold War rivalry and the lack of credible alternatives after the demise of great ideological projects.

Although these two points should have provided a more flexible, tolerant and sensitive framework within which political development and political modernisation could evolve, it proved in fact to be more stringent and uncompromising. Despite the powerful and justified critique levelled against political development and modernisation by dependency and 'Third World' scholars alike, it managed to survive the Cold War era and re-emerge under modernisation revisionism.

The anchor points of modernisation and modernisation revisionism are found both in their common ideological orientation (liberal democracy) and in the claim that political development is possible (modernisation/Westernisation). The main difference between the two is that modernisation revisionism assumes that classical political development theory is analytically and politically inadequate, and therefore requires some serious revision. In common with the current global democratisation and good governance projects, however, modernisation revisionism concedes that efficiency, accountability, transparency, legitimacy and political stability are noble ideals that must be nurtured in the transition from tradition to modernity.

It would be naïve to conclude that, because modernisation revisionism is premised on liberal democracy, it has an ideological coherence that would exclude counter ideologies. In fact, both liberal and various forms of socialist or Marxist ideologies are basically modernist in orientation. Tornqvist's (1999: 61–2) classification of modernisation revisionism is theoretically very useful, although its practical application amid the current universalising democratisation and good governance discourse is questionable. Tornqvist identifies four modernisation revisionist schools:

1) *Comparative historians* – the study of organised interests, dependency and conflicts of interests among different political actors;
2) *Clientalists* – critical of the universal usage of analytical frameworks based on the Western experience and the rigid dichotomy between traditional and modern, instead focusing on institutions and organisations that survived and yet changed in step with modernisation, such as ethnicity, patron–client relations, and patrimonial administration;
3) *Interventionists* – who question whether economic, social and cultural modernisation would promote political development, arguing that development is a contested and conflict-ridden activity, and
4) *Statists* – socialist or Marxist-inspired revisionism critical of the disappointing results of economic modernisation, hostile to neoliberalism, arguing that neither the bourgeoisie nor the working class could drive society forward alone. The state is the only institution that can bring changes across class and ethnic divide.

Interventionism, currently the most dominant modernisation revisionist variant, has not been greeted with the enthusiasm that its architects had anticipated. The interventionist paradigm is predicated on the belief that institutional and organisational changes are prerequisites to political order and economic growth. In this sense alone, modernisation revisionism echoes a debate that dominated the 1960s and 1970s, although the ideologically charged Cold War element is now missing. It is not difficult to conclude that the pragmatic rather than the opportunistic ethos of the Cold War era has vanished. However, where the initial triumph of liberalism over military and authoritarian one-party states was celebrated by reviving liberal political development theory, this time around, political development and modernisation are predicated on the triple heritage of modernisation revisionism – democratisation, good governance and human rights (Randall and Theobald 1998).

A common feature of most states that have embarked on political development using the neoliberal model is that development itself became a source of conflicts and a pressure point, resulting in the use of political coercion to impose development (or economic modernisation). Development is not only dependent or interdependent, it is oppressive, often evicting local communities from their sources of livelihood (see Chapter 3).

Two points deserve special attention here: that state repression is a direct outcome of dependent authoritarian development, and that democracy and authoritarian development are incompatible. A central question in the debate on authoritarianism and democracy is to what extent state repression is a function of political and economic development. We need a critical assessment of how the prevailing patterns of political development interventionism have failed to explain their relationship to state violence in the name of development. The earliest theories of political development, including dependency theories, which were also critical of liberal modernisation theories, paid scant attention to state violence in general and none to the repressive acts of the so-called developmental states in particular. Lopez and Stohl (1989) lamented that the 'political' critique of dependency theory paid little attention to the authoritarianism intrinsic in the development paradigm of the centralised states of the developing countries. Economic development was not indigenous to the post-independent states, but was under the control of external forces, over which the state was powerless. The prevalence of cash-crop production, a global trade regime that continued to exert pressure over subsistence economies, contributed to continuous cycles of poverty and violence against those who protested their impoverishment. The result has been dependent development at best and mal-development at worst, with increased state repression to quell the voices of protest that rose to challenge state authority:

> The management of dependent developing economy created the pressing need for new coalitions of ruling elite who would increasingly resort to harsh treatment of their own citizens in order to sustain the momentum on economic policies that were likely to attract dissent. Imposing development contributes to the creation of garrison states in which local elite opts for gain in conjunction with external patrons, all at the economic and political expense of the bulk of the citizenry. [Lopez and Stohl 1989: 1–2]

The global crusade for democratisation and good governance, its historical antecedent, has been echoed in the African literature. Most publications have adopted one of two dominant approaches: one explains the failure of the second wave of democratisation (early post-independence experiences) by the lack of a democratic tradition that could nurture the ethics of democratic governance (the lag in political culture); the other hinges on an economic explanation, apportioning blame equally between underdevelopment and poverty. These alternative approaches were explicitly used to defend two distinct forms of authoritarianism: military rule and one-party states.

The uniqueness of Diamond, Linz and Lipset's (1989) work stems from its strong theoretical and methodological approach, using comparative politics to explain the factors that contributed to democratic failure and success in five African countries: Nigeria, Senegal, Botswana, Zimbabwe and Uganda. Diamond, Linz and Lipset outlined seven factors which they considered responsible for democratic reversal in the Cold War era: 1) regime insecurity, 2) ethnic division, 3) weak political structures, 4) lack of legitimacy, 5) undermined and hence distorted local institutions, 6) state monopoly over economic development and a weak private sector, and 7) external pressures. These factors are still largely relevant to the post-Cold War democratic experience, albeit with some contextual differences. I illustrate this point below with reference to a number of the major contemporary works on African democracies. It seems that changes in the global context have not been matched by changes in the internal context of democratisation.

There are five dominant explanations of why Africa's democratic transition has been marred by constraints emanating from the socioeconomic and political context within which democratisation is practised. It is this context more than anything which determines whether the democratisation process is sustainable. The five explanations are as follows:

- The apparent failure of theories and concepts originating from outside Africa (mainly modernisation and dependency) to produce a body of knowledge consistent with and relevant to African reality. Among the authors of post-1990 contributions, Apter and Rosberg (1994) were the first to launch a stinging critique of political development within what they referred to as the new realism in Africa. According to them, this new realism was defined by Africa's harsh economic conditions and increasing external pressures to democratise. This realism (also defined as critical realism) challenges the entire corpus of past writing and theorising about Africa and looks instead for realistic African solutions to Africa's political, social and economic problems. The tone of Apter and Rosberg's argument is sympathetic to the possibility of the emergence of an African democratic tradition.

- The persistence of patrimonialism and its emergence in new forms. Bratton and van de Walle (1997) present a more pessimistic view by treating the democratisation process currently underway in Africa as no more than a transition from patrimonialism to neopatrimonialism. In their view, since the African transition to democracy is driven by neopatrimonialism, the outcome of the democratisation process will be determined more by social protest than by factors similar to those which shaped Western democracies. In other words, the possibility of strengthening civil society organisations as a prerequisite to democratic consolidation is unrealistic. In contrast to democratic transition in Western corporatist regimes, African democratic transition from neopatrimonialism to multi-party rule is characterised by the struggle over patronage rather than by the institutionalisation of democratic values.

- The surge of democratisation as an expression of people's yearning for development. The assumption here is that the democratic gains made by the African peoples will be consolidated by development. Wiseman (1995) concluded that although large numbers of Africans have long cherished the idea of democratic government, the goal received fresh impetus from the twin problems of economic decline and the crisis of legitimacy among the rulers of authoritarian states. The view that the surge of democratisation is enhanced by economic development is contested by some (e.g. Ake 1994; Mohamed Salih 1999a) who argue that the quality of development is more important than the incidence of development *per se*.

- The demand for democratisation and the rule of law arises largely from the failure of development strategies and the politics associated with them. The African elite has alienated the people by pursuing policies that project neither coherent national objectives nor plausible societal interests. These policies are so repressive that people began to see the state and its development agents as enemies to be avoided, cheated or defeated, as the circumstances permitted (Ake 1996).

• The absence of institutions capable of internalising the democratic values has made a mockery of democracy, contributing to the re-emergence of authoritarian leaders under the guise of multi-party democracy. Joseph (1999a, 1999b and 1999c) has succinctly explained the discrepancy between the form and substance of African democracy, arguing that within a few years of experience with multi-party systems, all but a handful of African countries have retained or re-elected former dictators, thus shifting power to authoritarian rulers. Donors and global actors accept 'virtual democracy' and the feigned conversion of African leaders, while factors that hinder substantive transition towards democratic consolidation and participatory democracy go unheeded (1999c).

There are many other contemporary contributions, such as Nyang'oro (1996), Mengisteab and Daddieh (1999), Kasfir (1998), Mohan and Zack-Williams (2000), among others, which deal with a variety of issues related to the debate on democratic transition, conflicts, institutional failures and the like. Comparative politics, clientalism and statism are the main theoretical strands informing the debate on the prospects of democratic consolidation in Africa.

What many of these contributions have in common is their concern with a civil society narrowly defined as interest associations or the modern forces of trade unions, professional associations, grassroots organisations, NGOs, etc. This leaves little or no room for the indigenous political institutions and fails to assign them any significant role in the governance debate. Using the classification provided by Tornqvist (1999), the major works on African democracies can be categorised as political history, interventionism, statism or clientism, each informed by conventional political development tradition.

With the exception of Ake (1996), almost all contributors to Africa's democratisation debate believe strongly in the need for an enlightened minority elite (or good governance) to nurture participatory democratic values and norms. This is more evident in the contributions of the 'establishment' scholarship for which the use of comparative politics is imperative to explain conformity or non-conformity of the developing countries to Western democratic standards. A handful of post-1990 contributions are overtly critical of the status quo and mindful of the obstacles confronting democratic transition. However, the belief that democratic consolidation is within reach is still the dominant trend, characterising a mode of thought that uncritically glorifies the so-called 'third wave of democracy' or the crusade towards a new political development paradigm. Some remain adamant that what is taking place in Africa represents the first steps on the long road to genuine democratic institutions similar to those prevalent in the West.

The academic debate on the state of democratisation in Africa is consistent with the policy objectives of multilateral development and finance agencies and their democracy and good governance project. This post-Cold War modernisation revisionism paradigm has its origins in the failed Cold War political development paradigm. Whether tampering with the association between economic growth and democracy will succeed this time is beyond the scope of this book. However, the signs are that democratisation is confronted with complex and difficult issues that cannot be resolved from within a good governance project which is divorced from the stark socioeconomic realities. Nurturing and internalising democratic values and norms is a function of the combination of complex realities with the internal capacity of transformation and renewal, and as such cannot be exported.

EXPORTING DEMOCRACY AND GOOD GOVERNANCE[1]

The previous section demonstrated that the current democratisation project originated from political development and modernisation under the guise of modernisation revisionism. I alluded to the emergence of interventionism as the most dominant strand of modernisation revisionism, and its resurrection in the democratisation and good governance project. This section focuses on the constituent elements of modernisation revisionism and the institutional and practical arrangements it uses to implement this project. However, the democratisation and good governance project cannot be fully understood without reference to its historical antecedents.

Historically, the desirability of an association between development and democracy, and the use of external interventions to make this possible, occurred in at least three distinct periods:

1) The height of the Cold War (1960s–1970s), which coincided with Africa's liberation and decolonisation struggle. Most development projects concentrated on human resources development in the field of public administration, legal development, development management and primary education. The general belief was that the last two decades of the colonial experience had left behind democratic govern-

ments that would continue to be dependent on the metropolis. During this period, although development aid was expected to result in growth and the adoption of Western-style democracies, in reality it provided support for a global anti-communism project.

2) During the early 1980s, an explicit Western interest in issues pertaining to the expansion of democratic values began to emerge. For the particular case of Africa: 'USAID [US Agency for International Development] was first hesitant about the new emphasis on promoting democracy in Africa. Over the previous two decades, USAID's Africa specialists became disillusioned about the possibility of working productively with African governments, in any fashion, and they were sceptical about political aid. Many of the specialists had consciously or unconsciously accepted the dogma of African exceptionalism and doubted that democracy was a feasible or even appropriate goal in the continent' (Carrothers 1999: 42). This is a far cry from USAID's current obsession with democratisation and good governance projects directly or indirectly involving 16 African countries.

3) With the end of the Cold War, multilateral agencies such as the World Bank, the UNDP (United Nations Development Programme), and the OECD (Organization for Economic Cooperation and Development), and the major bilateral development agencies, adopted what they considered to be a new conception of democracy and good governance, in a bid to foster the relationship between economic growth and democracy. The main assumption here is that democratic governance is self-reinforcing, so that democracy is good for economic growth, and vice versa. What is peculiar to this period is that development aid is used as both stick and carrot, rewarding countries that pronounce themselves democratic and denying development aid to countries that defy the will of a self-appointed 'international community'. Democratisation and good governance have become effective political instruments in the hands of donor agencies for short-listing deserving states, as well as black-listing pariahs, according to their position on the democratic scale.

The definitions of good governance introduced by multilateral development institutions are many, diverse and vague. For instance, the UNDP (1997) defines governance as 'the exercise of political, economic, and administrative authority to manage a nation's affairs'. For the World Bank (1989), 'governance is the way power is exercised in managing a country's economic and social resources for development'. In this sense, governance encompasses a wide range of government actions from exchange rate management to corruption in awarding of public contracts. For the OECD, governance policy makes a direct link between democracy and good governance. It purports that 'a vital connection exists between open, democratic and accountable governance and the respect for human rights, and the ability to achieve sustainable economic and social development' (OECD 1995: 5).

In 1989, the United Nations Economic Commission for Africa and the United Nations Development Programme sponsored a conference that put in place their general policy framework for governance. In fact, the framework is an abridged version of the UNDP's 1997 policy on governance. A broad consensus was reached on ten points which provide the common guidelines for developing good governance in Africa:

1. Transparency and accountability were agreed to be crucial elements for promoting development, and as such they should not be the sole concern of governments, but should also involve civil society organisations as well as Africans at large.
2. Note was taken that in almost all the countries represented, institutions and measures for improving accountability and transparency had been put in place. The problem remained how to transform them into more effective instruments. Functional problems existed at varying degrees in all the countries under consideration and include the need for more political will, resources and capacity.
3. The need to revisit African traditions and culture was recognised in the effort to reduce the perverse effects of an alien culture in post-colonial Africa.
4. The establishment of processes, operations and institutions were undermined by political and socioeconomic factors.
5. Both governments and civil society were responsible for the lack of transparency and accountability.
6. The application of sanctions alone would not be enough without appropriate incentives for transparency and accountability being put in place.
7. Transparency in decision making on macro-economic issues could enhance the practice of accountability. Conversely, accountability for public resources at the micro level was a requirement in setting up a credible system of transparency.
8. There needed to be a concerted effort to establish legislation for assets disclosure of all leaders in government, civil society and parliament. Enforcement mechanisms needed to be strengthened.
9. The possibility should be looked into for African governments to sign on to international conventions as in the OECD/DAC (Development Assistance Committee) countries.

10. The external dimension of problems of accountability and transparency required the cooperation of external partners in the search for appropriate solutions.

Guideline 3 is most intriguing, containing the only direct mention of 'the need to revisit African traditions and culture in the effort to reduce the perverse effects of an alien culture in post-colonial Africa'. In reality, neither the Economic Commission for Africa (ECA) nor the UNDP has devoted any effort to exploring how African traditions and culture could become vehicles for a democratisation project different from the globally sponsored one. In fact, ECA/UNDP are more inclined to pursue guideline 9, 'African governments signing on to international conventions as in the OECD/DAC countries'. This gives little comfort to Africans who wish to own the democratic process; rather, it subjects the democratisation process to unwanted external pressures that will stifle its ability to 'reduce the perverse effects of an alien culture in post-colonial Africa'. It will reinforce these effects and hence delay the whole process of democratic consolidation.

One of the bilateral international development organisations most active in the democratisation project is USAID, with its mission to further the United States' strategic long-term domestic and foreign policy objectives, which it believes are best served by enlarging the community of democratic nations worldwide. As part of this mission, it is entrusted with establishing democratic institutions, free and open markets, an informed and educated populace, a vibrant civil society, and a relationship between state and society that encourages pluralism, participation and peaceful conflict resolution – all of which contribute to the goal of establishing sustainable democracies. In implementing the objectives of this mission in Africa, USAID has supported the democratisation projects in several countries, including Eritrea, Ethiopia, Malawi, Mozambique, South Africa, Tanzania and Uganda, with mixed results and meagre signs of success.

If democracy is about expanding civil society's influence over state and public affairs through legitimate political institutional frameworks, then democratic governance better serves democracy. Democracy must enable society to hold responsible the triangulated components of the state. The functions, institutions and operators of the state – in fact, the entire machinery of the state, including the legislature, the judiciary, the executive, norms and values, laws and procedures by which the state operates – should all be accountable (Buzan 1991). Good governance and democracy are thus associated with society's capacity for self-governance, underlining how citizens govern themselves and the institutions of the state which they have sanctioned to govern their affairs.

Inclusive governance implies improved governance institutions, including improved government and the democratisation of the governing state and civil society. In essence, the creation or development of improved governance entails the gradual development of state and civil society from democracy to polyarchy (the type of political democracy prevalent in the West), and the quest for pluralism, accountable and transparent governance capable of responding to people's preferences. Polyarchy also entails polycentricity signified by the following: nested institutions of concurrent power centres; sovereignty vested in people and their institutions and organisations; overlapping problem-solving arenas and scenarios; state, economy and society that are mutually interdependent as institutional actors; self-governance, a key attribute of democracy; conditioning rules to specify commitments and to constrain deviant organisations, and finally, bottom-up lateral learning (Moore 1998).

Although there is nothing fundamentally wrong with aspiring to create democratic, accountable and transparent institutions in any society, the manner in which this endeavour has been pursued is a cause of concern. This donor-driven democratisation and good governance project has determined the fate of democracy in Africa by emphasising the form and neglecting the content. It insists on the replication of Western democratic experiences, at times without questioning their efficacy in the African context or asking what they would do to enhance the development of a truly African democracy.

THE STRUCTURE OF THE BOOK

This book applies a critical comparative method and offers a structural analysis of the socioeconomic and political processes within which power structures influence the outcomes of the current democratisation process. One important aspect of this method is that it exposes the role which political actors and institutions (traditional and modern) play in the democratisation process, stressing the capacity of power structures to subvert institutional politics. Implicit in this method is that the democratisation process, especially in societies where democratic forces are externally driven, often produces alternatives not initially contemplated by politicians or political analysts. This frees the analysis from being drawn by predetermined theoretical convention. It emphasises the socioeconomic and political context that empowers institutional mechanisms peculiar to the power structures in question. For instance, whereas ethnicity is usually treated as either instrumental or primordial, this method places ethnicity within the peculiarity of the context in which it exists rather than assigning it a predetermined role. The thrust of this method is that theory is context-specific and what may be a plausible explanation in one political structure may, in other circumstances, be rendered less useful or completely insignificant. For instance, ethnicity could constitute a dynamic modern institutional framework for the contestation of power (for instance, in ethnic political parties), a blend of 'traditional' and modern (for example in urban associations), or a mechanism for the organisation of production, consumption and the reproduction of traditional values and belief (as in most of rural Africa). Depending on the context within which ethnicity exists, it is in part old and in part new.

The critical comparative method challenges the orthodoxy of mainstream political theory, particularly the assumptions held by the modernisation revisionists' attempt to explain the political reality of developing countries. Contrary to the theoretical discussion that portrays modernisation revisionism as a vehicle for political modernisation, the case studies in this volume illustrate that democratic reversal, national disintegration, ethnic revival and institutional decay, rather than being exceptional, have developed into the norm. Political developments in Nigeria, Sierra Leone, Zimbabwe, Liberia and Sudan, for instance, reveal two contradictory tendencies: the shrinking of the modern political arena at the expense of ethnically based political organisations and institutions; and the expansion and intensification of violence and political activism, in both traditional and modern forms, including civil society's increasing impatience with authoritarian development and its outcome. The political, economic and social reality on the ground shows that the democratisation process which is underway has not yet fully absorbed the roles of ethnicity and religion, the position of minorities, and the potential role of political education.

Chapter 2 takes an unorthodox approach to ethnicity and treats it as a symptom of a much deeper socioeconomic and political crisis. Africa's political failings cannot be explained away in terms of ethnic conflicts or the non-amenability of ethnic groups to political change. Political scientists critical of ethnicity, as well as its apologists, have all failed to come up with a clear idea of what to do with ethnicity. Questions such as 'could ethnicity provide an institutional framework for enhancing the democratic process?', or 'if ethnicity is so divisive, how can its negative effects be redressed?' remain unanswered. Chapter 2 argues paradoxically that while the African elite/state deny ethnicity, they manipulate it for political gain, illustrating that the elite have succeeded in monopolising power and alienating local-level politicians, thus consolidating elite hegemony. A system that accommodates ethnic entities within modern political institutions might offer a fairer representation and hence reduce the negative consequences of political exclusion – one of the main sources of social discontent. Democracy exposes a myriad of weak institutions to ethnic, religious and regional pressures and claims, and to the contestation of power by class-based interest groups. This proposition may be controversial, but it deserves to be explored further, as ethnicity is no more controversial than class, elite or any other socioeconomic organisational forms.

Authoritarian development (top-down, centralised, disempowering and impoverishing) is not an aid to democracy. In Chapter 3, I argue that the way in which certain types of 'top-down development' have been implemented is largely authoritarian. It reinforces ethnicity, breeds insurgency and contributes to rebellion since this is the only institutional mechanism for collective action *vis-à-vis* the state. Post-independence African history has illustrated that some ethnic groups have organised in liberation movements and insurgency groups to resist authoritarian development. Democratising development is a neglected aspect in the externally driven democratisation project. Democrats and dictators alike have used development to justify their ascendance to power. In the circumstances, democracy has been used as an instrument of domination, for example, through the exclusion of minorities (see Chapter 9).

Education is one of the neglected areas in writing about democracy, particularly in the African context. Chapter 4 explores how authoritarian regimes use the educational establishment to strengthen their grip on power. It argues that the African educational establishment is authoritarian, and that an authoritarian educational establishment cannot nurture democratic values or produce democratic citizens. The tenet of the argument here is consistent with my critique of authoritarian development, since education is used synonymously with development. In other words, the democratisation of the African state and the advancement of the ethos of citizen politics are essential prerequisites of democratic consolidation. However, such a democratic ethos can come only from within Africa; the prospect of it being exported by multilateral development agencies is remote, if not impossible.

Chapters 5 to 8 consist of case studies, attempting to support the arguments raised in the first four chapters. The case studies can be divided into three broad categories: (1) countries that have been subjected to development conditionality as a result of their reversal from democratic to military rule (Nigeria, Sierra Leone and Sudan); (2) countries that have been rewarded by multilateral and bilateral development institutions for their compliance with the democratisation and good governance project (South Africa, Zambia and Zimbabwe) – these also fall under what Joseph (1999: 242) describes as 'virtual democracy'; (3) countries whose minorities have gained little dividend from the democratisation project

(Nigeria, Rwanda and Mali) or countries whose majorities have experienced profound changes due to the democratisation process (Ethiopia).

Chapter 5 describes Sudan as an authoritarian circus characterised by democratic bankruptcy and military coups. The National Islamic Front (NIF) began a process of political consolidation which resulted in the creation of the National Congress Party under the leadership of the Islamist Hassan Al Turabi, the mentor of the 1989 coup which brought the NIF to power. Internal opposition, civil war and political isolation and pressure forced the Sudanese regime to begin steps towards democratising the NIF's political establishment. With the enactment of the Political Organisation Act of March 2000, and the imminent return of the figures of the opposition to Sudan, one might ask whether the transition from NIF authoritarian rule to multi-party democracy is also imminent.

Even under the watchful eye of powerful multilateral and bilateral development institutions, Western-style democratisation has proved unattainable in Sierra Leone. The return of Sierra Leone to military rule in 1994 astounded many political analysts and observers. Democracy was restored in 1996, but Sierra Leone has hardly recovered from the consequences of a destructive civil war. In 1998 the Lome Agreement sponsored by the UN, the OAU (Organization of African Unity) and ECOMOG (the Economic Community of West Africa) came to effect. Chapter 6 attempts to expose the limits of democratising anarchy and the building of civil society. It challenges the conventional wisdom that an elite is essential for democratic consolidation and shows that in fact, in the case of Sierra Leone and possibly elsewhere, the elite had a minimal stake in democratisation. The Sierra Leone elite, at the expense of the poor, greedily sought diamonds, timber and other forms of wealth, in a context in which democracy became an instrument for self-enrichment. Chapter 6 offers a realistic critique of how the externally driven democratisation and good governance project failed even in Africa's oldest Westminster-styled democracy.

Since its return to democratic rule in 1999, Nigeria has been absorbed by religious violence following the introduction of the Islamic *sharia* laws in some northern states. Chapter 7 demonstrates that the flare-up of 'religious' violence in Nigeria actually has little to do with ethnicity or religion, both of which became effective political instruments used by the Nigerian political elite to pursue economic interests. Religious and ethnic violence instigated by the introduction of Islamic *sharia* laws during the transition to democracy became a tool for deporting southern Nigerians settled in the north – a desperate attempt by the northern political elite to maintain the status quo. The more Nigerians from the south settle in the north, the less ethnically inclined Nigerian politics will be, thus breaking the myth of a Hausa–Fulani Muslim alliance versus the Yoruba–Igbo Christian nexus. The politics of numbers militates against the integration of Muslims and Christians in northern Nigeria, with the northern Nigerian elite fearing that such integration would, in the long term, undermine their power base.

Southern Africa, particularly Botswana, South Africa, Zambia and Zimbabwe, represents a special case in African democracies and politics. Economically, this is the most developed region in the continent, with a special history which includes settler colonialism, apartheid, and one of Africa's most stable democracies. In this region, too, one finds Africa's most prominent case of racial tolerance, following the end of the apartheid regime in South Africa, and an example of the most unequal land distribution, in the case in Zimbabwe. This is a region with a sizeable white minority which has left its mark on the history of the continent, if not on the world's attitudes towards racial segregation. Despite its immense potential and resource endowment, the majority of the population in the region is poor, yet pinning much hope on democracy. Chapter 8 attempts to explain the substance of southern African democracies. Are they extensions of one-party regimes transformed to find a place in multi-party democracy (Zambia and Zimbabwe), or are their political parties – like those in the rest of the continent – ethnic political parties?

Finally, Chapter 9 addresses the role of minority groups in majoritarian democracies. It attempts to explain what it means to be a minority in multi-party democracy, and asks whether multi-party democracy improves their lot. The chapter revisits the majoritarian–populist debate and asks whether Western-style democracies serve majorities better. It introduces the cases of the Ogoni (Nigeria), Batwa (Rwanda), Tuareg (Mali) and the Southern Nations, Nationalities and Peoples of Southern Ethiopia. This chapter gives special attention to Ethiopia's experience with 'ethnic federalism' in order to explore whether this is a viable alternative to Western-style majoritarian democracies.

In short, this book attempts to explain the main factors which have contributed to the fate of democracy in Africa. It examines Africa's 'waves of democratisation' (colonial, early independence, post-independence and the 1990s), their failings and successes. It explores the efficacy of externally driven democratisation projects, and their promise for sustainable democratic consolidation. It asks why some cases of democratic reversal have occurred during the late 1990s and examines their potential ramifications for the future development of a home-grown African democratic tradition. In essence, it argues that democracy, particularly Western-style democracies, will not take root in Africa because of development conditionality, and the failure to take into consideration the specificities of the African continent. Traditional political institutions such as ethnicity, often shrugged off as archaic and non-democratic, may hold the key to an indigenous African democratic tradition. Modern political institutions such as elite-dominated political parties may, in the final analysis, be seen as an extension to ethnic politics and not an implant of Western democracy. Africa's ownership of the democratisation process is probably the key to democratic consolidation.

2
Ethnicity in Quasi-polyarchies

Polyarchies are regimes that have been substantially popularised and liberalised, are highly inclusive and extensively open to public contestation. A near-polyarchy can be relatively inclusive but with greater restrictions on public contestation than full polyarchy, or it might provide opportunities for public contestation comparable to those of a full polyarchy but be somewhat less inclusive (Dahl 1971: 8). In this sense, most democratic regimes that allow in some degree for the challenge of power by the public are, in fact, polyarchies or political democracies which fall short of the ideals of democracy. Dahl is also mindful of the differences in people's ability to formulate and signify their preferences and have those preferences weighed equally in the conduct of government. These are only part of what democracy implies.

However, Dahl's work on polyarchy is significant not only because it recognises that there are various degrees of adherence to the ideals of democracy, but also because it highlights two major possibilities: that polyarchy is a welcome development in countries where it signifies a move away from hegemonic regimes; and that in countries without recent experience in the operation of competitive politics, the transformation of hegemonic regimes into polyarchies is likely to remain a slow process, measured in generations (Dahl 1971: 47). The relevance of this to Africa and developing countries in general is that their democracies are most likely to exhibit characteristics unique to their political culture; the possibility of reproducing blueprints of western democracies, even hegemonic ones, is far-fetched.

African democracies are, by and large, elite-dominated democracies, which do exhibit some of the overt characteristics of what Dahl refers to as near-polyarchy. The aim of this chapter is to examine the role of ethnicity in the African democratisation process, to illustrate that some of the basic requirements of polyarchy are absent, in this case particularly the freedom to form and join organisations that are ethnically based. Although African political parties are themselves ethnically based, the African state and educated political elite denies people the right to create political organisations according to ethnic affiliation.

Ethnicity has been demonised and treated by most African states as a source of political instability, conflicts, genocide and other undesirable attributes. Even within the context of the democratisation process, most

African states ban the formation of ethnically based political parties and associations. Paradoxically, despite the elite's denial of ethnicity, the political parties they formed are by and large ethnically based. Hence, I argue that the failings of Africa's political development can be partly attributed to the political elite's misreading of anti-colonial nationalism. One of the consequences of this misreading has been the elite's continued desire to suppress ethnic consciousness in order to build nation states similar to those of the departing colonialists. Partly, this negativist paradigm continues to treat ethnicity as an archaic principle of political organisation that should be swept away through a progressive nation-building project. Recent and current events, however, reveal that ethnicity has not disappeared, and the nation-building project has not been realised.

This chapter explores the emancipatory potential of ethnicity against the backdrop of state oppression and authoritarian development. In reflecting on the democratisation process underway in Africa, the chapter concludes that the implications of not taking ethnicity seriously are immense. Hence 'another development and democracy' should attempt to unleash the liberatory potential of ethnicity in order to create the necessary political space for a truly participatory democracy.[1]

African nationalism emerged within the political confines of a reformed post-Second World War colonial state and its ability to train and hence co-opt a large number of politically aspirant western-educated African elite. Heralded by an elite unified by an apparent urge for decolonisation, and despite linguistic, cultural and religious diversity, and at times open ethnic antagonism, the struggle for independence was all-embracing. This unity of purpose gave some authors the impression that a genuine African nationalism had been born. However, some argued that while for the majority the liberation struggle was for independence, others were fighting for racial equality. Mazrui and Tidy (1984: 84–5) traced the origin of the anti-colonial struggle to African pre-colonial nations. In other words, the elite had reinvented African pre-colonial nations in order to reconstruct a glorious past enshrined in a pan-African ideology. They argued that 'nationalism was a strong feature of pre-colonial African civilisations. The colonial rule had the twin effects of weakening that nationalism and encouraging ethnic sub-nationalism' (p. 84). This view, plausible as it may be, has not been vindicated by the fact that Africa's new political nations have grown out of the colonial embryo as claimed by Mazrui and Tidy.

In my view, neither the origin nor the liberation objective of African's nationalism is traceable to pre-colonial states. The main objective of the educated African elite was limited and short-sighted. It was predicated on a genuine desire to replace the colonial bourgeois and military/civilian elite. To that extent, African nationalism originated in elite competition, that is, colonised versus coloniser, for the control of the state apparatus and institutions. In this competition, the African elite opted to take the reins of power from the colonial state without radically restructuring it. At least four factors support this view.

First, the independence movement was a modernisation movement inspired by Western-educated elite, typically civil servants, teachers, lawyers, doctors, journalists, intellectuals and an emerging national bourgeoisie. The immediate demands of the elite included better representation in the colonial state apparatus as well as better social services and job opportunities. At a later stage, elite-based demands were expanded to include self-rule and subsequently independence. By the late 1950s, African aspirations for independence had become widespread and apparently attracted the support of trade unions, industrial and agricultural labourers and peasants who opposed low wages, the expansion of plantations in African lands or unrewarding cash-crop pricing policies.

Second, owing to its emulation of Western political systems and institutions fomented by the desire to take over the reins of the colonial state, African nationalism was modern in its intent and purpose. The elite aspirations for independence were articulated, in most cases, through the creation of modern political parties and liberation movements, which were expected to see the continent through the transition to independence and self-managed modernity. African nationalism was associated, in the minds and hearts of many Africans, with what Smith (1998) calls modernity embedded in the Enlightenment, and the socioeconomic and political transformation they hoped would accompany it. Smith further characterises the paradigm of nationalism as a paradigm of classical modernism: 'nations and nationalism are intrinsic to the nature of the modern world and to the revolution of modernity. It achieved its canonical formulation in the 1960s, above all in the model of "nation-building"' (Smith 1998: 3). Hutchinson (1994: 12) echoes the view that 'the objectives of nationalism are essentially modernist: to secure a representative state for their community so that it might participate as an equal in the developing cosmopolitan rationalist civilisation.' Similarly in Africa, early nationalism meant progress and freedom. It started with African representation in the colonial state and eventually culminated in the agitation for independence from the colonial state. Doornbos describes ethnicity's potential as a liberating force. He argues that 'if ethnicity can indicate a route to the discovery of meaning, a recapturing of cultural identity and the recreation of solidarity, there can be no dispute about its enigmatic force and its liberating potential' (1998:

28). In Africa, elite and ethno-nationalists have done just that by developing ethnicity into a liberating force against colonialism and, after independence, against authoritarian states.

Third, far from being traditionalist or backward-looking movements hoping to reinvent African pre-colonial glory, the newly established political parties were in fact at loggerheads with traditional chiefs. The chiefs were treated by the state not only as agents of colonialism, but also as the guardians of traditionalism. To that extent, members of the Western-educated African elite behaved no differently in their struggles against colonialism or in their more recent antagonistic attitudes towards each other in the bid to secure or resist a representative state, or in conceding limited local autonomy for their ethnic groups. In fact, the elite contrived to take away even the limited sovereignty that the colonialists had accorded to local chiefs in running the affairs of their ethnic 'homelands'. The political culture of the new leadership was described as:

- Elitist – government was believed to possess a monopoly of wisdom and legitimacy, because there were few if any other social or political organisations that could compete with the concentration of professional knowledge that existed within government.

- Statist – state was regarded as the 'moderniser'. In the context of a weak private sector, powerful bureaucracy and sometimes socialist (*or militarist*) ideology, the state was seen as the agent of development.

- Nationalist – the leadership emphasises national unity as the paramount goal, condemning any subnational sentiment to tribe, religion, region or other centres of political attachment and loyalty as destructive of national integration. [Smith 1996: 207–8, emphasis added]

None of the above characteristics of the leaders of the independence movement is traditional or backward.

Fourth, Western education became an instrument for nation building, political indoctrination and the propagation of state ideology (socialism, capitalism, or military Marxism) in the bid to nurture the march to the promised nation state. In the long run, the nation-building policies have undermined Africans' capacity to start a soul-searching journey to devise political systems adaptable to African reality. The fact that the goal of the African elite struggle against colonialism was not to transform but to inherit the colonial state is evident in its persistent authoritarianism and disrespect for human and civil rights in the colonial and post-colonial states alike. The literature on the authoritarian nature of the post-colonial state is plentiful and I do not wish to dwell on this in the limited space available in this chapter.

In essence, Africans' agitation for independence comprised a temporary alliance of Western-educated elite supported by popular discontent premised on the hope that their own elite would deliver better institutions of governance than those imposed by colonial rule. While decolonisation had contributed to the creation of a short-lived African nationalism,[2] independence, on the contrary, contributed to the resurrection of ethnicity. This time round, ethnicity is incarnated as a modern form of political organisation.

As subsequent events have shown, a second wave of liberation has begun in earnest. Discontented ethnic groups who felt the brunt of political and economic exclusion took up arms in order to reconstruct the state thus forcing it to recognise their grievances. The goal of most ethnic-based liberation movements is to radically restructure the post-colonial state and with it the 'colonial element' of Africa's ruling elite. The struggle for the second liberation has been epitomised by the proliferation of insurgency, rebellion and liberation movements often led by those left with no other political option than armed struggle.[3] The second liberation has in some countries been extended to a continent-wide democratisation process in which both ethnicity and underdevelopment continue to haunt the emerging African democracies.

In short, the recent retreat of most African elite from nationalism to ethnicity is neither a retreat to traditionalism nor a retreat from the project of modernity, recently repackaged under the rubric of democratisation and good governance.[4] If nationalism is embedded in the paradigm of modernity, it is not plausible that the failure of one would herald the failure of the other. What is plausible, however, is that modernity can be reconstructed according to the meaning which people assign to it. In the process of reconstructing ethnicity, the political elite found little sense in staking their fortunes on 'nationalism' as an instrument for realising Africa's two most illusive projects, development and nation building. It is not surprising that ethnicity took over where nationalism stopped.

This chapter therefore explores state–civil society relations with specific reference to the relationship between ethnicity and the state in two inclusive spheres, democracy and development. It examines the intricate ways in which ethnicity continues to assume a significant role in African political life. I take a less common position by arguing that recognising rather than denying ethnicity may hold the key to democratising the state and development. Unless ethnicity is taken seriously, Africa's struggle to democratise the state and development will suffer no better a fate than that of an imagined nation state.[5] 'Another development and democracy' are rooted in democratic institutions that people can identify with, and in development that can bring tangible benefits.

ETHNICITY IN AUTHORITARIAN STATES

Ethnicity and the state are equally illusive concepts. Competing definitions of what ethnicity and state signify or claim to constitute are vast and cannot be covered in their entirety here. No matter whether ethnicity and state are real, imagined or social constructs, they constitute powerful institutions, which will continue to shape state–society relations in and between ethnically divided or ethnically homogeneous societies. As concepts, they circumscribe principles of political organisation and institutional mechanisms within which citizens articulate their political and other interests.

The inclusion of ethnicity in social science terminology began during the closing decades of colonialism, with concerns about the social units – tribe, ethnic group, nation, class, etc. – appropriate to the analysis of the socioeconomic and political processes taking place in Africa and elsewhere in the developing world:

> The debate contributed to the shift from the study of tribe to that of ethnicity, which was more than just a terminological shift. It was also a political and ideological shift signifying a powerful critique of the use of tribe, which Africans had historically considered Eurocentric, particularly its use to distinguish between civilised Europeans and the so-called primitive societies of the colonies. The deliberate shift to the use of ethnicity also implied that colonialism had succeeded in opening up the colonial societies for contacts with western civilisation, and that a certain degree of modernisation or 'westernization' had ensued. As a concept, ethnicity focuses on dynamics rather than statics and hence relativizes the boundaries between modern and tribal societies. [Eriksen 1998: 2, 37]

As I have argued in the Introduction, the African leaders, for their part, considered ethnicity equally primitive as an alternative to tribe. They opted for creating Western-style nation states and political institutions under the influence of modernisation theory, a choice that has in my view cost Africa dearly. Although state and ethnicity are the most ancient forms of political organisation, the African elite considered the nation state a generally superior system of political organisation.

'*Ethnie*, or ethnic community from which ethnicity is derived, may consist of named human populations with shared ancestry myths, histories and cultures, having an association with a specific territory and a sense of solidarity' (Smith 1996: 28–9). More than a historical event, Barth claims that one of the main objectives of ethnicity is 'boundary maintenance' by groups that feel threatened by other groups. Such groups 'are not givens, but are the product of ever changing situations' (Barth 1969: 2). Hence, ethnicity is an aspect of social relationships between agents who consider themselves culturally distinctive from members of other groups with whom they have a minimum of regular interaction.

In the African context, the 'boundary maintenance' function of ethnicity has, in most instances, been either exaggerated or rejected. In reality, there is no African ethnic group that can claim to be racially, culturally or linguistically 'pure', exclusive or unaffected by other ethnic groups, through intermarriages, trade, and administrative, economic and other forms of interaction. But even here the so-called ethnic boundaries are neither static nor exclusive. When the identity of one ethnic group is contrasted with that of other ethnic groups, ethnicity becomes a value-laden concept, with discernible political organisational principles. Politically, ethnicity can develop into a powerful ideological instrument for institutionalising political participation or mobilisation. Hence, 'the cultures, values and practices of ethnic groups become resources for elite in competition for political power and economic advantage. The cultural forms, values and practices of ethnic groups become symbols and reference points (ethnic markers so to speak) for identification members can call upon in order to create a collective political identity' (Brass 1991: 13–16). These, I would argue, are transformable and can be adapted to political circumstances and the limitations imposed by state authority.

Ethnicity enters the nation state debate not as autonomous, but as a representation of mutually interactive political entities that influence each other. Once the state becomes an extension of narrowly defined ethnic interests and/or an 'ethnic state', *ethnie* may assume the role of nation. Conversely, 'multi-ethnic states' often do not consider themselves multinational states, since this requires greater devolution of power, which is nearly impossible in states instituted on the principle of ethnic exclusion.

Like ethnicity, the state is an institutional mechanism for articulating social, economic, political and other claims and is often defined in relation to society. In this respect, Chandhoke's definition of state functions *vis-à-vis* society is illuminating. She laments: 'If we focus on the way state and society constitute and limit each other, then the state is the codified power of social formation.' This definition captures the organic relationship between state and society, but instead of collapsing one into the other, regards the two as analytically distinct:

1. Though the power of the state is in the first instance derived from society, it is itself a distinct and discrete organisation of power.

2. The state consists of a set of specific political practices that define and
   enforce binding decisions in the name of the collective interests ... In
   most societies the state is the ultimate and final repository of power.
3. The state monopolises the means of coercion in a way no other organisation in society does – a system of laws has always to be guaranteed
   by bodies of armed men [*sic*] able and willing to enforce the law, to
   catch and punish transgressors.
4. Since the state through a set of specifically political practices confers
   fixity to otherwise unstable power blocs in society, the social order is
   constituted through the state and exists within the parameters laid
   down by the state. [Chandhoke 1995: 66–8]

Certainly, because state functions are different from those of society,
conflicts often occur when certain sectors of society hijack and/or monopolise these functions to the exclusion of others.[6] Exclusion follows as the
political elite 'representing' these social forces treats the state with
contempt, forfeits its role as an arbiter of different ethnic claims or
perceives itself as an institutional mechanism designed to articulate the
interest of an exclusive class, gender or ethnic group, etc. In ethnically
divided societies, states that nurture such ethnically based exclusion
become a focus of conflict between the holders of power and those
excluded.

If the functions of state and society are different, does it really matter
if membership of the state (citizenship) is defined in terms of membership
of a nation or an ethnic group, since both underline what we perceive as
one of the primary principles relating citizens to the state? The current
stalemate in the debate over whether ethnic groups are nations or whether
the two are distinctively different raises two dilemmas: 1) if ethnic groups
are nations, the ultimate goal of most nations is to fulfil themselves in a
nation state; 2) if ethnic groups are not nations, the nation-state project of
the African-educated elite is based on a very shaky foundation.

Smith's earlier contributions are highly relevant to this debate. For
Smith (1971: 181–6), nations rather than tribes and ethnic groups possess
a particular set of characteristics. In other words, tribes and ethnic groups
may satisfy some, but not all the characteristics of nation, which are:

• Cultural differentiation
• Territorial contiguity with internal mobility
• A relatively large population
• External political relations
• Considerable group sentiment and loyalty
• Direct membership with equal citizen rights
• Vertical economic integration around a common system of labour.

According to Smith, tribes have only the first and the second of these characteristics. *Ethnie* has the first five. Nations have all seven. Although it is not difficult to criticise any typology for being simplistic, the one provided by Smith is useful in conveying at least three important and significant points: 1) none of the seven characteristics of nation, as described by Smith, is exclusively national – due to the expansion of various forms of modernity, the distinction between tribe and *ethnie* is blurred, particularly in terms of economic reach and external political relations; 2) there is nothing inevitable about ethnic groups becoming nations (Smith 1983; Brass 1991: 3) hence, ethno-nationalism is institutionally no less developed in articulating collective interests than any other form of nationalism.

If tribe, nation and state can be used interchangeably or simultaneously, at least in the political realm, *ethnie* is no less imagined a social construct than nation. While the latter uses ethnic ties in place of relations based on nation as a community, both can in fact be instruments for serving the political interests of the elite and not the immediate interests of nation or *ethnie* (see also Doornbos 1991 and Chazan et al. 1988). In Anderson's (1983) definition of nation as an imagined community, the African-educated political elite understood that if the nation is an imagined community, *ethnie* is even more so, particularly where nationalism has not matured beyond the confines of elitist or ethno-nationalism in multi-ethnic societies. Under certain historical conditions, both ethnic groups and nations qualify for Anderson's definition of an imagined political community.[7]

Paradoxically, the 'ethnicisation' of African politics has gone hand-in-hand with the African leadership's passionate public rebuke of 'tribal' or 'ethnic'-based political organisation. Not surprisingly, a modernist nation-building project based on the denial of ethnicity and a political mobilisation project based on ethnicity are on a collision course. Ethnicity, which is officially demonised and portrayed as a threat to 'national unity', a challenge to state security and an obstacle to political stability, has outlived nationalism. Far from disappearing, ethnicity has subsumed and duly subverted the political institutions of a truly imagined African nation state.

One of the main consequences of the denial of ethnicity is that African ethnic groups are thus deprived of the opportunity to secure recognised collective rights that would enable local governance institutions to take a more active role in democratising state and development. The African political elite's denial of ethnicity and its determination to prevent it from developing into a positive political force emanates from its fear of the capacity of ethnicity to produce alternative institutions of governance. A politically repudiated ethnicity is not a threat to the modern political elite's control over the modern institutions of power, including the state. An enlightened ethnicity is. The crux of the matter is that an enlightened ethnicity heralds a shift that would wrest power away from the monopoly of an exclusive political elite, and bring it closer to the people.

The denial of ethnicity is self-defeating, and has jeopardised Africa's opportunity to transform its ethnic groups into 'nations' with equal citizen rights – if that is what the elite really espouses to achieve. Instead of inclusion, ethnicity has become an instrument of exclusion. Ethnic groups have also been denied the opportunity to integrate across economic or regional rather than ethnic bases. This has prevented diverse ethnic groups from forming an inter-ethnic composite of a national culture through the agency of the modern state. By arguing that ethnicity is divisive and should be discouraged, the African elite has frustrated the paradigm of another genuinely African modernity in which African political culture is allowed to interact freely with other political cultures. Instead, the political elite has monopolised the space in which African and non-African political experiences might create contact points which could have produced a notion of nation and state relevant to the African experience.

The current debate on ethnicity and the state in Africa thus requires a serious re-reading: it offers little comfort to fill our library shelves with publications on ethnicity without attempting to answer the question whether it has any practical value other than being a destructive force. I raise this question because, currently, three main strands are dominating the debate:

- The first position is state-sponsored, which denies ethnic groups any officially recognised political role or collective rights. This position and the policies that support it have so far failed to envisage a role for ethnicity in a continent commonly described as overly ethnically inclined.
- The second position stresses ethnicity's negative contribution to Africa's 'political development'. Ethnicity is treated as the source of all evil, including the failure of the nation-building project, conflicts, war, genocide and underdevelopment.
- The third is an instrumentalist approach, which considers ethnicity an instrument for political manipulation enhanced by exclusion, uneven development and local animosities engendered by elite competition.

All three approaches are negativist in that they regard ethnicity as a constraint and as the cause rather than part of a solution to innumerable crises. In my view, the failure of the post-colonial state cannot be blamed on ethnicity, but on how ethnicity has been mismanaged by the African elite. Unfortunately, as a result of state mismanagement, ethnicity, which is the most powerful, widely spread, commonly known and practised principle of political organisation, has been denied the opportunity to develop into a people-centred governance institution.

The claims I have made thus far are serious enough to merit exposing them to the test of two main problem areas in contemporary Africa, development and democracy. My main premise here is that without assigning ethnic groups a greater role in Africa's economic and political transformation, the new initiatives on development and democracy are doomed to failure. 'Another development' is not just indigenous, but can also be modern and empowering in its capacity and formidable in its resolution to restore power to a disfranchised public.

POLITICAL ORGANISATION IN QUASI-POLYARCHY

Most contributions to the current debate are either critical or utterly dismissive of ethnicity's ability to generate political stability or sustainable multi-party democracy. Disillusionment with democracy's ability to contain ethnicity corresponds with the tendency to hold ethnicity responsible for development failure. This is hardly surprising since both political transformation and development are the main agents of the paradigm of modernity, which considers nation a more advanced political organisation than *ethnie* or ethnic community.[8] As in the case of development, the dominant paradigm has exhausted itself by denying African ethnic groups a role in the current debate on democracy and governance.[9]

The following section focuses on the structure and functions of African political parties in order to show that, although most authors describe ethnicity as a source of conflict and political instability, on the whole, political parties are actually ethnic parties. In another democratisation, ethnic groups should play a central role in the struggle for democracy and the rule of law. Before addressing this matter, however, I will review the current debate on ethnicity and democracy in Africa.

Most scholars consider ethnic heterogeneity a hindrance to stable democracy. For instance, Lijphart (1977) argues that social homogeneity and political consensus are prerequisites for, or factors strongly conducive to, stable democracy. In his view, the stability of culturally plural societies is threatened less by communalism *per se*, than by the failure of national institutions to explicitly recognise and accommodate existing communal divisions and interests. Horowitz (1994: 36) goes further, arguing that 'severely divided societies' represent a serious threat to democracy. In the particular case of Africa he asserts that 'most African countries remain severely divided, and ethnic divisions have proved a major impediment to the attainment of stable democracy all over the continent'.

Lijphart and Horowitz are not alone in expressing scepticism about the democratic credentials of ethnically divided societies. In the same vein, Rabushka and Shepsle (1990) argue that in the case of Africa and Asia, democracy is simply not viable in an environment of intense ethnic preference. Bratton and van de Walle (1997), discussing the role of ethnicity in regime transition, argue that African regime transition is constrained by neo-primordialism.[10]

Authors such as Sorensen (1993), Diamond and Plattner (1994), Wiseman (1995) and Joseph (1999b), among others, while recognising the role ethnicity plays in political change in Africa, seem to have no clear idea as to what do with it. Typically, African political institutions, actors and voting behaviour are presented as if they exist in a Western political milieu. Most recent publications make little or no reference to the ethnic background of the competing political parties, candidates and party functionaries though Donge (1995), Nnoli (1995) and Ottaway (1999a) deal with ethnicity and democracy more explicitly. These otherwise excellent contributions uncritically apply Western democratic theory in relation to a variety of normative theories of social choice. What they end up analysing is the form and not the content of what is a uniquely African democratisation experience.

In the following section, I intend to explore the ethnic element in African political parties in order to demonstrate that they are, by and large, ethnic political parties. I will then show how these parties fulfil functions similar to their Western counterparts, although they contrast with them in their tendency to assume the role and behaviour of the state. In other words, instead of acknowledging that the functions of state and society are different, African political parties seem to conflate these two functions. Once that happens, the state becomes the political expression of the ethnic group that forms the major constituency of a given political party. A brief commentary may clarify this point.

Most African political parties were established during the colonial period, and as such they were manifestations of what Mazrui and Tidy (1984: 84) call either multi-ethnic or ethnic nationalism. According to them, 'One factor which encouraged ethnic sub-nationalism in the decolonisation process was British eagerness to export to Africa their particular version of parliamentary government, with several political parties and organised opposition. In practice this development led to the emergence of numerous ethnically based parties in opposition to other ethnic parties' (p. 85).

A common feature of colonial and post-colonial African parties is elitism, with a less crucial role assigned to the relationship to the mass of Africans (Freund 1984: 245). This may well explain why jubilant crowds of well-wishers greeted any change of leadership, sometimes regardless of whether the leaders came to power through civilian or military means.[11] In the absence of a leadership accountable to citizens or strong democratic tradition, the nationalists' impatience with multi-party systems grew steadily. Calls for national unity and fears of national disintegration, weakened legislature, corruption and lack of transparency accompanied the appeal of one-party systems. The majority of one-party states were socialist, of various sub-ideological persuasions. The failure of Africa's first wave of democratic experience in the period immediately following independence can thus be attributed to a number of factors:[12]

- African political parties tend to be elitist, based on non-democratic structures and organisation, with irregular contacts with their electoral base. Contacts among party leadership are superficial due to the leadership's control over party management.
- The majority of party members are politically illiterate (that is, not aware of the ideological bases on which modern political parties are founded) and lack experience of how democratic institutions operate.
- Many of the parties were at an embryonic stage.
- The colonial rule from which Africa emerged was neither democratic nor based on 'one person one vote' or 'majority rule'. Africans' frustration with Western-style democracy and its long periods of consultation and consensus building, was rooted in the truism that 'democracy is neither about development nor justice'.
- With a few exceptions, most one-party system leaders ended up enriching themselves at the expense of the masses in whose name they seized power.
- The denial of ethnicity as a common principle of political organisation denied African ethnic groups the possibility of developing local accountable and democratic governance.

The first three points were commonly defended by one-party regimes to justify their existence. However, no matter how serious the factors which prompted the rise of one-party regimes in Africa, they do not constitute an excuse for human rights abuse or denial of civic and political rights. In fact, many of these regimes abused two of the main aspects of democracy – liberty and human rights, especially civil and political rights. This must call into question the way in which democracy has been conceived without serious recognition of the specificity of the African context within which it is being practised.[13]

The resurgence of multi-party democracy is a result of internal and external pressures as well as the end of the Cold War.[14] Political parties from colonial times and ruling parties during one-party systems have been resurrected. Some have actually contested and won elections. Others have conceded power to new political parties. Table 2.1 shows the political parties that have survived and those newly created. It is interesting to ask what the similarities and differences are between African and Western political parties. Randall (1988: 183–7) introduces four main functions of political parties:

- Endow regimes with legitimacy by providing ideologies, leadership or opportunities for political participation, or a combination of all three.
- Act as a medium for political recruitment, thus creating opportunities for upward social mobility.
- Provide opportunities for the formation of coalitions of powerful political interests to sustain government (interest aggregation), have major influences on policies as a result of devising programmes, supervise policy implementation, political socialisation or mobilisation of people to undertake self-help activities.
- Provide political stability in societies able to absorb increasing levels of political participation by the new social forces generated by modernisation.

Although African political parties are generally ethnically based, they assume similar functions and some have been able to maintain control over the personnel and policy of government through the elite who claim to represent their ethnic groups. They constitute institutional mechanisms for political organisation and articulation of political interests. Coleman and Rosberg (1964) describe political parties as associations formally organised with the explicit and declared purpose of acquiring and/or maintaining legal control, either singly or in coalition or electoral competition with other similar associations over the personnel and the policy of government of an actual or prospective sovereign state. Ethnic groups are informal associations, but because of an assumed dependence on collective rather than individual rights, support and preference.

Political party membership is based on shared ideology and objectives, although a political party can accommodate diverse individual interests. Ethnic political parties, on the other hand, are based on membership of an *ethnie* that may share an ancestry myth, collective memory, history and culture, has an association with a specific territory and a sense of solidarity (Smith 1998).

However, because ethnic groups assume permanence, their holding of power assumes a continuity of the political values enshrined in inter- and intra-ethnic politics. I have argued elsewhere (Mohamed Salih 1992) that ethnic group leadership is devoid of the concept of the circulation of the elite, which is central to Western democracy. While Western political elites may lose office upon failing to fulfil, without good reason, the promises they made to the electorate, tribal elites succeed to office not through achievement, but through predetermined rules of succession. African political parties do no better. According to Mwakyembe (1994), African parties are not democratic; they exclude people from the political process, are elitist and non-transparent. The situation is worse in the case of one-party states, which are non-competitive, have little or no room for political debate, and carry out unfair electoral practices. In some cases, non-elected organs and the state control the ruling party, thus creating an executive without legislative or political checks and balances.

If political parties are institutional mechanisms for capturing and maintaining power, elections are the institutional mechanism through which political parties compete for power. Elections are rightful political activities in which citizens exercise their sovereign will in selecting their representatives, who eventually form or select the personnel and policy of government. Furthermore, elections facilitate the orderly transfer of power according to the will of a sovereign citizenry. These practices and ideals are currently being implemented through ethnic-based political parties, with varying degrees of success. As with development, the failure or non-sustainability of democracy cannot be explained away by an ethnic group's inability to accommodate Western democratic values. Rather, Western-style democracies have been imposed on ethnic groups without due recognition of the latters' political values and aspirations.

The question that has eluded many observers of African democratic experience is whether or not voters are able to exercise, through their free will, their individual sovereign rights to elect their representatives to the legislature. While it is easy for Western political party members to change their allegiance from one political party to another, this is much more difficult for ethnic party members, who owe their allegiance to collective sentiments and values. If not properly managed, individual members of ethnic political parties could be subjected to psychical sanctions by invoking the morale of the collective – although this is not the case in all African countries. If political parties are ethnic political parties, 'elite pacts' are ethnic pacts. Moreover, minority ethnic groups have often allied themselves with other minority ethnic groups and formed coalitions, as in any other democracy. (See Mohamed Salih 1992, Ochola-Ayayo 1998, Donge 1995 and Ottaway 1995b for Sudan, Kenya, Zambia and Ethiopia, respectively.)

Table 2.1 shows the ethnic nature of political parties and voting behaviour in 16 African countries. It also exposes the diversity of the bases on which membership recruitment occurs. Although the table suggests very complex processes, it does reveal at least four significant points about the ethnic nature of Africa's political parties.

Table 2.1
Ethnic voter behaviour in elections in ten African states 1995–99

Country	Date of elections	Type of election	Remarks
Ghana	7 Dec. 1996 8 Dec. 1996	Presidential Parliament	National Democratic Congress (66% of vote), which secured Akan/Ewe support, but also gained support from a variety of smaller ethnic groups
Kenya	29–30 Dec. 1997	Presidential and National Assembly	Kenya African National Union (51.6% of votes), elite pact, alliance of small ethnic groups, with larger ones (i.e. Lou and Kikuyu)
Lesotho	23 May 1998	National Assembly and Senate	Lesotho Congress for Democracy (60.7% of votes) and Basotho National Party. Basotho formally Basutholand National Party
Malawi	17 May 1994	Presidential and National Assembly	United Democratic Front (46.4% of votes). Chewa, Nyanja, Tumbuko, Yao, Lomwe, Sena, Tonga, Ngoni, Ngonde
Mali	4 May 1997 20 July and 3 Aug. 1997	Presidential National Assembly	Alliance for Democracy in Mali (87% of votes). Bambari, Fulani, Songhai, opposition, mainly Tuareg, Moors and Bella
Niger	23 Nov. 1996 and 19 Jan. 1997 7–8 July 1996	National Assembly Presidential	National Independent Union for Democratic Renewal (70% of votes). Hausa and Djerma

Country	Date of elections	Type of election	Remarks
Nigeria	27 Feb. 1999	Presidential House of Representatives	People's Democratic Party (57.2%) although mainly Yuroba/Igbo. Opposition consists of a Fulani/Huasa-dominated alliance of All People's Party and Alliance for Democracy
	20 Feb. and 20–7 March 1999	Senate	
Sierra Leone	26–27 Feb. 1996	House of Representatives	Sierra Leone People's Party (36.1%), United National People's Party (21.6%) and People's Democratic Party (15.3%) of the votes. Temne, Mende, Creole
Zambia	18 Nov. 1996	General	Movement for Multi-party Democracy (MMD) (60.8% of votes). Main ethnic groups include Bemba and Luapula, on the one hand, and Chinyanaia, Lozi and Tonga, with different constellations of party support
Zimbabwe	8–9 April 1995	House of Assembly	Zimbabwe African National Union-Patriotic Front (82.3% of votes). Ethnic divisions emanating from the late years of independence (Shona with whom power rest versus Ndbele)

Sources: compiled by author from case studies in Wiseman (1995); case studies in Joseph (1999b); Buitenhuijs and Thiriot (1995); Europa Publications (1999); Electronic publications (Election results Africa): <http:/gkgvot.com/Govt/Africa.htm>

First, although each political party has an ethnic base or is part of a pact of ethnic groups, ethnicity is more prominent in some countries than others. The manifestations of ethnicity also differ greatly. We can find examples of religious, regional and linguistic manifestations, such as minority ethnic groups within the same region (north versus south in Sudan), or language base (Amhara versus Oromo in Ethiopia). In politicised ethnicity, the identity of ethnic groups is not necessarily racial; during elections ethnic groups tend to forge regional, linguistic or religious identities.

Second, apart from Lesotho (Basotho National Party) and Ethiopia's coalition of ethnically based political parties (EPRDF), African political parties tend not to use the names of the ethnic group or groups which make up the majority of their constituencies. The party name reflects an ideological orientation (socialist, social democratic, liberal or conservative) but not an ethnic one.

Third, countries with strong ethnic majorities (such as Mauritania, Zimbabwe and Nigeria) are not politically more (or less) stable than countries with several ethnic groups (such as Benin, Kenya, Tanzania or Sierra Leone).

Finally, the dominance of elite pacts is also a reflection of ethnic group pacts. While elections are fought on the basis of the support which chiefs lend to one political party or another, after the elections, political pacts or coalitions are forged without reference to the constituencies. Given the lack of commitment to political programmes, elite pacts can be created even between ideologically irreconcilable political parties.

The point I am driving at is that although African political parties are modern, they appeal to ethnicity – referred to, at the state level, as backward. It is unlikely that the political elite is unaware of the fact that the political base of their modern political parties is ethnic. Hence the elite's selective ethnicisation of politics represents an opportunistic appeal to collective ethnic sentiments. In essence, the African political elite denies ethnic groups any collective rights, while at the same time manipulating ethnic groups' collective sentiments and collective allegiance. African political parties and their non-democratic organisation exploit their ethnic groups in a classic populist fashion. This has, in a sense, denied the ethnic groups the opportunity to develop the capacity to handle democracy or their local affairs. This poses a major constraint to democratising African polity. Taking ethnicity seriously in another democracy means creating a political space for African ethnic groups to play a positive role in democratising state and development.

In short, the African political elite's misreading of the political meaning of early nationalism, which shaped their agitation for independence, continues to frustrate their efforts to come to terms with ethnicity. While ethnicity is officially demonised, in reality it provides a widely shared value system through which people are able to articulate their grievances and take collective actions against an oppressive post-colonial state. The current democratisation process makes it possible for people to organise more freely, for instance in grassroots associations, community-based and non-governmental organisations. In the urban centres, the majority of these organisations are not ethnically based. However, at the national and regional levels, ethnicity is the main principle of political organisation. Ethnic solidarity and collective action have become the most effective means for coping with economic hardship and for resisting impoverishment resulting from ill-defined authoritarian development. The elite's monopoly of the democratic process, through non-democratic structures, has strengthened its control over the state and development. Rather than being democratised, state and development have become instruments for the political legitimisation of an exclusive political elite.

The democratisation process currently underway in Africa is elite dominated to the extent that civil society is narrowly defined as the 'modern forces' – of private business, non-state institutions, trade unions, church organisations, social movements, pressure groups, etc. Because the state does not consider them part of these modern forces, ethnic groups, which constitute the political parties both in government and opposition, are not considered part of civil society (see also Rothchild and Chazan 1988, Haynes 1997). In fact, as part of the nation-building project, African states (with the exception of Ethiopia) ban the formation of ethnically based political parties. This narrow definition of civil society as the modern forces comprising the political space for which government and opposition compete in order to secure the support necessary to control the state, denies ethnic groups the democratic right to organise freely. However, as we have already seen, ethnicity is a function of elite competition for the control of the state power and resources. In this context, banning the formation of ethnically based political parties, or describing ethnicity as an archaic principle of political organisation, are strategies employed by the elite to suppress ethnic consciousness and hence maintain their own grip on power. As events have shown worldwide, suppressing ethnic or national consciousness is a futile endeavour, frequently leading to popular discontent or violent conflicts that often prove extremely difficult to control.

Elite-dominated quasi-polyarchies, such as those of Africa, are restrictive (Dahl 1971: 8) in a sense that they respond only to the sectors of civil society that are of immediate consequence to the elite's holding of power, that is, the modern forces. In the long run, this will hamper Africa's democratic development from transition to consolidation. Democratic consolidation cannot be realised unless the majority of the people internalise the ethos enshrined in the democratic process through genuine participation. In the absence of consolidation, the African democratic experience runs the risk of being haunted by military coups and popular insurgency, for example, the military coups that ousted democratically elected governments in Sudan (1989), Gambia (1996), Sierra Leone (1994), and recently Niger (1999).

In order to democratise state and development, it is therefore imperative to widen the political space through an enlightened accommodation of ethnicity in a manner attuned to Africa's political culture and institutional structures. This would eventually allow for a power shift from exclusion to inclusion, where genuinely people-centred democratic institutions, values and practices could be enshrined. An all-encompassing participatory democracy cannot be realised in an exclusive elite-dominated democracy. Another development and democracy should be built on inclusive principles that take seriously both ethnicity and the political culture that comes with it.

On account of their severe division by ethnic, linguistic, cultural, economic, regional and other attributes, near-polyarchies and quasi-polyarchies rather than democracies are the norm in African countries today. This does not in itself mean that African democratic experiences are quantitatively different from others. What it does mean is that the consequences that accrue to the people are qualitatively less tangible than in countries that have lengthy experiences with polyarchy.

The following chapter demonstrates that the denial of ethnicity is an inseparable part of authoritarian development policies that have unwittingly created a space for ethnicity to be used as an alternative framework for political organising *vis-à-vis* the state hegemony. Instead of creating political autonomy – an important factor in consolidating democracy – authoritarian development reinforces dependence on ethnicity as a liberating force in the bid to resist the state's ill-conceived development policies.

3
Harnessing Authoritarian Development

This chapter is not about introducing competing definitions of Western democracies and then attempting to show whether one democratic theory is more capable than another of promoting development. Nor is it about the ability of democracy to promote social welfare, human rights and political stability. These issues and more have been the subject of many publications (see, among others, Bagchai 1995, Roemer 1995, Bauzon 1992). For instance, in assessing the relationship between democracy and development, Bagchai (1995) and Bauzon (1992) commonly argue that there is no strong evidence that democracy promotes development or vice versa, although they concede that well-established democratic states are highly industrialised with higher per capita income. Because most industrially advanced countries adopt Western-style democracy (with the exception of China), most authors draw the simple conclusion that there is a strong correlation between democracy and development, even if measured in terms of economic growth and per capita income (with the exception of India). Others (including Sorensen 1993) have tried to illustrate that human rights are an important consequence of democracy and that human rights are more respected in democratic than authoritarian regimes. According to Roemer (1995), human rights are abused both in democratic and non-democratic states: the only difference is the magnitude of abuse and the accountability of the abusers. None the less, there are fewer human rights abuses in democratic than in authoritarian regimes, and fewer cases of human rights abuses in industrially advanced than in underdeveloped countries: 'Stable and consolidated democracy correlates with a higher respect for human rights. Likewise, democracy offers the possibility of political stability and with it the opportunity to redirect resources and build institutions that can foster the cause of development through fairer competition, participation and the respect of civil and political liberties' (Sorensen 1993: 88).

I would suggest that, in attempting to correlate the incidence of democracy and development in the advanced industrial countries, we should be mindful of the fact that these countries were industrialised centuries ago and did not attain economic prosperity through democratic means. Serfdom and exploitation at home, reinforced by the slave trade and colonialism abroad, were characteristics of most, if not all, of today's industrially advanced societies. In the post-colonial state, dependent

Box 3.1
Fulani pastoralists of northern Nigeria

Most of the Fulani of Nigeria inhabit the northern states, especially Sokoto, Kano, northern Kaduna, Katsina and Borno. Agriculture and livestock production constitute the main sources of subsistence, and both respond negatively to drought. Rainfall is unpredictable. The Fulani are a demographic minority comprising about eight million people (that is, less than 8 per cent of the Nigerian population). Politically, however, the Fulani–Hausa alliance constitutes a political majority, which has provided most of the presidents of post-independence Nigeria.

Beginning in the early 1970s, the Nigerian government introduced large-scale mechanised schemes for the production of cash crops such as cotton and tobacco and food crops such as wheat and sorghum. The schemes were located in the northern states, where high human and livestock population density prevail. Irrigation schemes were expanded at the expense of the Fulani pastures and thus created conflicts between the pastoralists and the cultivators. By the end of the 1990s, Fulani grazing lands had been transformed into arable lands owned by wealthy farmers who consistently excluded the Fulani pastoralists from using the dry-season pastures on the river banks, thus making them more vulnerable to drought and famine. The ultimate result of this ill-conceived development was that the Fulani became impoverished landless labourers working for the business elite.

A possible solution for this situation was sought in the establishment of grazing reserves. However, only 22 million hectares of land (25 per cent of the land pledged for the project) has been acquired and demarcated as grazing reserves. None the less, the grazing reserves infuriated Hausa farming communities, which perceived southward Fulani migration as a threat to their land and future farm expansion. Hausa farmers continued farming on their old farms within the grazing reserves, thus igniting conflicts with the Fulani.

From the Fulani viewpoint, this type of development is impoverishing and disempowering. It is centralised, top-down and favours the more politically vocal, wealthy and powerful urban elite. The Nigerian state is controlled by a power elite which thrives at the expense of the poor, even if these poor belong to its own ethnic group. There has been no participation or consultation on how local resources are distributed, or on how to attain particular development objectives. This is an example of authoritarian development at work. [Mohamed Salih 1992]

development is neither indigenous nor free of powerful global interests that control and monopolise the direction of development. Dependent development is based on the extraction of natural resources by larger states in which cash-crop production dominates over subsistence economies. The penetration of capital markets by foreign investors who take advantage of under-valued commodities and cheap wage labour contribute to perpetuating the vicious cycle of poverty.

Lopez and Stohl push the dependent development debate further by arguing that although the overt political institutions that sustained colonial and imperial rule have vanished, the stranglehold of state domination remains in the form of trade, technology and capital dependence. The result is dependent development at best and mal-development at worst, with increased state repression to quell the voices of protest that challenge state authority:

> In the drive towards modernity, the social mobilisation of various groups would produce unprecedented demands on governments with limited capacity to respond effectively. Under such conditions, and until social institutions could arise and government capacity improves to meet such pressures, the governing elite would opt for older, lest whatever economic progress had been made would deteriorate in the ensuing political violence and instability. [Lopez and Stohl, 1989: 3–4]

In other works, I have attempted to delineate how authoritarian exploitative states, and private and transnational economic interests have contributed to the impoverishment and displacement of millions of peasants, pastoralists, forest dwellers and fisher folk from their lands in the name of development (Mohamed Salih 1987, 1994 and 1999b). My argument is that global and developing world business elites used state power to control resources (such as land, water, minerals, oil, etc.) by evicting local communities and refusing them access to resources essential for their survival, often without consultation or compensation. Authoritarian development denies peoples the right to livelihood resources in the name of progress.

Authoritarian development represents a brutal attack on people's sources of sustenance. Among the major features of authoritarian development are the following:

(1) It serves interests other than those of the intended beneficiaries (that is, it serves transnational capital or national private interests) to the detriment of local communities.

(2) It is top-down and is implemented without consultation or involvement of the local communities.

(3) It uses force and coercion including the police and the army to evict those who oppose evacuation.

(4) Those evicted are often not compensated, but are left to fend for themselves after having been stripped of the land on which they depend for their survival.

(5) It represents a gross abuse of the human rights of those evicted by force and denies them the right to self-development.

Human-induced displacement and resource scarcity contribute to conflict and political coercion that invite counter-insurgency and authoritarianism.

In other words, authoritarianism breeds violence and invites more authoritarianism and increasingly brutal ways of using the state's monopoly over the use of power and coercion to legitimise its holding on that power.

In this chapter, I intend to develop the debate on authoritarian development further by showing that it is dominant both in democratic and non-democratic African states. Development – or at least the way it is being practised today – is authoritarian. Instead of arguing that the democratic crisis in Africa is a result of underdevelopment, I argue that the dominant development paradigm is non-democratic and should be seen as a major cause of democratic reversals in Africa.

DEFINING AUTHORITARIAN DEVELOPMENT

A closer look at the literature on democratisation in Africa reveals that the authoritarian nature of development has not been given sufficient attention. Five main areas have so far dominated the literature:

- Constructing or reconstructing democratic institutions such as political parties, associations and civil society institutions.
- Consolidating democratic gains through constitutional and electoral reforms.
- Campaigning for improvements in human rights through lobbying, advocacy and legal literacy.
- Taming the state by reinforcing the role of the legislature, and by global governance's imposition of economic and political conditionalities.
- Supporting non-governmental organisations (NGOs) and the private sector in order to strengthen a narrow and misconceived concept of civil society.

However, the debate on democracy and underdevelopment has lagged behind, for a number of reasons. As argued at the beginning of this chapter, development – both as concept and practice – boasts meagre democratic credentials. In fact, the way development has been practised during the last fifty years or so can largely be described as authoritarian, disempowering, top-down and highly centralised. There is a heightened tension between democracy and development that is often ignored by private development agents and the political elite interested in securing political gain at any expense. Three factors can explain this tendency:

- The lack of creative and new thinking on development objectives combined with the resistance of the development establishment to structural change in the way it operates, means that a 'business as usual' approach has continued to usher in only cosmetic changes.

Bilateral and multilateral development agents and agencies have internalised the ethos of conventional development.

- The use of development in a carrot-and-stick formula designed to impose conditionality on non-democratising states makes a mockery of both development and democracy. As a result, democracy has become an externally driven project, with authoritarian development used as an instrument to achieve supposedly democratic objectives.
- The rolling-back of the African state and the temporary (Uganda, Mozambique, Chad, Central Africa) or long-term collapse (Somalia, Liberia, Sierra Leone) of some states has created an institutional vacuum that inadequate and fragmented NGO efforts and a weak private sector have failed to fill.

This chapter is not intended to be an introduction to competing definitions of Western democracies and their suitability (or unsuitability) to Africa; nor is it an attempt to ameliorate the current trends, which espouse to demonstrate that Western democracy is capable of promoting development. Two concepts developed by Rao (1984) in this regard are instructive: the necessity to understand the resource endowments, the level of historical development, the motivation of economic agents and the relative strength of different social classes in developing societies; and the need to identify the nature of goals, including the rates of aggregate growth and income distribution. Rao (1984) also comments on the linkages between democracy and the level of economic development, arguing that the capacity of a democratic framework to achieve its goals is a measure of the extent to which democracy and development are compatible.

Africa is generally characterised by highly skewed income distribution and concentrated political power. The prevalence of low literacy rates, poverty and lack of political education make a small minority elite vastly powerful. When the state colludes with this dominant minority, the results will benefit mostly the upper classes, and democratic institutions will be used to perpetuate hegemony rather than to advance liberty. Moreover, African leadership often claims that it has been compelled to adopt non-democratic measures to achieve development objectives. The situation in most African countries has been succinctly diagnosed:

> The struggle for power was so absorbing that everything, including development was marginalized ... Besieged by a multitude of hostile forces that their authoritarianism and exploitative practices had engendered those in power were so involved in the struggle for survival that they could not address the problem of development. Nor could they

abandon it. For one thing, development was an attractive idea for forging a sense of common cause and for bringing some coherence to the fragmented political system. More important, it could not be abandoned because it was the ideology by which the political elite hoped to survive and to reproduce its domination. [Ake 1996: 7]

The gist of the argument here is that the interest in augmenting the embryonic African democratic process will bear no fruit unless development itself is democratised. If development is to succeed, it must be participatory, and no genuine participation in development can be secured without adherence to democratic principles. In this respect, the consequences of non-democratic development in Africa are clear to see in the failures that beset many well-intentioned efforts to develop the continent's resources for the benefit of its impoverished population.

The relationships between the citizen, the state and education have become increasingly locked into the market, frequently creating competing imperatives detrimental to the democratic process – food riots, student unrest, an increase in crime and other social problems. Mamdani (1995) focuses on some of the intricate problems of marketisation, democracy and late colonialism in Africa, arguing that: 'For democracy to have any meaning, African Governments must be accountable to African peoples, not only for the resources they receive and spend, but for the very policies they formulate and execute' (Mamdani 1995: 22).

In my view, this type of government requires a particular type of leadership, which currently exists in only a handful of African states. The case for political education on issues pertaining to the empowerment of civil society, democracy and development should be part of an all-embracing package of structural reforms.

FACES OF AUTHORITARIAN DEVELOPMENT

The following section introduces two trajectories: the first explores the relationship between authoritarian agricultural modernisation and the resultant resource conflicts; the second examines how ethnic and multi-ethnic community-based, grassroots and non-governmental organisations coexist. The question that I attempt to answer is why ethnicity is still the main principle of organisation in regional and national-level politics, but less so in community-based development and social welfare initiatives.

Most of rural Africa is still divided into ethnic territories (homelands) or enclaves inhabited by one or more dominant ethnic group(s). Originating in pre-colonial Africa, this pattern was reinforced by colonial and post-colonial policies as well as by socioeconomic circumstances, which forced people to settle in tribal homelands. Ethnic (or primary) affiliations still provide the basis on which individuals and groups gain access to land. Ethnic groups also provide security against cattle rustling and land grabbing by neighbouring ethnic groups, insurance against damage (payment of blood-money) and means for meeting social obligations (payment of bride-wealth), among others.

Agricultural investment in Africa has been lopsided, most resources being allocated to the modern cash-crop sub-sector, while the traditional sub-sector, which supports the majority of the population, is neglected.[1] Such bias is not just a matter of favouring investment in one sector over another; it is also a matter of expanding the modern farming sector at the expense of subsistence producers. Elsewhere, I have described as authoritarian and disempowering the process of agricultural transformation that thrives on land alienation and the eviction of peasants, pastoralists, hunters and gatherers, and other such impoverished groups, from their main sources of livelihood: authoritarian because of the use of brute force to evict people from their lands, and disempowering because it impairs their ability to eke out a living (Mohamed Salih 1999b).

The majority of African states have introduced a highly centralised administrative structure in order to ensure that decisions over land administration and allocation are centrally controlled, and to put in place agents who make sure that state policies are implemented. This strategy takes away from ethnic groups and their representatives any control over decisions vital to their survival and denies them the possibility of democratically deciding how to manage their resources. As will be discussed further below, political and administrative centralisation have strengthened the state's assault on ethnically based associations and attempts at local development, in a deliberate act to control local development initiatives and institutions, including local government. Olowu (1999: 285–6) makes the point that, 'the years immediately following independence were often golden years for local government in Africa ... However, as African national governments increasingly perceived themselves as the sole modernising agent in society, they took over the functions and resources of local governments.'

If local governments in rural Africa are expressions of territorial administrative units occupied by ethnic groups, the weakening of local government institutions can be seen as a *de facto* policy decision to reduce the capacity of those ethnic groups to manage local financial and natural resources. In re-reading Olowu's remarks, the decision to take over local government functions and curtail the authority vested in local governance was a deliberate act aimed at rooting out ethnic groups and denying them access to the state's institutions. Some countries considered

Box 3.2
The Nuba peoples of the Sudan

Numbering over one million people, the Nuba are the indigenous inhabitants of the Nuba Mountains of western Sudan. They are politically and economically marginalised and have suffered under both colonial and post-colonial regimes. Currently, the Nuba Mountains area is undergoing a sinister campaign of human rights abuse by the Sudanese state, including genocide and ethnocide (or cultural genocide) under the fundamentalist National Islamic Front regime. Between 1973 and 1994, the Sudanese government introduced large-scale, privately owned agricultural schemes in the Nuba Mountains, about 2000 km southwest of the capital, Khartoum. People's attempts to relocate in new areas were hampered by the state. The large-scale mechanised farms exclude small peasants, while their location in the intermediate land between the semi-arid zone and the rich savannah is a potential source of conflict between pastoralists and farmers.

The appropriation of Nuba land by a privileged political and business elite in the name of development has occurred under both democratically elected and non-democratic Sudanese governments. They have perceived the Nuba as an ally of the Sudan People's Liberation Army (SPLA) and its political wing, the Sudan People's Liberation Movement (SPLM). This has led the governments to apply oppressive measures indiscriminately against all Nuba, including Nuba Muslims, although many of them have no connection to the SPLA/SPLM.

In the 1986 national elections, the Umma Party lost several seats to the Nuba-backed Nuba Mountains General Union and the Sudan Nation Party. In retaliation, the Sudan government turned a blind eye to a series of atrocities committed jointly by the national army and the government-supported militia, the Popular Defence Force (PDF), against Nuba villages which they claimed had pledged support to the SPLA/SPLM.

By 1999, over 100,000 people had been forcibly evicted or displaced by these private agricultural schemes. In a startling example of state oppression, millions of victims of the 1983/85 drought and famine who were trying to find possible survival alternatives by moving into new fertile lands, were stopped in their tracks by state authorities who staunchly opposed their migration, claiming that these areas were demarcated for the future expansion of large-scale private mechanised farms.

The displaced peoples moved from the rural to the urban areas, only to be confronted by a myriad of problems, such as lack of employment opportunities, due both to economic recession and to their inadequacies in skills and education; inadequate health services; poor water and sanitation provisioning, and housing problems. Town Planning Authorities consider the displaced people's settlement illegal and use the police and the army to demolish their houses and repatriate them to the very conditions which caused them to migrate in the first place. The struggle here is between urban refugees, whose main concern is with physical survival, and the political survival of those in power, who fear that poverty and deprivation may contribute to political uprisings, leading to a social revolution. [Mohamed Salih 1999b]

the weakening of local institutions a prerequisite for modernisation whereby the chief's traditional authority ought to be replaced by a modern educated elite from the ruling 'ethnicity', the ruling party or both. (See Mamdani's (1996) work on citizens and subjects.)

Peasants, pastoralists and other subsistence producers whose lives have been ruined by ill-conceived agricultural modernisation are right to associate state and development with authoritarianism. In most cases, state and development constitute the main contributing factors to the deterioration of the socioeconomic and environmental conditions which affect the impoverished and famine-stricken rural communities.[2] Ethnic groups whose land has been appropriated often become part of an organised opposition against the state. As I have argued elsewhere, ill-defined development policies have resulted in widespread discontent and in some cases have contributed to the emergence of national or regional liberation movements and insurgency groups (Mohamed Salih 1999b).

As if the political coercion and economic ruin that beset Africa's rural communities were not enough, by the end of the 1990s, most African states (under considerable economic pressure) had joined the ill-fated structural adjustment programmes (SAPs) of the World Bank and International Monetary Fund (IMF). Of particular interest here is agricultural adjustment which further entrenched the private sector and large-scale private farming. Agricultural adjustment is based on two principles: market liberalisation and the privatisation of public enterprises, including state farms and agricultural marketing boards; and the promotion of private property rights regimes, including a liberalised land market (Gibbon et al. 1993, Mou 1993). Obviously, land privatisation opposes both state (public) land ownership, as well as common property regimes. The World Bank argues that such policy reforms provide security of tenure as a stimulus contributing to price incentives induced by a wide range of liberalisation policies (World Bank 1981, 1989, 1994).

Corina and Strickland (1991) report that, as a result of these policies, landlessness in Africa increased by 15 per cent during the 1980s and the 1990s, and near-landlessness by 30 per cent. Knowing that there are few, if any, employment opportunities in the urban areas to which displaced peoples tend to move (Mohamed Salih 1994, Baker and Aina 1995), it can be inferred that those displaced peasants and pastoralists have, by and large, joined the urban or the rural poor. Contrary to the declared policies of stimulating economic recovery, agricultural adjustment not only failed to assist impoverished rural communities to improve their lot, but actually made many of them landless.

Rural resistance to state oppression is thus not only an expression of discontent, but also represents a struggle to gain access to state power, and to use that power to rid themselves of authoritarian development. Because it controls the production and distribution of material and social resources, the state wields power over the welfare of its subjects. Access to state power and resources has never been equally available to all ethnic groups, and to many it has never been available at all: 'Since those who control the state have used its power to defend their own privileged position, the state has become an object of conflict as well as an opportunity for further political claims. Those left out of the control of the state seek to restructure it in order to gain access to power and resources' (Mohamed Salih and Markakis 1998). The secondary objective is to gain autonomy or independence from what is perceived as a 'non-provisioning state' or 'irrelevant state' as far as the victims of authoritarian development are concerned.[3]

One serious implication of the above discussion is that there is nothing like a unified all-embracing definition of ethnicity and its social functions. The content of ethnicity and its potential mobilisation is contextually determined thus, illustrating its continued viability as an analytical tool. However, beyond the analysis and social functions of ethnicity, there lies another important political function pertaining to its use to protect real or imagined ethnic political claims. In this sense alone, ethnicity can be described as emancipatory, a force to reckon with in resisting state repression or harmful interventions in the name of development, or what I refer to below as an escape route from authoritarian development.

ETHNIC ESCAPE ROUTES FROM
AUTHORITARIAN DEVELOPMENT

While resistance against authoritarian development takes the form of collective action waged by ethnic, liberation and environmental movements, livelihood struggles in the more ethnically heterogeneous urban centres involve both ethnic and multi-ethnic community-based associations. One of the problems for social scientists of all persuasions is ethnicity's ability to coexist with and influence modern institutions. This issue arose during the colonial period when African migrants began to establish urban associations and reinvent 'traditional institutions'. In the circumstances, rural–urban migration (in search of employment and seeking alternative means of livelihood) produced some unexpected social and political dynamics. Immigrants often organised themselves in self-help, community-based organisations and practised rural values in order to support each other through difficult times. For example, given the prominence of ethnicity in most African towns, Shaw (1986) doubted whether the onset of modernity would reduce the value of ethnicity as a viable analytical tool. He describes ethnicity as 'the resilient paradigm', distinguishing between 'old' and 'new' ethnicity. New ethnicity, according to Shaw, is associated with the retreat from urban decline to rural survival in ethnic homelands. New ethnicity engulfs gender and class, and is largely informed by the relative decline of food security and household income. In the face of Africa's economic crisis, ethnic ties offer survival possibilities and linkages between town and countryside (Southall 1988, Baker and Aina 1995), thus making its presence felt all the more.

The emergence of ethnically based associations and community self-help organisations is not new to urban Africa. The literature on the colonial period demonstrates that most African immigrants and job seekers organised themselves in such associations. Banton's (1957) study of urban associations in Free Town reveals the complexity of African urban life and the multitude of strategies that people use to adapt themselves to it. People create ethnic associations in order to recreate aspects of rural life essential for the reproduction of social organisation (such as marriage and death ceremonies). Immigrants are also involved in professional and occupational associations, which are part of the urban milieu in which they find themselves.

Social networks exist which are capable of supplying material goods and services, facilitating remittances and investment to the home areas, and fostering political gains, as well as providing a forum for the exchange of information about job opportunities and public amenities. A number of studies provide testimony to vibrant social, economic and political processes that are traditional in form, but modern in content. Mitchell (1975) studied social networks in an urban situation and analysed personal relationships in central African towns, concluding that social networks based on kinship are essential for the reproduction of rural values in African towns. These networks also perform an important role in enhancing personal political status, as well as economic ties and gains. Ross's (1975) research on grassroots and political behaviour in Nairobi challenged the 'melting pot' theory, demonstrating that modernisation had failed to loosen ethnic ties. In fact, Ross argued, the harsh urban environment forced people to maintain closer links than ever with their kinsfolk.

Furthermore, as demonstrated by Cohen (1977), there is an interaction between formal and informal institutions which extends to the intersection between ethnic and class interests. Doornbos (1998: 22) argues 'there has been rapidly accelerating urban and rural class differentiation in most parts of Africa, at times articulated with ethnic differentiation generally cutting across the ethnic matrix'. In the Ethiopian context, Markakis (1998: 145) observed that, with the recognition of ethnicity as a base of what is now known as ethnic federalism, 'the value of ethnicity attracted numerous ethnic entrepreneurs eager to turn it into political capital. They came from the same merchant sector that previously had stayed clear of political involvement, but who now took up the task of weaving identities.'

To recapitulate, ethnicity is not only a rural phenomenon, but also an urban phenomenon in which associations, social networks and grassroots organisations have been developed to provide services and cater for needs that cannot be satisfied by individuals alone. Research interest has largely shifted to the study of foreign NGOs, however, and where urban studies continue, there tends to be a focus on poverty, the informal sector, or on the application of one of a host of theories of development, such as dependency theory or neo-Marxism.

With the onset of democratisation, the state has allowed people's organisations supporting local development initiatives to operate in their home areas. Ethnic groups supported those political representatives who appeared to be most capable of lobbying the state to secure public amenities. With the drastic decline in their socioeconomic conditions, people began to fall back on traditional institutions and survival strategies in order to eke out a living. Rural, community-based and grassroots organisations played an important role in empowering people and hence enabling them to fend for themselves, thus contributing to the emergence of modern NGOs. (The study by Tidemand et al. (1994) of the new local-level politics in Uganda, Tanzania and Kenya provides an excellent illustration of this point.)

Another important factor in this development was the economic crisis which hit Africa. Failed development, land alienation, destitution and mass impoverishment all stimulate the resurgence not only of social conflicts, but also of ethnically based associations, self-help groups, networks and NGOs. With the beginning of the democratisation process in the late 1980s and early 1990s, and the collapse of the one-party regimes, most African states have loosened their grip on people's organisations.

With the lifting of the restrictions earlier imposed on people's organisations, Africa witnessed a steady increase in the number of non-governmental development organisations, pressure groups and human rights activists. The main activities in which these organisations are involved include community and rural development, environmental rehabilitation, health services, shelter, advocacy, legal aid and human rights, family planning and literacy (see Table 3.1). Material from the United Nations Commission for Africa (1996) shows that ethnically based associations represent less than 1 per cent of the 4,231 people's associations included in Table 3.1. This finding may tempt the reader to jump to the conclusion that ethnicity is no longer an important factor in the way people organise for development.

In explaining this discrepancy, there are a number of factors to take into account. In the first place, due to government regulations, some countries are still suspicious of ethnic-based associations. Some ethnic groups get around this by avoiding giving ethnic names to their non-governmental or

Table 3.1
Approximate number of major NGOs, by country

Country	No. of NGOs	(1)	(2)	(3)	(4)	(5)	(6)
Angola	47	23	10	8	–	4	2
Benin	144	60	30	31	10	4	9
Botswana	43	24	4	2	5	–	8
Burkina Faso	172	90	12	32	17	9	12
Cameroon	89	40	6	23	4	7	9
Central African Republic	86	33	12	16	7	8	10
Côte D'Ivoire	47	22	5	7	3	6	4
Ethiopia	150	39	57	29	5	8	12
Eritrea	16	3	4	3	–	2	4
Gambia	81	31	23	7	4	7	9
Ghana	206	79	57	29	15	12	14
Guinea Bissau	43	27	9	3	–	2	2
Kenya	268	94	78	34	27	12	23
Lesotho	76	36	20	7	3	4	6
Liberia	43	15	5	4	–	6	13
Malawi	98	34	19	4	12	12	17
Mozambique	40	13	7	6	3	4	7
Mali	216	110	28	45	5	5	23
Namibia	150	67	45	16	12	2	8
Niger	69	39	12	4	2	7	5
Nigeria	4,028	1,670	845	345	327	252	589
Rwanda	75	30	19	7	4	6	9
Senegal	144	64	37	14	13	9	7
Sierra Leone	80	41	9	6	–	7	17
Sudan	71	19	24	8	–	19	4
Swaziland	47	29	7	1	–	4	6
Tanzania	147	47	62	9	9	7	13
Uganda	130	56	31	4	17	7	15
Zambia	143	59	37	10	6	8	23
Zimbabwe	289	132	86	17	30	4	20
Total	7,238	3,026	1,600	731	540	444	900

Key: (1) Community development, education; (2) Women, family planning and child care; (3) Community health, environment, water, sanitation and shelter; (4) Legal help, advocacy and human rights networking; (5) Relief/emergency; (6) Religious.

community-based organisations. This is particularly true in squatter settlements and rural areas. Second, modern professional and occupational associations are by nature ethnically heterogeneous. The ethnic factor is less visible here than in the case of non-professional community-based associations in the poor quarters of the urban centres. Third, some urban associations, community-based organisations and NGOs represent a continuous link between modern and traditional community-based organisations. Although the latter are larger in number and more widely spread than modern associations and NGOs, they do not feature prominently in official statistics. Most large squatter settlements are divided into ethnic or semi-ethnic neighbourhoods. Studies have shown that these are less ethnically heterogeneous than the modern residential areas which are mostly inhabited by the upper middle class and other well-to-do classes.

Although the material presented here shows that ethnicity is not just a traditional but also a modern phenomenon, and that ethnic groups organise for development in community-based, grassroots associations, there is no agreement on whether ethnicity is an impediment or an aid to development. As argued in the previous chapter, however, much current development practice treats ethnic affiliation as a backward institutional framework for political organisation.

By inference, development cannot be entrusted to ethnic groups but should be the monopoly of the state, a modern arbiter of different ethnic, religious, economic and other claims. The fact that ethnic groups were so rarely consulted before or after development projects shows not only the denial of ethnicity, but also the authoritarian nature of centralised, top-down, non-participatory development. Community-based organisations and local NGOs took over where the state failed. They are more multi-ethnic and participatory without overdoing the ethos of participatory development, which is often used as an instrument to co-opt rather than to create a space for people to participate in self-development of their own accord.

Ironically, one of the main outcomes of authoritarian development has been the unwitting reinforcement of ethnicity as a countervailing force. Instead of ethnicity being weakened, it has been used by those displaced through authoritarian development as an institutional framework to confront state development policies.

ETHNICITY AND AUTHORITARIAN DEVELOPMENT

One of the main features of authoritarian development is excessive centralisation, with development treated as a monopoly of the state. In fact, the denial of ethnicity by the authoritarian nation-state project is extended to the denial of local community capacity for self-organisation for development. The authoritarianism of the central organs of the state is also reflected in the way in which development is defined in terms inconsistent with the interests of the local peoples. In the face of the appropriation of local community land under authoritarian development, ethnic affiliations become a major institutional framework for protecting common interests and channelling resentment against poverty-inducing development policies. For its part, the state perceives local communities' survival concerns and livelihood struggles as testimony to the misconception that ethnicity is a hindrance to development and an archaic institutional framework for political organisation. Authoritarian developmentalists treat ethnicity as an obstacle to development and a source of conflicts detrimental to development.

In treating ethnicity as an obstacle to development, three factors are commonly stressed. First, ethnically based community organisations are considered a hindrance to national integration; they create independent, self-sustaining socioeconomic communities that show little concern for other similar communities. Second, ethnically based community organisations foster exclusion, nepotism and unfair play in the economic and political distribution of the factors of development. Such organisations have also been charged with the abuse of 'national' resources for narrowly defined ethnic goals. Third, ethnically defined resources (such as ethnic or tribal lands) limit the capacity of the state to intervene for the public good. It is often claimed that agricultural modernisation in many states has been hampered by ethnic claims over lands allocated by the state for national or privately owned projects. The resultant conflicts involving ethnic groups, state agents or the private sector result in political instability, which often frustrates development and discourages 'developers'.

However, it can also be argued that ethnicity is a catalyst for development. In the first place, ethnically based community organisations accept some responsibility for ethnic group members. Such associations are sometimes able to intervene in areas where the state has failed or has been unable to reach out to disenfranchised or impoverished ethnic communities. In many countries, immigrant networks and Diaspora communities have been able to send remittances to support projects such as school building and providing health services. Second, ethnic solidarity can be seen as a motivating factor through which some communities have been able to defend their rights, and support the weak and the needy, thus securing better (re)distribution mechanisms than state-based institutions. Furthermore, ethnically based associations are often much closer to people, more participatory in their operations, in a better position to respond directly to their members' felt needs, and more flexible in redefining priorities and objectives according to changing local circumstances.

I would argue that organising along ethnic lines during periods of hardship or in order to pool efforts for the public good is not an impediment to development. In rural Africa, the existence of ethnically based organisations tends to be more spontaneous than planned. Not all urban community-based, grassroots and non-governmental organisations recruit their membership along ethnic lines; in most cases, people have ethnic and multi-ethnic affiliations. Ethnic and multi-ethnic associations coexist. While it is true that the majority of residents in squatter settlements organise themselves along ethnic lines, this is not to suggest that the poor are ethnicists while the educated are not. I have demonstrated earlier that the African elite has misused ethnicity for narrowly defined political gains.

In contrast to the dominant multi-ethnic nature of community-based associations, at the national and regional levels mono-ethnicity invokes the need for collective action in defence of livelihood, particularly over land. In societies where land is more than an individual property, the struggle over land often takes the form of liberation struggles, insurgency and social movements (see Mohamed Salih 1987, 1994, 1999b). The reliance of the African-educated political elite on ethnicity as a useful political instrument also explains how authoritarian development re-inforces ethnic sentiments. The African political elites have adapted a Western-style, narrowly defined democratic ethos that considers ethnic and local political organisations and aspirations to be obstacles to development. Authoritarian development, as this chapter has shown, is practised both by authoritarian and democratic political regimes. The political elite's dependence on ethnicity as a political resource is duly informed by the nature of the post-colonial state and its inability to create a space for people's political participation.

The relationship between authoritarianism and failed development is all too obvious. With the failure of the state to become an engine of development, the use of force and coercion to secure political legitimacy became a dominant feature of authoritarian development. In the circumstances, both democratic and authoritarian states in Africa have been compelled to shift their main objectives away from development to simply managing and maintaining peace and order. In response, the people's recipe for humanising development is to democratise the state.

POLITICAL RECONSTRUCTION OF AUTHORITARIAN DEVELOPMENT

The current democratisation process is based on the assumption that it is possible to restructure authoritarian development and to put in place a more responsive people-centred development. Three major schools of thought are at play here. The first is modernisation theory in its current incarnation in the trio consisting of democratisation, human rights and good governance. With all their different persuasions, the main advocates of the current strand of modernisation hold on to four axioms:

1. Only an elite committed to and sufficiently aware of the positive consequences of democracy can advance Western-style democracy. In other words, democracy cannot be brought about by uneducated masses; see my earlier critique of the notion of civil society as used in the African context (that is, the modern political forces).
2. There must be a political culture conducive to democratic principles, rules and institutions. This reverts back to an age-old convention that modernisation refers to the institutionalisation of Western values and beliefs in traditional, pre-literate and technologically backward societies.
3. External economic pressure and conditionality are capable of pressurising non-democratic governments out of office through international isolation (for instance, Bashir's Sudan, Nigeria during General Abacha's military rule, and Sierra Leone during the military regime of General Johnny Koromo).
4. A vibrant and politically active civil society is necessary, defined here as modern forces, trade unions, professional associations and pressure groups, human rights activists, an organised opposition, religious groups (church and mosque), etc.

The second and third schools are enlightened dependency theory and, at the left of the school of social democracy, progressive theory. According to these schools of thought, democracy should be defined to include social and economic rights as well as political rights; they forcefully denounce the assumptions put forward by modernisation theory. In their view, democracy cannot thrive under conditions of rampant poverty, illiteracy, underdevelopment and exploitation by advanced capitalist countries. In other words, economic well-being is a prerequisite for the consolidation of democracy.

The trouble with all three theories – modernisation, dependency and progressive – is that they all advocate top-down democratic restructuring and consolidation projects. They miss completely Sen's argument that there are a number of interconnected and mutually reinforcing freedoms that influence and are influenced by development: 'These are: 1) political freedoms, 2) economic facilities, 3) social opportunities, 4) transparency guarantees and 5) protective security.' According to Sen, these instrumental freedoms 'tend to contribute to the general capability of a person to live more freely, but they also serve to complement one another ... The claim that freedom is not only the primary object of freedom but also its principal means relates particularly to these linkages' (1999: 38).

In a sense, restructuring authoritarian development means redefining the meaning and content of development from simple increases in per capita income or high rates of growth, to a comprehensive perspective that incorporates political, economic, social, protective security and transparency guarantees, as suggested by Sen. The implication of this approach is that the fate of democracy has already been decided by the prevalence of authoritarian-dependent development. This development is incapable of either advancing freedom from poverty or offering new development ethics that would create opportunities, transparency guarantees and social security. According to Khotari, the alternative agenda that would thus emerge

> ... is not spectacular or revolutionary capture of power with a view to producing a national utopia. It is, instead, far more mundane yet far more basic – of taking the people seriously, respecting their thinking and wisdom, producing structures and institutions and technologies that can respond to their needs, and adopting attitudes and values that respond to their voices. Voices from below, voices of the powerless who have so often entrusted power to a political party or a set of parties within the parliamentary framework but whose expectations have all along been belied. [1993: 123]

In Africa, as in most developing countries, the dominant free market forces that negate all that is humanly possible structurally determine democracy's fate. People's voices are either selectively heard or systematically silenced using democracy as an instrument of oppression. An authoritarian circus rotating between military and civilian politicians fosters the circulation of authoritarian development benefits. Thus, like authoritarianism, democracy under conditions of extreme poverty opens wide the space for the enrichment of a politically vocal, educated, mostly urban, rent-seeking and land-based elite (see Chapters 5 and 8).

Restructuring authoritarian development means reversing the logic of exclusion and marginalisation of the poor, and encouraging the empowerment of the institutions that foster distributive justice and enables the poor to access resources vital to their survival such as land, water, forest. These are the very resources that authoritarian development appropriates as an exclusive domain for its destructive interventions. True democracy is akin to true development and both should ideally be responsive to people's needs, and particularly to the needs of the majority, if majority rule and preference are an essential part of a meaningful definition of democracy.

4
The Potential Role of Democratic Political Education

The point of departure of this chapter is that there are compelling reasons to seek a better understanding of the linkages between the current democratisation process and the need to enhance the role of education in political transformation. At least two factors support the quest for envisaging a conscious and deliberate role for political education in the current democratisation drive. The first is the need to create critical awareness of political phenomena by facilitating an open and balanced discussion, and analysis of a range of opinions and problem-solving scenarios. The second is awareness (or increased consciousness) of positive political values pertaining to liberty, justice, equity, respect for the law and authority, participation and enhanced personal and collective obligations for the public good (Harber 1997).

The democratic political education which this chapter defends presents a critique to conventional concepts of political education in populist regimes premised on the pretence of knowing what is good for the people and therefore demanding unconditional obedience and loyalty to authority. In fact, populist political education, according to Komba, 'tended to support, reinforce and legitimate the existing political system; the content emphasised factual knowledge of existing institutions of government, while its teaching methods were characterised by a devaluation of discussion of controversial topics' (1999: 69).

One of the questions this chapter grapples with is how to tread the thin line between emancipatory political education for democratic consolidation, and the fear that such an education could be used as an instrument of political indoctrination. This is a legitimate question, considering that one of the main negative features of authoritarian political education was intolerance to dissenting views and constructive critique. Such authoritarian political education had failed its objectives in advancing the state cause as (a) a credible guardian of the public good, (b) an engine of development and (c) a legitimate and democratic expression of people's preferences.

However, with the creation of a democratic educational establishment and political institutions which respect human rights, political education can play a vital role in advancing the democratic process. As I will argue below, the African educational establishment itself is authoritarian and must be liberated from the stranglehold of a hegemonic statist ideology in order to be able to play a positive role in enhancing the drive towards desirable democratic values and practices.

The democratic political education this chapter advocates draws its tenets and strength from a conception of democracy based on the tripartite relationship between society, state and education. This tripartite relationship is informed by the conviction that the role of education is to assist citizens to understand and negotiate their interests *vis-à-vis* the state, without losing the possibility of integrating that role into the normative system of the state. As part of the nation, the citizen is expected to contribute to national integration and to extend solidarity to encompass positive regional sentiments. Therefore, the purpose of political education should be incorporated in the principles of social science pedagogy as well as being an inseparable part of a distinct notion of civic education. In this way, political education is expected to increase political awareness, often measured by political participation, information, media exposure and engagement in politics. The general tendency, according to Zaller (1990), should be to explain rather than indoctrinate normative tendencies and regularities of political awareness, including attitude stability, support of people-centred policies and consistency of ideology and political practice.

Most African post-colonial states have developed a hegemonic and intolerant notion of political education based on a narrow, state-driven nation-building project. This project has unfortunately been inspired by intolerant attitudes towards other 'national' cultures, languages, religions and ethnic groups. In these circumstances, political education is considered part of the overall objective of the educational establishment, which has explicitly been used as an oppressive political instrument to further the official ideology of the state.

POLITICS OF EDUCATION: COLONIAL AND POST-COLONIAL

The penetration of Western education in Africa began during the colonial period, initially by missionaries and in the later part of the nineteenth century through formal education. The latter development was motivated by the introduction of colonial administration and the expansion of commercial firms which, according to Cowan et al. (1965: 4), 'sought indigenous auxiliaries to fill the lower posts, since they were less expensive than expatriates'. A major development in education occurred after the Second World War when secular education began to expand throughout the African colonies.

The first meeting of African education experts was held in 1961 in Addis Ababa, Ethiopia, with the main objective of articulating the role that education should play in independent Africa. Although the delegates were critical of the literary and humanistic nature of the colonial education, they conceded that 'it had provided an introduction to liberal political philosophy of the West' (Cowan et al. 1965: 14). Cowan and associates also add that, with the beginning of African agitation for independence, there was an articulate, well-organised group of African politicians who were generally the products of the best schools in their own countries and who had often been educated in European and North American universities. In the same vein:

> As Africa entered the decade of independence in the 1960s, the number of politicians with experience in teaching was striking. In Ghana and Nigeria thirty percent of the members of the legislatures were teachers. Most of them were drawn from rural areas ... The high prestige inherent in the new Western-style secular education, as well as the prerequisite of the English language for national political career, converted teachers into highly eligible parliamentarians. [Mazrui 1978: 3]

Admittedly, the colonial education had awakened the African's voiced agitation for independence. The African-educated elite had discovered that they could ameliorate the administrative skills of their colonial counterparts and that they were eligible to take part in the political structures of the colonial state. In pursuance of this objective, African professional and ethnic associations and trade unions were established and soon transformed into organic structures of political parties and pressure groups. The downside of Western-style education was that it inculcated into the minds of the African-educated political elite a sense of superiority over their own people. Even African independence leaders have done little to emancipate their own minds from the bondage of Western education. As indicated in Chapter 2, the educated African elite has kept intact an education system that fosters dependence and cherishes authoritarianism.

Shortly after independence, education was expected to grease the machinery of development by producing skilled human resources. Education was thus used to achieve the twin projects of the post-independence state: socioeconomic development and nation building. We have already looked at the former; the latter shows that the relationship between politics and education could also be exploited to achieve national integration among diverse linguistic, ethnic and cultural groups. Hence the need for political education emerges as an instrument for confronting 'ethnicity' by promoting a 'national culture'. There was a sense of urgency in the post-colonial state's deliberate intervention to transform schools and universities into melting pots, an extension of the political institutions responsible for cultivating a national identity devoid of ethnic schism. Education in that sense was used as an instrument for aggregating national interests expressed in the ideological strands and political preferences of those who controlled the state.

Ironically, the nation-building project has undermined its own mission from within, by emphasising a homogenising educational system which denies people the right to use their own vernacular languages or publicly exhibit their pride in ethnic belonging and cultures. The nation-building project has developed into a nation-demolishing project, particularly where the state has failed to meet people's aspirations for development and for an improvement in their standards of living. In some cases, ethnic groups opted out of the state and turned to the very ethnic institutions which the nation-building project conspired to subvert. Today, the grand aim of developing the nation-building project into a nation-state project has been confronted by massive problems, which are symptomatic of the failure of that particular notion of political education.

The unholy alliance between the official state ideology and education created an oppressive system of education, that treated the opposition forces or those who entertain alternative political thought as enemies of the state. Education became an instrument for teaching and learning the official ideology, for internalising the political ideology of the state. For instance, the courses commonly taught in socialist states were on the fundamentals of Marxism-Leninism. This ideological and political education was a key aspect in forming the socialist personality, with the aim of transforming party members into political subjects or ideologues. Similar associations between political education and the state ideology were rampant in African socialist states as well as in various forms of military and authoritarian regimes. Pro-Western states had likewise taught modernisation theory and a devout critique of communism and the Marxist-Leninist thought associated with it. For example, in the particular case of political science teaching, Oyugi contrasts the situation of socialist Tanzania with that of pro-Western Kenya, arguing that:

The Marxist political economy emerged when there was a lot of talk about the need to Africanize the discipline (political science) – especially after the founding of the African Association of Political Science (AASPS) in 1973 in Dar es Salaam. Unlike Dar es Salaam, there were no ideological debates in Nairobi surrounding the introduction of the political economy course and the movement captured neither the other sub-disciplines of political science nor extended to other social science disciplines. The social sciences remained as 'bourgeois' as they had been before. [1989: 3–4]

In authoritarian political regimes, political education meant political indoctrination, and that is certainly not the type of political education that this chapter advocates. Populist political education has done more harm than good to the nation-building project. It has undermined the development of democratic institutions and suppressed people's aspirations for representative political organisations. This is mainly because, in most African states, the concept of nation building has been abused by authoritarian regimes intolerant to dissenting voices.

The basic features of the political orientation of education can also be captured from the policy statements of some states. For instance, Tanzania's education for self-reliance was predicated on 'developing political consciousness among the pupils to enable them to understand and facilitate the implementation of the country's policy of socialism and self-reliance. Pupils are therefore required to understand and implement party resolutions and government policies in their environment' (Tanzania Ministry of Education 1980: 9).

In Ethiopia, the objective of education was 'to reflect socialist principles of pedagogy whereby education is defined to aim at raising political consciousness of the masses, at promoting research, and at enhancing individual productivity which would in turn positively influence the overall level of production' (Provisional Military Government of Socialist Ethiopia 1984: 134).

Similarly, the declared policy of Sudan's Ministry of Education (1971: 3) was to 'promote socialist thought in conformity with the aims and principles of the May Revolution, awakening of the working people to take part in national and socialist action as well as promoting people's social, cultural, economic and spiritual life'.

Although there is nothing basically wrong with assigning education a national mission in order to improve the quality of life and expand citizens' social, economic and political well-being, the question is whether education has really been used for these noble goals. In the ten countries (Ethiopia, Ghana, Kenya, Nigeria, Tanzania, Sierra Leone, Somalia, Sudan, Uganda and Zambia) whose education policy I reviewed for the purpose of writing this chapter, education was used as an instrument for political indoctrination rather than for promoting democratic values. The educational orientation of these countries was also subject to changes according to shifts in state ideology, and external relations according to the prevalent East–West political divide (for an Africa-wide perspective see Nweke's 1992 contribution on political education for collective self-reliance in Africa).

However, it is important to emphasise that the objectives of political education in these countries differ not only between socialist and procapitalist oriented regimes, but also in the degree of political pluralism each political regime would allow. For instance, although governed by a one-party state, Tanzania has been less repressive than other one-party states such as Ethiopia, Kenya and Somalia, despite their different ideological orientation.

The end of the Cold War and the introduction of political pluralism have been greeted by attempts to project the nature of political change and its desired influence on the new orientation of education policy. This trend has taken two broad routes: the restructuring of national education policy to enhance the propagation of democratic political culture; and the emergence of informal education institutions operated by civil society activists training their membership in legal advocacy and human rights education. The latter is funded through special development allocation projects designed to propel the capacity of civil society to articulate its position *vis-à-vis* the state (elaborated in Chapter 1). These two dominant trends and their contribution to democratic consolidation will be examined below.

DEMOCRATISATION AND POLITICAL EDUCATION

In this section I take the Tanzanian case in detail to illustrate how education has been used in order to socialise students and teachers to democratic values. Tanzania was in a sense blessed with a leader like Nyerere who through his vision of Ujama and the quest for self-reliance was able to position education in a very privileged position.[1] But as many authors have shown (Boesen et al. 1977, *Ujamaa: Socialism from Above*, among others), his vision was populist and bureaucratic and gave the state agents and the party functionaries much power over the people. The democratic education instilled, including the concept of education for self-reliance (see the concise summary of the concept in Ishumi 1988) by the party and its political education was far from democratic. The school was shared by ideologues and party slogans and gave little room for the type of democratic political education this chapter proposes. In the democratisation process the government of Tanzania has given attention to the political role of education as will be critically demonstrated.

In the build-up to multi-party democracy, Tanzania established special commissions to look into the future of the one-party system. In 1991, the Presidential Commission on the Future of Tanzania's Political System (known also as the Nyalali Commission and referred to here forthwith as the Presidential Commission) reported its findings. Although the report is about the future of the one-party system, it emphasised that in order to change people's attitudes from those informed by an authoritarian political environment to those consistent with political openness, they should be encouraged to nurture critical thinking.

The Presidential Commission also laid great significance on the importance of linking political reform (that is, multi-party system and democratisation) to educational reform. The educational recommendations in the report aim at ensuring that

> Tanzanians build a new political culture of opposition without violence and of criticism without rebuke. This culture should be promoted during the period of transition (to democracy) through a strategy of education about the Constitution and about national values for the general public, in schools, colleges, institutions and universities. Such a culture must recognise that opposition is not treason. Therefore the commission recommends that the parliament/council should have a recognised Leader of the Opposition. [Government of Tanzania 1991: 7–81]

Komba, in his succinct contribution to the debate on choosing between civic or political education, laments,

> Tanzanian's education establishment was less enthusiastic about political education and its emancipatory potential and therefore resorted to the teaching of civics, a more neutral and consensual subject ... Moreover, the political learning is undermined even further by the use of medium English which is less familiar to the students. Thus, there is a wide gap between the vision of Nyalali Report which envisages a politically charged curriculum, and the vision of the curriculum specialists who want to suppress politics. [1999: 60]

Theoretically, the attitude of Tanzania's educational establishment towards political education is no different from what recent studies of political education have revealed. Political education enables citizens to further understand, among other political concerns, public policy processes and the political mechanisms through which the processes are generated. It socialises the young to become natural defenders of democracy, liberty and rights. However, defending democracy, liberty and rights in situations where the leadership's lust for power is pursued irrespective of constitutional norms, is an unwelcome pursuit from that leadership's perspective (for a fuller account of democracy and education in Tanzania see Nyerere 1973 and 1968a, Buchert 1994, and Harber 1997).

The Tanzanian political and educational establishments' resistance to integrating political education in the curriculum and its substitution with the study of civics shows its approach towards bringing about a structural change of political attitudes. If political education is to address issues relevant to political literacy, then Gale (1994) is right in defending it by arguing that political literacy confronts and responds to the question: 'What is required of the citizens of a democracy to ensure their individual and social rights?' Gale answers this question by saying that citizens must be so educated as to have an intellectual awareness of the inherently political nature of public life and their relationship with the state. Gale calls for changes in the way the public is educated about the justice system, given the risk of complacency in this crucial area of public life. This is one of the ways in which progressive political education should take root, for it is not in the interest of the dominant classes that benefit from an educational establishment premised on domesticating citizens to serve their interests below:

> It is not important whether educators are conscious of following a domesticating practice, since the essential point is the manipulative dimension between education and learners, by which the latter are made passive objects of action by the former. As passive individuals, they are not invited to participate creatively in the process of their learning; instead they are 'filled' by the educators' words. Within the cultural framework of this practice, educators are presented to learners as though the latter were separated from life, as though language-thought were possible without reality. In such educational practice, the social structures are never discussed as a problem that needs to be revealed. Quite contrary, these structures are made obscure by different forms of action that reinforce the learners' 'false consciousness'. It would be extremely naive to expect the dominant classes to develop a type of education that would enable the subordinate classes to perceive social injustices critically. [Freire 1985: 101–2]

Evidently, political education without improvement in people's standards of living could instil apathy and could likewise undermine the positive aspects of political activities designed to ensure state legitimacy. In responding to such claims often made by populists, Boyle and Mulcahy (1993) make the point that the quality of freedom and democracy is directly linked to the level of knowledge and education of citizens. The question then becomes: if we cannot be ignorant and free, how smart do we have to be to keep our freedom? The answer they gave: we should be pretty smart and getting smarter every day. To be a citizen means to be a lifelong student; but the ultimate pay-off is a more enlightened populace and a democratic society that works better.

Although it is obvious that education is politics, the role of political education is not only strictly political; it also has ultimate linkages to other life pursuits, including legal advocacy, social development, empowerment, subversion of exclusionist practices, conscientisation and so on. Democratic political education has an important role to play in explaining the nature of political reforms and transition, management of political parties, electoral education and reform and the creation of citizen politics. However, the manner in which this can be achieved differs from one country to another; it is therefore necessary to caution against any blueprints and readily transferable packages.

DEMOCRATISING AFRICA'S EDUCATIONAL ESTABLISHMENT

The education policies of most African countries reveal that the educational establishment cannot be entrusted with the burdensome task of consolidating the democratisation processes under way. Both in policy and practice, the behaviour of the educational establishment demonstrates that while they are comfortable with teaching civics, they are deeply uncomfortable with political education which calls for democratising the educational establishment itself. Unfortunately, the African educational establishment has internalised, through a long history of serving dictators and one-party states, authoritarian values that are not easy to eradicate in a short period of time.

The institutionalisation of a liberating democratic political education is possible only when the educational establishment itself is democratic and not fearful of empowering the younger generation whom it has to prepare for the future. Conventional, backward-looking educational establishments must be liberated before they can be entrusted with the task of generating democratic citizens. Authoritarian educational establishments can hardly be expected to enhance the spread of democratic values or increase political awareness to emancipate citizens or encourage their free engagement in public life and public policy setting.

Without democratising the educational establishment from its inherent position as the guardian of the status quo, social transformation and the accompanying political emancipation will be impossible. If left as it is, it will fail to fulfil its role in advancing individual liberty or societal interest in democratic governance and non-authoritarian political values. If education passes on the notion that non-conformity is politically unacceptable or socially unjustified, it will lose its ability to challenge the genesis of political apathy and instead will foster those values that encourage control and domination. Such an educational establishment could even usher in the Marcusian (1972: 23) contention that, 'an abstract liberty can be made into a powerful instrument of domination based on the absence of basic liberties'.

The main question here is, how can an educational establishment that served dictators through most of the post-independence period also be made useful in serving the conception of a society experiencing democratic transition based on the principles of advancing liberty and citizen-focused politics? No matter how the educational establishment may attempt to rethink its mission, the formalising role of education must be challenged in order to give way to an essentially different social and political order. Exposing and clarifying the national or regional and even universal goals and strategic objectives of people as sovereign citizens cannot be achieved by the negation of the status quo alone, although this is vital. Such a persuasion would fall short of creating a political space for the participation of informed people in democratic activities, as a prerequisite for consolidating democratic values. An educational mission that is based on the ability to express only that which is taught, is a system which falls short of decolonising the imaginative and creative faculties of those on whom the educational mission is focused. Such education betrays society and merely reproduces intellectual fads; it is tantamount to the subversion of societal goals, particularly the democratic values that are based on the negotiation, debate and discussion of multiple scenarios of problem solving.

The mismatch between education and the democratic values which society is eager to embrace is particularly clear in the educator–student relationship. In most of Africa, the distance between educator and student is so wide that accessibility to the educator becomes impossible. Cases of critical thinking being repressed, silenced or treated as troublesome are common. It is impossible to imagine that a non-democratic educational experience can yield democratic results or help foster the goals of democracy. Democracy has to be practised by educators who are themselves supposed to uphold the higher values that they teach and propagate. An authoritarian educational system is apt to produce an authoritarian society, particularly in the form of an educated elite which generally forms the future leadership. Education can and has been used as a means of control and an instrument to achieve undemocratic political goals by authoritarian regimes and one-party states. The institutionalisation of democratic values needs a solid basis: a democratic, non-authoritarian educational system and a democratic society are mutually reinforcing.

Evidence of the educational establishment's failure to achieve its mission can be found in the current resurgence of ethnic identities hostile to the state. As I argued in Chapter 2, ethnicity has outlived nationalism. The educational establishment could thus be seen as having failed in its historic nation-building mission (Mohamed Salih 1996). Education is the main instrument to create nation states in those states which contain groups of diverse ethnicities and nationalities. Because the nation-building project was itself authoritarian, it therefore needed an authoritarian educational establishment to implement it. The relationship between the conditions of rational action and the conditions of social rationalisation has been grossly distorted, with state interests parting company from societal goals. Instead of a society-in-state scenario (Migdal et al. 1994), societal demands are expressed in terms of state interests and not in terms of the state as a medium for social interaction between diverse social forces. The rationalisation of world-views in the Weberian sense is far from being self-evidently rational. Habermas (1990) is of the view that the life-world is a correlate of the concept of communicative action, referring to collectively shared basic convictions, to a defused, unproblematic horizon within which actors communicate with one another and seek to reach an understanding. In my view, this however does not deny that the actors may have some serious differences within each collective, no matter how we define it. Seen from a theoretical perspective, the critique of the educational establishment relates to its failure to aid the nation-building project in at least two respects:

- In most of Africa, more than forty years after independence, communicative action still occurs within communities whose cultural tradition, social integration and personal identity are those of the ethnic group or the locality.
- Actions are not only embedded in the symbolic space of the life-world, in Habermas' sense, but are also organised into functional systems. Those functional systems have not, in most cases, been allowed to engage in a meaningful communication of interests with the dominant state institutions and policy orientations. No wonder that the failure of the nation-building project has produced, in some cases, political disintegration and in most other cases a sense of political apathy.

Instead of creating a political space for enhancing communicative action, education has become a communicative barrier through the use of foreign languages and foreign symbols, intended to suppress national languages and centuries-old traditions and ethnic symbols. In essence, the inner colonisation of the life-world means that any attempt to replace primordial communicative action with a superficial nation-building action will produce secondary or pathological effects (Habermas 1990). In that respect, the African nation-building project has produced secondary and artificial national as well as personal identities which oscillate between modernism, which is taught, and traditionalism as the prescient constituent of a life-world's communicative action.

There is compelling evidence showing that there is a growing schism between objectives of African education and the interests of the African people. Recently research on endogenisation and African universities concluded that:

> It was, however, the lack of progress toward Africanization since independence that most marked the interviews and research. Both the political models dominating the post-colonial African scene, Enlightenment-inspired Western democratic capitalism and Marxism, have neglected – if not suppressed – domestic awareness of ethnic and cultural aspects of social life. Further, what African (political) schools of thought arose have favoured the building of nation state, or even pan-African consciousness, over the promotion of ethnically charged endogenous realities. [Crossman and Devisch 1999: 8]

Based on field research, a review of teaching materials and education policy documents, this conclusion is testimony to the urgent need for the educational establishment to undergo a liberating process to rid itself of the remnants of colonial education. My own experience in this regard is no different, demonstrating clearly that the African educational establishment largely operates with dictates and with little room for manoeuvre *vis-à-vis* the state.

To liberate the educational establishment is to redefine the goal of education and to develop it into a citizen-responsive system with democratic meanings attached to its mission. An oppressive educational establishment does not support democracy; rather, the 'pedagogy of oppression' presents a false and oppressive notion of political education, with a coercive populist pursuit:

> The pedagogy of the oppressed animated by authentic humanism (not humanitarianism) generosity presents itself as pedagogy of man [*sic*]. Pedagogy which begins with the egoistic interests of the oppressors (an egoism cloaked in the false generosity of paternalism) and makes of the oppressed the objects of its humanitarianism, itself maintains and embodies oppression. It is an instrument of oppression. [Freire 1972: 39]

I would therefore emphasise the need for what Gramsci (1971) calls an alternative educational revolution that conceives of change not as a mere seizure of power by democrats but as the building of a new culture of counter-hegemony into a historical bloc which, over time, becomes the democratic state of citizens. A recent commentary by Cohen (1995) on this powerful statement emphasises the importance of Gramsci's work for education as a life-long process with a vital political purpose, particularly in an information-based society where hegemony may take new, invisible forms. Since these different forms may range from the politically overt to subtle forms of domination, counter-hegemony must also take different forms (for the debate on this subject see Gorham 1992, Garnham 1993).

Hence, I do not subscribe to a rational explanation of a consciousness change among citizens and institutions, nor do I advocate a populist political education, the politicisation of the educational establishment, or a presupposed notion of moral education. What I have attempted to explore is the possibility of introducing a positive and desirable change of political attitudes through sustained efforts to be exerted on and eventually replaced by an alternative educational establishment. One measure short of democratising the educational establishment is the creation, outside the educational establishment, of an alternative venue for political education fully committed to citizen-focused politics.

THE STAKEHOLDERS IN DEMOCRATIC POLITICAL EDUCATION

The educational establishment is still largely preoccupied with conventional methods, which at best foster compliance, and at worst obedience. This is particularly so in societies which have recently emerged from one-party systems where education was used as a tool for political indoctrination. In most such countries, the educational establishment itself was non-democratic. Transition to democracy, educational reforms and the values that political transformation enhance have thus often been resisted by the vestiges of the authoritarian education establishment which feared that such democratic values may herald the relinquishing of what is left of their claim to power.

When the educational establishment is nothing more than one of the institutions entrusted by the state operators with maintaining the status quo, it is difficult to achieve much in the way of consolidating the democratisation process. If political expediency within the educational establishment rules over the perspective of citizen-politics, it is likely to hamper any attempts to break the well-established alliance between power and knowledge (Foucault 1980). Described by Finnegan (1994) as close-knit, full-time, localised, long-lasting and exclusive, the so-called academic community is more resistant to changes in privilege than any other community. Privilege here refers not only to financial benefits:

knowledge itself is probably the greatest of all privileges. Notwithstanding the financial difficulties which the educational system is undergoing, it is clearly the most suitable institution for subverting the pedagogy of oppression, and encouraging new democratic values.

Do I seem to be suggesting that African democratisation should be guided, beyond the watchful eye of the 'international community', in order to allow people to reap the benefits of political participation and to further the call for people-centred institutions of governance? Citizen politics, action and practice, without democratic institutions and political awareness, are doomed to failure, incapable of delivering results or internalising the political values enshrined in the pursuit of democracy. Nor would democratic slogans such as participation, accountability, transparency, good governance, expanding the public space, and so on, be able on their own to head off the twin effects of political ignorance and lack of information on which citizens can base their own opinions about public life and the organisational parameters within which responsibility towards the private and public good needs to be constructed (Boyle and Mulcahy 1993). In my view, progressive political education should assert citizens' rights to free expression of political views and ideas, the right to organise and develop a critical understanding of public policy. If only for this reason, there is a need for citizen politics with an empowering and an emancipatory role, leading to engagement at local, national and regional levels.

Without citizens' participation, therefore, the defining moments of 'citizen politics' can easily be appropriated by a small number of political-actor-operators who monopolise agenda setting and political issue-making. In this respect, one of the essential ingredients of public policy education is to help the emergence of a new generation who think and act as liberated citizens emancipated from the fear of performing new roles and setting new agendas for 'social progress'. That agenda should be advanced with an understanding of what responsible and engaged citizenship implies at the local, national and regional levels. In my view, this type of new citizenship should be conceived within the overall democratic process which should ideally assist people to discover the true meaning and benefits of positive, but self-chosen, political participation.

The stakeholders in political education are those who have a stake in the current democratic process: the present generations who heralded the transition, and the younger generations whom we hope will carry the torch and internalise the democratic values for which it stands. Its mission is not only the creation of a vibrant civil society (political parties, opposition groups, grassroots organisations, indigenous people's groups, trade unions, women, youth, professional associations, the alternative media and so on), but also the consolidation of the transition to democracy. It should also spark discussions beyond the political arena to provide leadership in all the walks of life which involve civil society. The African state and the educational establishment must certainly have a stake in political education, given its role in providing people with pedagogy in constitutional literacy and public policy awareness. The real stakeholders, however, are the younger generations who will be better prepared for the future.

INTERGENERATIONAL ASPECTS OF
GOVERNANCE AND LEADERSHIP

Leadership/governance encompasses a broad spectrum of political, social, economic, recreational, professional, entrepreneurial and other leadership domains. In other words, it does not refer to the narrow definition of a leader as a holder of a political position such as president or minister. Leadership here includes the politically delegated or economically, recreationally or socially recognised agency of individuals, groups and associations. The current debate on the need to empower civil society and strengthen its capacity to generate legitimate and accountable governance pays more attention to how to reform or change leadership and less attention to intergenerational aspects of leadership. Such an approach could be described as a statist approach, which assumes that the reform of the state will result in the reform of the system of governance. Implicit in this approach is the possibility of ensuring political change by changing the state ideology or reducing the level of state hegemony over civil society. Although it is possible to achieve change in situations where the democratic principles and values of political expression and practice are internalised by civil society, results might not be uniform or identical in different societies. Indeed, it is doubtful whether a leadership that holds itself accountable to the people would automatically spring from the wreckage of a previous regime. Recent African history bears testimony to the fact that, even when a political regime is ousted, the new power holders may either lack a new vision or prove incapable of providing responsible and accountable leadership.

While intragenerational concerns with governance can be understood at the level of contingency and short-term needs, intergenerational processes are more important and essential in situations where leadership failures are apparent. Hence the moral basis for intergenerational considerations go beyond the argument that younger generations should be prepared for the future, whatever that future may be, to one that recognises the fact that today's youth constitute the future generation of governance. More than any political processes, generations have to be aware of the burdensome task of assuming leadership and aspiring to create a better system of governance (see Gorham 1992 on citizenship and political education, and Jenniages 1993 on education and political development among adults). As already noted, leadership/governance not only transcends political leadership, but also encompasses the need for responsible governance and citizens in all walks of life.

The systems of governance Africa inherited from the colonial regimes call for what Ake (1994) describes as the second liberation of Africa from the stranglehold of an oppressive authoritarian leadership. Leadership forums have been useful intragenerational exercises, but have fallen short of becoming a forum for intergenerational dialogue on the issues that concern the younger generation and potential leadership/governance. Responses to issues of necessity (democracy, the rule of law, good governance and development) and those of opportunity (social development, growth, environment and social justice) require more than discussion for the sake of discussion; they require political realism with relevant and engaging debates, explanations, political imagination and even crude predictions.

It has been argued that the contextual, localising approach adopted in analysing the meaning of democracy provides an orientation toward inquiry, but not an assured set of options (Boyle and Mulcahy 1993). A perspective on governance and democracy needs to be worked out in response to specific situations as interpreted by those participating (civil society and state) in the political processes. The cumulative impact of this on the younger generation is enriching in at least two ways. First, the particularity of the national situation or governance crisis does not imply that there is nothing in common in terms of objectives, aspirations and outcomes of political processes. Second, informed inspirational principles, associated with the understanding that systems of governance overlap and carry certain universal underpinnings, are necessary and compelling whether the point of reference is democracy, human rights or people-centred governance institutions.

In a sense, great visionary opportunities for the enhancement of the human condition are contained within the fluidity of circumstances that make this period of history turbulent and fraught with contradictions and surprise (Falk 1995). However, even the project of strengthening critical civil society cannot succeed if the genesis of today's turbulent conditions is not consciously and deliberately treated as an aggregation of turbulent conditions suffered by localities and communities. The empowerment of present and future citizens should build on local, national and regional strengths before such great visionary opportunities are embraced. It is difficult for generations that, in the twenty-first century, will live in a global village to be confronted by narrow meanings, mistrusts and political constraints attached to the regional reach. Despair, given the chance, will work its way towards diminishing hope, despite the possibilities and hope that live in the minds and hearts of the younger members of civil society.

At a more practical level, the younger generations and youthful members of civil society hardly know each other. Economic crises and decades of hostilities have contributed to the suspension of exchange programmes, study visits and other forms of interuniversity educational and cultural programmes. Despite talk of globalisation and the emergence of a global civil society, regional integration is yet to become a shared dream. The defining forces of the current regional order are beset by mistrust. The influence of the political elite is yet to be exerted at the national level, while the regional level is still open to 'common risks and fears': displacement, insurgency, famine, environmental degradation and poverty. It is difficult to be a visionary without having a stake in the future. Political education should take over where the universities have stopped – from education to empowerment and engagement in public issues. It should provide a regional forum, which could be expanded in the future to further extend the role of civil society and its capacity to generate accountable and people-centred governance. This is a local, national, regional and global imperative in which the youthful sections of global societies should be encouraged to participate.

There are discernible links between the objectives, functions and mission of education and wider societal goals which go far beyond classroom instruction to create a platform for dialogue and self-discovery. African state and civil society are increasingly discovering the startling realities of a democratic era in which education in all its forms could be used as an instrument for empowerment. The case for political education, with special emphasis on consolidating the current democratic transition, is justified on several grounds. In the democratisation process which is sweeping the region (with a few exceptions), both state operators and civil society are experimenting with political organisations and practices with little knowledge of the rights, obligations and responsibilities of citizens. Many citizens' organisations and democratic institutions are run by a small number of political operators who often know next to nothing about how to empower their constituency or give guidance on the basic rights of the citizens living in democratic societies. Others have opted out of state-sponsored political activities altogether, to the extent that they lose any influence on the essential public policies that affect their lives in a very profound way.

There is a fine dividing line between, on the one hand, loyal opposition, the politics of accommodation and dispensation and, on the other, confrontational, conflictual and violent politics with its far-reaching negative ramifications. In the quest for quick results, democracy is often sacrificed and civil dictatorships have in some instances replaced military rule. Not only does the educational establishment need to be liberated – it is financially bankrupt and needs to be rehabilitated before it can take on citizen-centred functions. Entrenching education in governance, democracy and development will enable future generations to revitalise the regional sentiments that have been lost by decades of subregional conflicts and wrangling. It will provide an opportunity for the future leaders of the continent to get to know each other and discover how similar they are, with the ultimate goal of increasing political, cultural, social and economic regional interaction and regional awareness within and between states.

In short, it is worth exploring the democratic potential of political education, given that it should not be used for the inculcation of a particular state ideology. It should instead address the need for participation, the rule of law, human rights, accountability, and responsible and transparent governance. Political education ought to be a facilitating vehicle for consolidating the fragile democratic gains African civil society has managed to bring about after bitter struggles and sacrifices. Following on from this, it is therefore necessary to restructure the role of education so that it becomes democratic and capable of empowering civil society. In view of the pressures which civil society has to confront in order to provide a new type of leadership in all walks of life, people-centred political education could play a pivotal role in consolidating democracy and enhancing respect for human rights.

The main obstacle to democratic political education is the fact that most African leaders still fear their people, and therefore concentrate on maintaining the status quo. In democracies without democrats the fate of democracy is often decided by the very elements that use it as an instrument of political domination – a less risky route to positions of power and influence than outright dictatorship.

In essence, all explanation of the current challenges to African democratic transition is bent on the role of a dominant educated political elite. Unfortunately, as the following chapters will reveal, this political elite is at the core of the political problems from which the African continent has suffered. The option here is either we pursue a business-as-usual approach by assuming that education has no social purpose, or else search out for ways to democratise the education establishment for a more sustainable democratic tradition. Such an education should, by and large, be based on political values closer to the people in order to enhance their participation in developing an African democratic experience peculiar to the region and its diverse socioeconomic contexts and political cultures.

5
An Authoritarian Circus: Sudan from NIF to Multi-Party Democracy?

More than any other former British colony, Sudan had a relatively long and ironically positive experience of multi-party democracy prior to independence. During the closing decade of colonial rule, the Sudanese educated political elite appeared modernist in attitude and action. They established a wide spectrum of political parties ranging from the far-left Sudanese Communist Party to the far-right Umma (Nation) Party, and including the moderate Nationalist Unionist Party (today the Democratic Nationalist Party). As in most of colonial Africa, Sudan had its share of the 'first wave of democracy', and witnessed the emergence of political parties and fronts with strong connections to the Egyptian Islamic movement, particularly the Muslim Brotherhood (today the National Islamic Front – NIF, with its political offshoot, the Sudan National Party).

However, this early start with multi-party democracy and the relatively orderly transition from colonial to national rule did not prevent Sudan from drifting into various forms of authoritarian rule, successive military coups, one-party regimes and civil dictatorships. Sudan's democratic reversals have taken on the form of a vicious circle of successive democratic–military–democratic–military governments. The political consciousness of Sudan's governing elite has been frozen in the ethos and nostalgia of pre-independence political dispensations, remaining under the shadow of political institutions that were originally created to maintain the status quo. In a sense, the Sudanese political elite became prisoners of their own creation – political parties and organisations premised on harnessing political modernisation to the interests of a minority class, insensitive to the aspirations of the populace. The 'bewitchment of reason' became so entrenched in the Sudanese political establishment that it was believed to be the only substitute for alternative politics. The call for democracy is therefore structured around regimes of truth premised on a 'legitimation crisis' rather than on people's aspirations for a more representative system of government (see Beck 1995 and Habermas 1972). Alternative regimes of truth that might contribute to a power shift from the elite to a people-dominated democracy are rejected in favour of the glorification of political genealogies founded on pre-independence struggles or God-given spiritual qualities, both of which largely ignore people's call for more workable alternatives. The struggle against an authoritarianism that was originally motivated by the political elite's disrespect for the institutions of democracy has become the one political asset that they hope can bring them back to power. The struggle for democracy by an elite that has little to show in terms of socioeconomic or political achievements has become a hallmark of Sudanese politics. While they gain credibility through the struggle for democracy, they simultaneously lose that same credibility by failing to heed democracy's call for responsible governance.

Obviously, the Sudanese political elite is comfortable with the regimes of truth that it has nurtured in order to be able to maintain the status quo, sometimes at any cost. Ironically, that same elite is desperate to understand the political sentiments and appreciate the political aspirations of a populace that long ago lost faith in the elite's capacity to learn from past mistakes. Political engagement is therefore seen as relocating their political energy from authoritarianism to democracy, where short-lived democratic regimes are successively followed by long-term authoritarianism. It is even more ironic that Sudanese elite of different political persuasions still use the discourse of independence, the events that had shaped it and the configuration of political life that ensued, to claim and justify their right to rule. As a result they have offered virtually no new visions of governance, or alternative institutional arrangements.

This chapter introduces the concept of circular reversal and looks at its relationship to political decay and the failure of the political elite to deliver the minimum requirement of democratic rule or to create sustainable democratic institutions. It traces the various waves of democracy in Sudan from pre-independence to independence in an attempt to understand why circular authoritarianism has thrived in one of Africa's earliest democratising states.

PRELUDE TO WESTMINSTER-STYLE, MULTI-PARTY DEMOCRACY

Although the history of the Sudanese struggle against Anglo-Egyptian rule is well documented, its development from rural insurgency to urban educated elite-based struggle began to emerge only during the early 1920s. The struggle itself was inseparable from the increase in people's aspirations, fomented by an apparent improvement in Sudanese access to Western education. To that extent, British colonial rule had sown the seeds of resistance in an energetic and largely outward-looking middle class which found in education a resourceful instrument for resisting the British. Many authors have shown that the late 1920s represented a period of undeniable transformation of the rural-based Sudanese economy and society as they were increasingly exposed to Western influences, including modern education, health facilities, transport and communication, as well as limited industrialisation.

Unusually, the army was also one of the main modernising forces as well as being among the first to resist the British rule under the Egyptian influence. For instance, on 9 August 1924, the cadets of the Military School staged a demonstration in support of the White Flag League and in protest against the arrest of Ali Abdel Latif. They carried with them the green Egyptian Flag and a photograph of King Fuad of Egypt (Beshir 1974: 81). One result of the implication of Egypt in the protest against British rule was the withdrawal of Egyptian officials and troops and the removal of militant nationalists from Sudan. A Sudan Defence Force, paid for by Egypt, came into existence in 1925.

The linkages between the spread of Western education and the birth of a Sudanese national consciousness should not be underestimated. With the spread of modern education, post secondary school graduates began to entertain the idea of creating a Sudanese political identity independent of Egypt and Britain. In 1937, the Graduates Congress was created, at Omdurman Graduates Club. The Congress was welcomed by the colonial government, which hoped to establish an Advisory Council in which graduates were represented. The British looked upon the Congress as an embryonic form of Sudanese nationalism and a vehicle for developing a Sudanese political identity separate from Egypt. In fact the objectives of the Congress were more mundane: to protect the economic interests of its members and to bring their problems to the attention of the government. In 1941, the politicisation of the Graduates Congress began in earnest when seemingly non-political demands such as the call for the expansion of education and the increase of development projects in line with national interests began to show some signs of growing nationalism. (See Beshir 1969 and Woodward 1990 for more details on the general issues surrounding the birth of a modern Sudanese intelligentsia.)

By 1941, the Congress began to polarize into advocates of cooperation with the government, particularly those with neo-Mahdist inclinations, and Egypt-loyalists who invited the involvement of Sayyid Abdel Rahman (the leader of the Ansar) and Sayyid Ali Al Mirghani (the leader of the Khatmyia). With the departure of the pro-cooperation group, those left in the Congress established the Ashigga political party, supported by Sayyid Ali Al Mirghani and the Khatmyia sect. In response to this, the section of the Congress supported by Sayyid Abdel Rahman Al Mahdi established the Umma Party, supported by the Ansar sect (Abdel Rahim 1969).

From then on, the Congress became the battleground between these two leaders, who subsequently found wider support among educated Sudanese. The graduates were divided into two main religio-political groups: the Khatmyia religious sect and its leader Sayyid Ali Al Mirghani who, by forging an alliance with Egypt, took a stand of opposition to and non-cooperation with the British administration; and the Ansar religious sect under the leadership of Sayyid Abdel Rahman, who became committed to a policy of cooperation, if not collaboration, with the British (Beshir 1974: 168).

The 1940s thus witnessed the emergence of the Sudanese political parties which continued to shape the political destiny of the country, with varying degrees of success and failure. The fact that these political parties were created within the confines of the Sudanese historical religious families meant that their political support base remained largely religious. This also implies that Islam was part of the Sudanese political equation much earlier than contemporary writings would suggest, identifying political Islam with the National Islamic Front which was created in 1985 – more on this later. Let me first briefly introduce the context within which these political parties emerged, and their role in the pre-independence wave of democratisation.

The Umma Party was established in 1945 by Sayyid Abdel Rahman Al Mahdi, the son of the Mahdi, the leader of the Mahdiya revolt against Turco-Egyptian rule (1881–98). The *ansar* (literally 'followers') of the Mahdi constituted its main political base, and it was premised on an anti-Egyptian stance. In fact, Sayyid Abdel Rahman went as far as denouncing the White Flag League (the Sudanese officers' rebellion against British rule) and other pro-Egyptian elements like Sayyid Ali Al Mirghani, the leader of the Khatmyia religious sect, as offshoots of Egyptian nationalism. As the founding father of neo-Mahdism, Sayyid Abdel Rahman relied on his father's nineteenth-century ideological creed: the *ratib* (book of prayers) and *manshurat* (proclamations). *Shabab Al Ansar* (the Ansar Youth), armed with the *ratib* and the *manshurat*, constituted a paramilitary organisation in the tradition of Islamic *jihad* (holy war). However, putting a non-militant gloss on *shabab Al Ansar*, Sayyid Abdel Rahman described its mission as one for *jihad al nafs* (within one's self) and not for waging holy wars against the infidels. Sayyid Abdel Rahman became the first Imam of the *Ansar* and, by demanding *bya* (an oath of allegiance), he was able to gather considerable support from a large number of people previously part of the Mahdiya movement. The *bya*, *ratib* and *manshurat* became the ideological symbols that united the *Ansar* regardless of their ethnic diversity, with groups ranging from the Baggara of Kordofan and Darfur to the populations of central and northern Sudan (Warburg 1978: 21–4).

Sayyid Abdel Rahman reconstructed *gezira* (island) Aba, where his father had begun his rebellion against Turco-Egyptian rule in 1881. Together with the Mahdi tomb in Omdurman, Aba Island became a destination of *muhajirin*, holy pilgrimage. Shabab Al Ansar provided labour and a contingent of political support. Warburg describes the Ansar as 'the only organisation in the Sudan, before World War II which enjoyed mass support based on its popular Islamic mission, and at the same time sought to assume a leading political role'. Moreover, 'the choice of name Umma is significant as it suggested a link with 19th century Mahdism and its belief in the establishment of an Islamic Community (*Umma*). It was also significant in the political sense as it implies adherence to the concept of Islamic unity and to anti-sectarianism, while advocating a separate Sudanese national entity' (1978: 41).

From the time of its establishment, the Umma Party championed Sudan's full independence under the slogan 'Sudan for Sudanese'. This could be explained in terms of its followers, the majority of whom were not riverine Sudanese; and its suspicion of Khatmyia and its leader Ali Al Mirghani's strong relationship with Egypt. The following sections illustrate how the events which surrounded the establishment of the Umma Party and its position in the debate over independence continue to influence the processes that shape current political developments in Sudan.

During the colonial period, most of rural Sudan was self-governed under the Native Administration system, which was tribal in outlook. The rise of nationalism (including the White Flag and the Graduates Congress, supported by various organisations and intellectuals), an apparent increase in political consciousness among the educated elite, and aspirations for self-rule among the public convinced the British administration that a modern system of government was needed to succeed the tribally based Native Administration. The enactment of the Local Government (Municipalities, Towns and Rural Areas) Ordinance (1937) was a testimony to this new, more liberal orientation, and a move away from 'divide and rule' to a more comprehensive system of government with fewer British administrative personnel (see Howell 1972).

Although riddled with rules which excluded Sudanese from fully participating in the democratic process and which assigned crucial executive and legislative powers to the Governor General, the British opened a narrow political space for Sudanese political parties to operate, even if it was within a limited dispensation. I refer here particularly to the British decision to devolve further power to the Sudanese. This intention became a reality when devolution was confirmed by the promulgation of the Advisory Council for Northern Sudan Order (1943). In comparison with other colonies, the Advisory Council gave northern Sudanese politicians a considerable say in how the country was governed. In fact, that influence has never diminished since then.

Besides the President (Governor-General) and Vice-President (Civil Secretary), the Council consisted of 28 members, 18 of whom were ordinary members appointed from Province Advisory Councils. Three Sudanese from each of the six northern provinces of Blue Nile, Darfur, Kassala, Kordofan, Khartoum, and the Northern Province participated in the Advisory Council, selected either by direct elections or recommendation of the Governor. The remaining ten members were appointed at the discretion of the Governor-General; of these, it was stipulated that two should be of Sudanese origin. It was also stipulated that honorary and extraordinary members could be appointed to the Council: these would be individuals who wished to attend or present informed views to the Council. Sayyid Abdel Rahman Al Mahdi and Sayyid Ali Al Mirghani were appointed in the category of 'distinguished Sudanese notables'.

Although the Advisory Council was not free to decide on all issues, and although the Civil Secretary (as Chair of the Council) was authorised to suspend the discussion at any time and on any matter that was deemed sensitive, the Council provided the participating Sudanese with a first glimpse of how modern government institutions operate. Some might say that the Sudanese were to learn from colonialists who came from one of the world's better-known modern democracies. Others might claim, conversely, that the Sudanese elite learnt their early political lessons on government from colonialists – individuals who, by the very nature of their colonial creed, proved themselves second-rate democrats.

Either way, it can certainly be argued that some of the worst lessons that the Sudanese political elite learnt from their early exposure to modern political institutions persisted and, in so many ways, continued to haunt them after independence. One example was the granting of privileges to the leaders of the largest political parties (Unionists and Umma), whose claims to power continued to derive legitimacy from the role their ancestors played in that particular period. The sons and grandsons of Ali Al Mirghani and Sayyid Abdel Rahman still demand to be treated, if not as holy, at least as a category of extraordinary personalities.

Other negative political ramifications that were particular to the Advisory Council included the selective manner in which issues were presented for debate, some issues being thoroughly discussed and resolutions passed in adopting them, while others were not fully discussed or were passed without a resolution. Abdel Rahim laments that 'The powers of the Council were entirely advisory; advice, however, could only be given within certain limits and in accordance with strict rules which were set out, in considerable detail, in the order' (1969: 139).

Following the end of the Second World War in late 1945, Egypt (the junior colonial partner) and Britain announced their intention to enter into negotiations to grant self-government to Sudan, leading to independence. The Sudanese political elite was divided on whether Sudan should break all ties with Egypt (Umma Party and Independence Front) or unite with Egypt (Unionists and Ashigga). Soon, the country was embroiled in violent demonstrations and clashes between the supporters of independence and the supporters of unity with Egypt. On 17 April 1946, the Governor-General declared that Sudan should define its relationship with Britain and Egypt after and not before independence.

During the early preparations for Sudanese independence, the public mood was for expanding the Advisory Council into a national representative Council. Mindful of the criticisms levelled against the Advisory Council, the Sudan Administration Conference (22 April 1946) made the recommendation that a Legislative Assembly of elected Sudanese members from the whole of Sudan should be established. The Legislative Assembly's functions would include the exercise of legislative, financial and general administrative functions in conjunction with a newly constituted Executive Council, which would replace the Governor-General's Council (Abdel Rahim 1969: 160). After considerable wrangling between the British and Egyptian colonial powers, the Executive Council and Legislative Assembly Ordinance was endorsed in its final form on 19 June 1948.

Less than two years after the establishment of the Executive Council and the Legislative Assembly, the Sudanese political elite decided that it wanted more powers *vis-à-vis* the British Governor-General. This is well illustrated by the Khatmyia petition of March 1950, for the Amendment of the Executive Council and Legislative Assembly Ordinance, and particularly the call for direct elections, and the demand to vest the Assembly with legislative and financial powers that should be binding on the Executive Council. For its part, the Umma Party petitioned for full independence. After considerable objections by Egypt and in spite of Britain's attempt to secure a deal that would serve its interests in Sudan, the Constitution Commission was established to transfer power to the Sudanese. Independence seemed within the grasp of the Sudanese elite, which was still divided between supporters of complete independence and advocates of unity with Egypt. The dissolution of the Constitution Amendment Commission on 26 November 1952, and the abrogation of the Anglo-Egyptian Condominium rule following the Anglo-Egyptian Agreement of 1953 made Sudan's chances of gaining independence even more real.

At this point we may recall the debate mentioned in Chapter 2 on nationalism and the political nature of African political parties. The Sudan case illuminates that discussion on at least four points. First, it provides an example of the existence of African political parties prior to independence, and shows their limited representation in the political structures created by the colonial administration. Second, the role of these political parties (or at least their leaders) was purely consultative, with the colonial powers in full control over decision making. In this way, they were 'token' political parties, although none the less important in fulfilling a necessary sociali-sation function. Third, the colonial experience gave rise to elite-dominated democracies that refused to recognise the right of the masses to hold the political leadership responsible and accountable. In fact, the colonialists feared the masses more than the educated elite who were created by them. Fourth, the colonial powers sanctioned the emergence of ethnically based political parties because ethnicity was the most visible and most common form of political organisation.

Unfortunately, the independence of Sudan in January 1956 was consummated in blood. The religious, ethnic and linguistic divisions already in place during the colonial era became the spirits that haunted the independence leadership and those that succeeded it. A combination of religious sectarianism, ethnically based regionalism and war became the symbols of Sudanese political instability. The war which had begun in August 1955 continued unabated, costing millions of lives and contributing to the collapse of least three consecutive democratic govern-ments, as the following section of this chapter will illustrate.

DEMOCRATIC PRACTICE UNDER NATIONAL RULE

One of the fates of democracy is that it is often hindered by complex conflicts that create conditions not conducive to its practice. In war-torn countries, questions of physical survival develop their own dynamics, often working against normal political practice. Even in normal circum-stances, adherence to democratic principles can be affected by the intensity of ethnic and religious tensions created by competition over resources. Sudan combines both a tense war situation and ethnic and religious differences that have occupied much of the debate on the civil war.

The ethnic and religious complexity of Sudan is mind-boggling: 56 ethnic groups are divided into 597 subgroups speaking some 115 major languages. Islam and Christianity are the main religions, with 27 different religious sects and Sufi orders and at least five Christian denominations. While the North is predominantly Muslim, the South is mainly Christian, with some traditional religions still practised by large numbers of the population (see Beshir et al. 1985).

Although ethnic and religious diversity are not unique to Sudan, and are not necessarily a cause of war, ethnicity and religion have exhibited particularly destructive forces that have contributed to fuelling one of the longest civil wars in Africa. However, ethnicity and religion alone are not sufficient explanations: in my view, the South–North conflict is a result of the long history of mutual hostility characterised by northern domination over the South. The North is relatively more developed than the South and, because the South has suffered from almost four decades of war (1955–1972, and 1983 to the present), it has lost most of the education, health and administrative infrastructures that were created in the pre-war era.

Sudan's first democratic election was announced on 25 March 1953, just four days after promulgation of the Self-government Statute. The election was organised by the Sudanese and was held over a protracted period of time (2 November–10 December 1953). It was declared by the Electoral Commission to have been generally peaceful, fair and free, although some complaints were filed against 'corrupt' practices. Of the 97 seats in the House of Representatives, the Nationalist Unionist Party won 51, the Umma Party won 22, the Republican Socialist Party 3, the Southern Party 9, independent candidates 11, and the Anti-Imperialist (that is, clandestine Communist Party) won 1. Of the 30 electoral seats in the Senate, the Nationalist Unionist Party won 22; it also accounted for 10 of the 20 members appointed by the Governor-General.

The Constituent Assembly could count amongst its achievements the 1953 elections, the establishment of the parliament, the approval of the Transitional Constitution, and the declaration on 31 December 1955 of 1 January 1956 as Sudan's Independence Day. One of the first priorities of the independent Sudanese state was to develop a home-grown parliamentary constitution capable of accommodating the aspirations of its peoples with their diverse cultural, religious and ethnic backgrounds, and socioeconomic expectations.

Sudan's first national government and multi-party democratic system were born in crisis. Just three weeks into independence, the government led by the Nationalist Unionist Party failed to pass the budget, and less than two weeks later the Prime Minister (Al Azhari) barely survived a vote of no confidence. To make things worse, 21 members of the Nationalist Unionist Party, with the support of Al Mirghani, created a new political party called the People's Democratic Party. The political party with the largest number of members of parliament was thus divided into two distinct groupings (the Nationalist Unionist Party and the People's Democratic Party), and coalition politics became inevitable. In 1956, an Umma Party-led government, supported by members of the People's Democratic Party, was sworn in under the premiership of Abdalla Khalil:

This coalition was strictly a marriage of convenience of two partners with opposite foreign and domestic political interests save one: to exclude their NUP rivals from office. In that latter goal they succeeded, and even managed to perpetuate themselves at least temporarily by extending the life of the Constituent Assembly until summer 1957, when a new parliamentary Election Act was adopted. This Act called for general elections in early 1958. [Bechtold 1976: 188]

Polling for the second parliamentary elections took place between 27 February and 8 March 1958. The number of constituencies was increased to 173 for the House of Representatives and 30 for the Senate. According to Bechtold: 'There were no disturbances on polling day and it is to the credit of the organization and the performance of the electoral commission that no serious complaints were lodged against it. Eyewitness reporters were overwhelmed by the orderliness of the voters at the polling stations and by their evident dedication to pass this "test of nation-building"' (1976: 190).

The 1958 parliamentary election was the first election for which two political parties (Umma and the People's Democratic Party) were able to form a pre-election coalition, pooling their resources. The election results were a reversal of the 1953 results. They gave the Umma Party the largest number of seats in parliament (63) and in the Senate (14). With its ally, the PDP, winning 26 parliamentary and 4 senate seats, and with the Southern Liberal bloc – a loose association of southern Sudanese – easily won over, the coalition had secured a majority, and an Umma–PDP government was sworn in.

The Umma–PDP alliance certainly inherited a weak economic base, but it added to the problem by failing to diversify the country's monocultural economy that depended on cotton as its main export crop. The government expanded the Gezira Scheme by half a million acres, actually increasing the economy's cotton-dependence. The situation was further aggravated by low production and falling international prices for cotton. The government's counter-measure was to offer the Gezira Scheme tenants a minimum price for their cotton, resulting in huge unsold stocks (Holt and Daly 1979: 169).

The Umma–PDP coalition began to unravel when it was rumoured, in October 1958, that a PDP–NUP reconciliation was imminent, under the auspices of Nasser of Egypt. The implication of a PDP–NUP coalition for the Umma Party was its exclusion from power. To pre-empt this possibility, the then Prime Minister Abdalla Khalil prompted his schoolmate, General Ibrahim Aboud, to assume power. The military coup of 17 November 1958 was thus instigated by the Umma Party, although the

Mahdi family managed to distance itself from the event. The coup was also noteworthy for the lack of popular support ready to defend Sudan's new and fragile democracy. The main reasons for this are summarised by Holt and Daly:

By mid-1958 the position of the government was fast becoming intolerable. Deteriorating economic conditions were underlined by the obvious incapacity of the political parties to cope with them. Serious national issues were seen to be subordinate to increasingly hectic maneuvers necessitated by the unworkable Umma-Peoples Democratic Party. Political machinations reached a finale in the late summer when the Umma leadership began actively to explore the possibility of coalition with Azhari's Nationalist Unionist Party. This was complicated by reports of a possible Nationalist Unionist Party-Peoples Democratic Party alliance, which, if consummated, would remove the Umma from power in yet another bizarre maneuver. Before any of these plans could be fulfilled, however, the army stepped in and swept away parties, politicians and the parliamentary regime itself. [1979: 170–1]

Bechtold argues that:

The capriciousness of party politics in 1958 was distasteful enough for the majority of the ordinary Sudanese. But when it became compounded by economic reversals, the atmosphere changed from distasteful to unbearable. Foreign exchange reserves had dwindled from 62 million Pounds Sterling to 8 million, and the balance of trade continued in a negative spiral with no relief in sight following a poor cotton crop harvest. Import restrictions on important consumer items added to the open grumbling; and soon public demonstrations ensued. The lack of systematic management and public order was patently clear and could not even be ignored by the well-disciplined military. [1976: 197]

Three important lessons can be drawn from Sudan's first post-independence democratic experience. First, the Sudanese political elite continued their wrangling over office and prestige often at the expense of pressing national issues. They failed in the first instance to prove to the public that they were trustworthier than the colonial administration. Their failure in this respect and the general impression they left among the public was that they were disorganised and cared less for public interests than for consolidating their own power positions. Second, political proliferation and the newly created offshoots of the conventional political parties and factions had barely transcended the sectarianism of the political parties they rejected. Some of these divisions remained loyal to the leaders of the two main religious sects, because of their material and ideological dependence on them. Third, the military extension of political rule has become a norm (as will also be illustrated in the case of Nigeria and Sierra Leone). As the Umma Party had invited the army to take power in 1958, so did the National Islamic Front, which master-minded the 1989 military coup. These three lessons show that Sudan's political elite sowed the seeds of democratic failure during the first decade of independence and has, since then, continued to harvest the agony of its own creation.

SECOND WAVE OF DEMOCRACY AND
THE PERIL OF SECTARIAN PARTY POLITICS

General Aboud's military regime (1958–64) has been described by many commentators as politically stable, with considerable economic success and the highest level of economic prosperity ever experienced by the Sudanese. However, the regime curbed people's freedoms by banning political organisation, trade unions, strikes, and freedom of the press and speech, and suspending the constitution. In the words of Bechtold (1976: 203): 'the civilians' mistrust of the military manifested itself by popular refusal to give credit to the military for the accomplished economic progress.'

The Aboud regime was confronted by the war in southern Sudan. In the southern Sudanese daily reality, the British seemed to have been replaced by northern Sudanese colonialists: the administration, the army, the police and all symbols of a foreign occupation force remained intact. Apparently determined to use brute force to achieve national integration, the military regime stepped up the military campaign, backed by policies of Arabisation and Islamisation. These policies included the promulgation of the Missionary Societies Act of 1962 and the expulsion of foreign Christian missionaries from southern Sudan.

The beginning of the end of Aboud's regime was sparked in mid-October 1964, when the Khartoum University Students' Union organised a rally to discuss the problem of southern Sudan. The death of a student in confrontations between the riot police and the students galvanised the national resistance against the military. The Front for the Professional Organisations, a broad-based alliance of political organisations and professionals, was established; a general strike was organised and in less than two weeks Aboud announced the dissolution of the Military Supreme Council, thus signalling the end of the first military regime in Sudan.

A transitional period was necessary to enable political parties to prepare to re-enter political life after a number of years of suspension. This transition period lasted until February 1965 when the second national election after independence was held. The election was contested by the Umma Party, Nationalist Unionist Party, People's Democratic Party, Communist Party, Islamic Charter Front, the Socialist Democratic Congress and other minor political parties. It was also at this time that a number of regional political organisations such as the Beja Congress and the General Union of the Nuba Mountains emerged. These regional political organisations were to play an important role in the post-1965 political development of the Sudan, as will be demonstrated in the following sections of this chapter.

Of the 158 territorial constituencies, the Umma Party won 76, the Nationalist Unionist Party 52, the Islamic Charter Front and the People's Democratic Party 3 each. The Nuba Mountains Union, the Beja Congress, and the independent candidates won 24 seats. The Umma Party and the independent candidates did not win any of the 15 graduate constituencies; the Nationalist Unionist Party and Islamic Charter Front won 2 seats each, the People's Democratic Party won 8, and the Communists and their sympathisers won 3 seats.

The Constituent Assembly was convened on 10 June 1965 to approve the NUP–Umma coalition, with Mahjoub as prime minister. The coalition lasted for just one year. In 1966, Al Sadig Al Mahdi was sworn in as prime minister when Mahjoub was forced out of office by a vote of no confidence. Al Sadig's government did little better, and in March 1967 Mahjoub was returned to office after yet another vote of no confidence, heading a coalition of NUP, PDP and three Southern groupings. This politically fragile coalition lasted to the end of 1967 when a new parliamentary election was announced for early 1968.

Some commentators describe the 1965–68 period as the worst in Sudan's experience with parliamentary democracy. Sudan's democratic practices were characterised by political factionalism, nepotism, corruption and unprecedented personalisation of state power and misuse of political authority. There was also a general neglect of pressing national issues, particularly the civil war in the South, worsening economic conditions, and high unemployment among school leavers and university graduates alike.

With the unification of NUP and PDP under a new name, the Democratic Unionist Party, they won the largest number of parliamentary seats (101) in the 1968 election, followed by the Umma Party, which by then had split into two factions under Al Sadig and his uncle (Al Hadi) who won 36 and 30 seats, respectively. This election demonstrated a strong showing for southern Sudanese political parties. For instance, the Sudan National Africa Union (SANU) won 15 seats and the Southern Front (SF) won 10 seats. The Beja Congress, the Political Union of the Nuba Mountains and the Islamic Charter Front lost ground, winning 3, 3 and 2 seats, respectively. The rest of the 218 seats went to smaller political groupings, including the Communist Party which, since it was banned in 1967, had to camouflage its candidates among the independents.

A coalition between the Umma (Al Hadi faction) and the Democratic Unionists assumed power under the premiership of Mahjoub amid political intrigues and constant fear of counter-coalition and loss of personal power. Poor government performance, political intrigues, factionalism, contradictions between stated policies and actions, and the absence of any sense of direction prompted Sudan's second military *coup d'état* on 25 May 1969.

NIMEIRI: FROM SOCIALISM TO ISLAM

The May 1969 military coup was led by Colonel Jaafar Nimeiri, the leader of the Free Officers movement within the army. That the Communist Party was heavily implicated in the coup was evident in the fact that in the ensuing Revolutionary Command Council, four of the ten members were communists. While all political parties were banned and their leaders arrested, Abdel Ghaliq Mahjoub, the Secretary General of the Sudanese Communist Party, not only remained free, he also addressed political rallies in support of the government. However, the honeymoon – or rather, the reluctant alliance between Nimeiri and the Communist Party – was shattered by a failed military coup engineered by officers loyal to the Communist Party on 19 July 1971. (For more information on the Communist military coup against Nimeiri and its repercussions see Warburg 1978 and Niblock 1987.)

After the failure of the Communist Party coup, Nimeiri's economic policies were largely influenced by the brand of Arab socialism developed by Gamal Abdel Nasser with its strong emphasis on central planning and state ownership of the means of production. Politically, Nimeiri's aim was to eliminate the influence of the sectarian political parties in Sudanese political life and to create a secular socialist state. To achieve this goal, Nimeiri chose to create a one-party state under the political guidance of the Sudanese Socialist Union (SSU), a union of the working peoples (farmers, workers, professionals, intellectuals and the army). The structures of the SSU and those put in place by the newly instituted People's Local Government Act of 1971 were identical. Among the main objectives of the SSU was the creation of a secular socialist national identity. Linked to this was the aim of bringing government closer to the people by stripping the sectarian parties of their tribal base which was inherent in the Native Administration System (1921) established during colonial rule.

For their part, the sectarian political parties (Umma and Democratic Nationalist Union) and the Muslim Brotherhood were not going to stand idly by and wait for their political foundations to be dismantled by the Sudanese Socialist Union. They organised themselves under the umbrella of the National Front, a marriage of convenience, with the overthrow of the Nimeiri regime as its main objective. The National Front was able to organise several demonstrations and stage a series of military coups, all of which ended in failure. The most serious of these was the 1976 coup attempt, supported by a 3,000-strong invading National Front force from military bases in Libya.

Following the 1976 coup attempt, Nimeiri and his opponents adopted more conciliatory policies. In early 1977, government officials met with the National Front in London, and arranged for a conference between Nimeiri and Al Sadig Al Mahdi in Port Sudan. In what became known as the 'national reconciliation', the two leaders signed an eight-point agreement that readmitted the opposition to political life in return for the dissolution of the National Front. The agreement also included the restoration of civil liberties, the freeing of political prisoners, reaffirmation of Sudan's non-aligned foreign policy, and a promise to reform local government. The SSU also admitted former supporters of the National Front to its ranks, including Al Sadig Al Mahdi and Hassan Al Turabi. Al Turabi became the Attorney General under whose advice Nimeiri introduced Islamic *sharia* laws in September 1983, while Al Sadig became a member of the Central Committee of the SSU.

Prominent members of the dissolved National Front contested the 1978 National Assembly elections as independent candidates and between them won 140 of the 304 seats. In observing those elections, it became clear that the SSU was, for the first time, divided between conservatives who supported the continuity of its socialist tradition, and radicals whose intention was to steer the government away from its socialist orientation. Others, particularly the sectarian parties and the Muslim Brothers, saw these developments as an opportunity to enhance their own political interests, to weaken the SSU from inside in a bid to take over power when the time was ripe. Many SSU veterans felt that the SSU had lost its ideological, political and social purpose with the inclusion of the very forces that had fought for its demise.

Nimeiri's greatest triumph during his first ten years in power was the Addis Ababa Agreement. After 17 years of civil war between the North and the South, the Addis Ababa Agreement was signed in 1972, between the Sudan Government and the main southern rebel group, the *Anya Nya* Movement (the poisonous snake) or Southern Sudan Liberation Movement (SSLM). The Addis Ababa Agreement brought peace and granted the South regional autonomy within a united Sudan. After the Addis Ababa Agreement, the South was ruled under the Regional Self-government Act for the Southern Provinces until the promulgation of the Regional Government Act in 1983.

Nimeiri's move away from socialism, or socialist rhetoric, and towards Islam came in September 1983, when he announced the introduction of the Islamic law (*sharia*), which became better known as 'September laws'. Hassan Al Turabi, then Nimeiri's attorney general, presided over a thoroughgoing reform of the judicial system and its harmonisation with the principles of Islamic law. In the South, full-scale civil war erupted again as a reaction to the introduction of Islamic laws by the northern-dominated government, and the division of the South into three regions (which undermined the Addis Ababa Agreement) in a typical 'divide and rule' policy. The Sudan People's Liberation Army (SPLA) and its political wing Sudan People's Liberation Movement (SPLM), were established in 1983, perceived by its leaders as an all-Sudanese national movement. The combination of the South's redivision, the introduction throughout the country of the *sharia*, the renewed civil war, and growing economic problems eventually contributed to Nimeiri's demise.

In Sudan's highly charged political and social milieu, the use of ethnicity and religion as well as economic and political leverage have produced one of Africa's longest civil wars. In such a turbulent political reality, democracy can be used as an instrument of dominance. Large ethnic groups can always secure the votes of their ethnic constituencies and, in alliance with other ethnic groups that have similar religious affiliations, can control the state.

By early 1985, public anger and disappointment with the Nimeiri regime reached uncontrollable proportions. Political unrest was characterised by sporadic strikes and protests over pay, while high prices for consumer goods, a deteriorating situation in the health service, regular power cuts and petrol shortages, an inadequate supply of drinking water, and high unemployment all fuelled public anger. Sudan's usual answer to political stalemate struck again.

On 6 April 1985, a group of military officers, led by Lieutenant General Abd-Al Rahman Siwar Al Dahab, overthrew Nimeiri while he was on a visit to the United States (he later took refuge in Egypt). A Transitional Military Council (TMC) came to power with a pledge to return Sudan to democratic rule. Like all military governments, the TMC suspended the constitution, dissolved the SSU, the secret police, and the parliament and regional assemblies, dismissed regional governors and their ministers, and released hundreds of political prisoners.

Siwar Al Dahab's short reign of power will be remembered by Sudanese on both sides of the political and religious divide for its failure to repeal the Islamic *sharia* laws, a major factor in the failure to reach any meaningful dialogue with the SPLA/SPLM leadership. As later events would show, the southern Sudan and the question of Islamic *sharia* law were among the main factors behind the demise of Sudan's third wave of multi-party democracy.

SUDAN'S THIRD WAVE OF PARLIAMENTARY DEMOCRACY

In March 1986, the Sudanese government and the SPLM produced the Koka Dam Declaration, which called for a Sudan 'free from racism, tribalism, sectarianism and all causes of discrimination and disparity'. The declaration also demanded the repeal of Islamic *sharia* laws and the opening of a constitutional conference. All major political parties and organisations, with the exception of the Democratic Unionist Party (DUP) and the National Islamic Front (NIF), supported the Koka Dam Declaration. To avoid a confrontation with the DUP and the NIF, Siwar Al Dahab decided to leave the *sharia* question to the new civilian government.

Sudan's multi-party general elections, following 18 years of rule under Numeiri, took place in April 1986, and forty political parties contested the elections. Among the main new players was the National Islamic Front, an alliance of social forces with Islamic orientation, including the Muslim Brotherhood organisation and its surrogate organisation, the Islamic Charter Front. The election results confirmed a strong showing for the National Islamic Front, which won 51 seats. The Umma Party won the largest number of seats (99), followed by the Democratic Unionist Party (64). The regional parties such as the Nuba Mountains General Union, Sudan National Party, and the Beja Congress won 13 seats, while the Communist Party suffered the worst defeat in its political history with only one member of parliament elected.

In June 1986, Al Sadig Al Mahdi as Prime Minister headed a coalition government, with the DUP, the NIF and four southern parties. The question of whether to repeal or codify the Islamic *sharia* laws came to haunt Al Sadig's government, which failed to achieve any of its pledges to the electorate. The old curses of Sudanese multi-party democracy returned in full force, including intrigue, nepotism and personalised state authority, leading to political instability and public discontent. In less than a year, Al Sadig Al Mahdi had dismissed the government and formed a new coalition with DUP and the southern political parties.

In my view, the second Umma–DUP coalition was a non-starter. It reimposed the state of emergency in July 1987, it failed to reach even a workable understanding let alone an agreement with the SPLA/SPLM leadership concerning the war in southern Sudan, while the economic crisis was intensifying with no end in sight. As a result of disagreements about how to proceed in all the above fronts, the DUP withdrew from Al Sadig's government, while the NIF refused to join any coalition while the state of emergency was in place.

Al Sadig presided over a government in limbo. It took him more than six months (until May 1988) to pull together another coalition, consisting of the Umma, NIF, DUP and some southern parties. Within another six months, in November 1988, this coalition too became unworkable, particularly when Al Mirghani, the DUP leader, as well as the SPLA/SPLM and other political parties signed the Koka Dam Declaration in Addis Ababa. The Koka Dam Declaration demanded, among other things, the convening of a National Constitutional Conference, a cease-fire, the suspension of the Islamic *sharia* laws and lifting of the state of emergency. Initially, the Umma Party sided with the NIF in opposing the Koka Dam Declaration, the former on the grounds that it would boost the image of its coalition partner and its leader Al Mirghani, the latter on the grounds that the suspension of the *sharia* laws may be a step towards their total repeal in the future.

The political stalemate was further complicated by an ultimatum issued by the Commander-in-Chief of the Sudan Armed Forces, Lieutenant General Fathi Ahmad Ali, in which 150 senior military officers demanded that Al Sadig Al Mahdi should establish a government of national unity and take serious steps towards negotiating a peaceful solution to the civil war. On 11 March 1989, Al Sadig responded to this pressure by dissolving the government. Without the participation of the NIF, a new coalition comprising the Umma–DUP, southern parties and the trade unions took the reins of power amid fears of a military coup and serious food shortages, particularly in war-torn southern Sudan. The government's chances of being seen in a positive light were improved by the reluctant acceptance by Al Sadig Al Mahdi of the November 1988 DUP–SPLM agreement, which meant that the NIF was the only major political entity left out of the new political arrangements.

On 30 June 1989, Al Sadig was overthrown by an NIF-instigated military coup when his government was preparing to enter into discussions with the SPLA/SPLM. Colonel (later Lieutenant General) Omar Hassan Ahmad Al Bashir headed a 15-member Revolutionary Command Council (RCC) for National Salvation; the constitution and the National Assembly were suspended, political parties were banned and freedom of organisation, speech and the press were curbed. The fact that the NIF leadership was behind this military coup became clear only at a later stage, in revelations made by its leadership.

Strategically, the Revolutionary Command Council needed a social force to legitimise its seizing of power, while the NIF was ready to lend that support in exchange for the advancement of its Islamisation programme. Small wonder that Al Turabi became the political ideologue of the RCC–NIF alliance, reinforcing the Islamic *sharia* laws and presenting Sudan as the centre of Islamic resistance against Western hegemony. In the process, Khartoum became the meeting place of various Islamic organisations, while the Afghan and Pakistani Mujhidin became involved in the civil war in southern Sudan. (See El Affendi (1991) on the role of the National Islamic Front in the 1989 coup.)

DEMOCRATISING POLITICAL ISLAM

Like all other Sudanese military rulers, Bashir, supported by the NIF, began a political normalisation process, including the dissolution of the Revolutionary Command Council. In February 1992, Bashir and the ruling NIF established a 300-member Transitional National Assembly with the aim of filling the vacuum created by the banning of the political parties. The dissolution of the RCC in mid-October 1993 paved the way for presidential and parliamentary elections conducted simultaneously in March 1996. Although all candidates contested the elections on an individual basis, since political parties were banned, the NIF was better prepared and produced the majority of candidates and winners. Bashir won the presidential election, securing 75.7 per cent of the vote against 40 contenders who together managed only 24.3 per cent of the vote. Some 900 individuals contested 375 National Assembly seats, while 125 Assembly members were appointed by a national conference in February. Al Turabi was elected speaker of the National Assembly. A Presidential Committee drafted a new constitution, which was approved by referendum and was enacted in June 1998.

Article 26 (1) and (2) of the Sudan Constitution of 1998 guarantees freedom of association and organisation as follows:

26(1) Citizens shall have the right of association and organisation for cultural, social, economic, professional or trade union purposes without restriction save in accordance with the law. (2) There shall be guaranteed for citizens the right to organise political association; and shall not be restricted save by the condition of consultative decision making and democracy in the leadership of the organisation, and use of propagation not material force in competition [*sic*] and abiding by the fundamentals of the Constitution, that as regulated by law.

Article 67 (1), (2) and (3) of the Constitution provides for the establishment of a National Assembly. Article 67 (1) reads that there shall be established an elected National Assembly to assume the legislative authority and any other powers by virtue of the Constitution. Article 67 (2) describes the composition of the National Assembly of a number of members, elected by direct, special or indirect general election as follows:

(a) seventy five per cent (75%), of full membership by way of general direct suffrage from the geographical constituencies which are divided by fair representation of the population in the country; (b) twenty five per cent (25%), of full membership by special or indirect suffrage in representation of women and scientific and professional classes representing States or national electoral colleges, as may be prescribed by law.

According to Article 67 (3): 'where it is not possible by decision of the General Elections Board to conduct elections for the National Assembly for compelling security reasons in any constituency or college, the President of the Republic may appoint a member to occupy the seat in the National Assembly pending conducting elections as urgently as possible.' Article 10 provides that:

The Court shall be competent to hear and determine any matter concerning the following: (a) Interpretation of the constitution when requested to do so by the President of the Republic, the National Assembly, half of the Governors of the states or half of the State Assemblies. (b) Suits from any aggrieved person to protect the freedoms and rights guaranteed by the Constitution after exhausting the executive and administrative remedies available. (c) Suits concerning jurisdictional conflicts between national and federal bodies. (d) Criminal procedures against the President of the Republic and the Governors under the Constitution or the laws. (e) Objections concerning the acts of the President of the Republic, the Council of Ministers or a National or Federal Minister if the objection concerns any infringement of the national constitutional system or the constitutional inviolable freedoms or rights. (f) Any other matters determined to be within the competence of the Constitutional Court.

Articles 11.1, 11.2, and 11.3 state that the powers of the Constitutional Court are as follows:

Article (11.1) the Court shall, for the purpose of exercising the jurisdiction provided for in article 11, exercise all powers to hear and determine a case, to declare any law, judgment, or order unconstitutional, and to restore the right of an aggrieved person and to compensate him. Article (11.2), the Court has the power to issue an order to any authority to prevent it from doing any act in respect of a matter before it, to transfer a matter to the Court, to issue an immediate order to any authority to prevent that authority from disposing of a matter in a specific way, to take specific action, or to bring the matter before the Court so that its constitutionality may be examined, or to issue an order to any authority or person to bring a detainee before the Court to examine the constitutionality of the detention of that person. Failure to obey an order of the Court shall incur personal responsibility. Article (11.3), the Court shall exercise the procedural powers of a criminal court in any criminal case against the President of The Republic or the government.

On 24 November 1998 the National Assembly passed, in accordance with the provisions of the Constitution, an Act allowing the organisation of political associations, called *tawali* in Arabic (that is, 'association'). By naming the bill *tawali*, Al Turabi meant to show his disdain for Western-style multi-party democracy. However, the provisions of the Political Organisations Act 1998, which came into force on 1 January 1999, were revolutionary by Sudanese political standards. For the first time in Sudan's history, a legal bill was introduced to organise political parties and to make these political parties legally responsible to their membership and the Constitutional Court. Given the mistrust between government and opposition, however, this Act was severely criticised from the beginning. Let us look at the main provisions of this Act.

The Political Organisations Act provided for 'organisation' – in other words, a combination of persons could, by voluntary affiliation, join together for the purpose of political expression and/or to compete in elections for public authority in accordance with the law. According to section (7):

> political Parties can register and thereof be bound in its form by freedom, *Shura* (consultation) and democracy and that shall be: (a) by free and voluntary choice of to join as a member, through the advice of members and through direct and indirect election for federal, state and local bureau's and supreme commanders. (b) No one shall be compelled to join, purchase or tempted by money to support or be bound by the organisation, nor shall they be discriminated against on

the basis of colour, origin, social status, ascendancy, sex, prestige or locality.

Article (3.2) on the organisation of political parties states that they 'shall be bound by the fundamentals relating to the principles and provisions of the Constitution and laws and shall not adopt any methods or measures for the purposes of realising any doctrine to amend such fundamentals save by the manner and proceeding required by the Constitution or legal provisions'. Article (3.3) stipulates that 'the relationship between organisations shall be based on competition for the purposes of manifesting opinions and/or taking over authority and shall be restricted to safe and peaceful means and ... shall be peaceful without recourse to violence, force, aggression or tyranny which is in contravention with the rule of law, for the purpose of achieving any competition or political victory'. The minimum number of people to organise in a political party is, according to Article (4): 'any number no less than one hundred citizens having the right to vote in elections according to law and the leader of the organisation according to section (1), may establish an organisation and submit the application of its registration in accordance with the provisions of this law'.

Lt.-Gen. Al Bashir officially invited the exiled opposition and political parties to contribute to a committee headed by Abdel-Aziz Shidu, a former Minister of Justice entrusted with the task of reviewing the *tawali* bill. However, all political parties rejected the bill, accusing the Al Bashir government of trying to gain legitimacy by pretending that it aimed at restoring political freedoms. The bill was criticised in opposition circles for empowering the Registrar of Political Associations to accept or reject any political associations, and to monitor their membership and sources of finance. Another criticism was the introduction of the term *al-muhtasib*, which means that any citizen may, under oath, contest the legality of the registration of any party or political association.

Despite the criticism of opposition forces, particularly the National Democratic Alliance (NDA) based in Eritrea, 19 political parties have registered inside the Sudan and have begun to agitate for amendments to the Political Parties Act in order to allow for free association and organisation of political parties. The question that continues to haunt many Sudan analysts is whether Al Bashir's moves towards allowing greater freedom than ever before in his government's eleven-year history is a genuine desire to return to democracy, or political manoeuvring to prolong the life of one of the most hated Sudanese regimes. Or perhaps Al Bashir came to realise that the odds against the survival of the regime were mounting.

ISLAMIC FACTIONALISM: AL BASHIR VERSUS AL TURABI

Despite opposition doubts about the constitutional and other legislative provisions that allowed a degree of political participation, they began to show some immediate results. Al Turabi's underestimation of how even limited democratic dispensations can lead to quite momentous changes and develop their own dynamics contributed to his own political marginalisation. Realising Al Turabi's intentions to manipulate the governing National Congress Party in order to restrict his authority, Al Bashir introduced a state of emergency on 12 December 1999 and dissolved the National Assembly (Parliament) in order to end what he called the duality of decision making in government. Al Bashir claimed that Al Turabi, the Speaker of the Parliament, had begun to interfere in the appointment of the Federal States Governors in order to influence the forthcoming presidential elections. Al Bashir was also under tremendous internal and external pressure to distance himself from Al Turabi, who was seen as the Islamic ideologue behind the regime, and the cause of Sudan's external isolation, particularly in its relationship with its neighbours (Eritrea, Ethiopia and Uganda). In February 2000, Al Turabi was officially banned from addressing public meetings and rallies for fear that he would incite some of his devout followers to disturb the peace.

Lt.-Gen. Al Bashir's move produced an immediate political dividend. It gave the Constitutional Court an opportunity to exercise its duties as provided for by the Constitution. A number of Al Turabi's supporters filed a suit alleging that the imposition of the state of emergency and the dissolution of the parliament by Al Bashir were unconstitutional, but the Court ruled on 8 March 2000 that the President had acted within the powers vested in him by the Constitution. This ruling paved the way for extending the state of emergency to the end of the year.

Table 5.1 shows the names and political orientations of the main registered political parties which resulted from the constitutional provisions and acts allowing the freedom of organisation. A number of observations deserve serious consideration here.

First, Sudan's two largest opposition parties and members of the National Democratic Alliance have registered and operate from their offices in Sudan. These are the Unionist Democratic Party and the Umma Party. This illustrates that opposition is now tolerated, particularly after the marginalisation of Al Turabi and his subsequent arrest in February. These two parties will certainly participate in the next elections, as they already have representation inside the country. This makes something of a mockery of their criticisms of the new constitutional provisions allowing for the formation of political parties; indeed, their intention was to apply maximum pressure to secure more concessions from Al Bashir's government before they returned to Sudan.

Second, the conventional Islamic movement parties are now more divided than ever before. Three main political parties associated with the Muslim movement have registered: the Muslim Brothers, the National Islamic Front and the National Congress Party. The current power struggle between these forces holds the key to political reforms in the Sudan. However, new Islamic-oriented political parties have also emerged as a result of dissatisfaction with the conventional Islamic political parties, both sectarian and orthodox. These include the United Democratic Salvation Front, National Reform Congress, the Umma Islamic Party and the National Patriotic Coalition for South Sudan. In any future elections, it is likely that this proliferation of Islamic political parties and organisations will weaken their electability, splitting the Islamic vote among so many candidates.

Third, three political parties which have close associations with Egypt and which are calling for unification between Sudan and Egypt have emerged. These political parties are supported by a large number of Sudanese migrant workers and exiles as well as businessmen and women with close economic, political and social ties to Egypt. Interestingly, some of the founding members of these political parties were traditionally supporters of the Unionist Democratic Party, with affiliations with Egypt dating back to the last decades of Sudan's struggle for independence.

Fourth, the Sudanese Socialist Union, which governed Sudan between 1972 and 1985, registered under the Alliance of the Forces of Working Peoples; it is headed by ex-President Numeiri who returned to Sudan in 1999, receiving a hero's welcome from high government representatives. The question is whether Abul Gassim Mohamed Ibrahim, known as Numeiri's ex-aide and the Secretary of the Sudanese Socialist Union, currently the Minister of Health, is in the government in his individual capacity or as a representative of the Alliance of the Forces of the Working People.

Fifth, three regional parties representing southern and western Sudan have also registered: the Islamist 'National Reform Congress' (NRC) for western Sudan and 'National Patriotic Coalition for South Sudan' (NPCSS) and 'Free Sudan National Party' (FSNP) for the Nuba Mountains. The NRC and NPCSS are also Islamist in their ideological orientation and call for the application of the Islamic *sharia* laws, while the FSNP is secular.

Sixth, there are four political parties which are Arabist in their orientation and either advocate unification with Egypt, or take a pro-Libya stance including Sudan's adherence to Gadafi's Green Book, which calls

Table 5.1
Registered political parties in Sudan (25 November 1999)

Political party	Political orientation
1. Unionist Democratic Party (UDP)	Second largest political party before 1989 coup, sectarian, pro-Egypt
2. National Congress Party (NCP)	Succeeded National Islamic Front (NIF), Islamist
3. Muslim Brothers (MBs)	Gave birth to National Islamic Front and NCP, respectively, Islamist
4. United Democratic Salvation Front (UDSF)	Southern Sudanese based, unitary Sudan
5. Sudanese Central Movement (SCM)	New political party, Arab unity, secular
6. National Reform Congress (NRC)	New political party, regional (western Sudan), quasi-Islamist
7. Sudan National Front (SNF)	New political party, off-shoot of traditionalist party members, Islamist
8. Umma Party (UP)	The largest political party before 1989 coup. Led by Al Sadig Al Mahdi, Islamist
9. Nile Valley Congress (NVC)	Offshoot of Al Ashiga, unity between Egypt and Sudan, secular
10. Free Sudan National Party (FSNP)	Succeeded the Nuba-based Sudan National Party. Led by Father Philip Abas Ghaboush
11. Nile Valley Unity Party (NVUP)	New political party. Unity between Egypt and Sudan, secular
12. Sudan Labour National Democratic Party (SLNDP)	New political party, liberal-democratic
13. National Islamic Front (NIF)	Originally The Muslim Brothers. An accomplice to the military coup which brought Bashir to power, Islamist
14. Umma Islamic Party (UIP)	Offshoot of the Umma Party, Islamist
15. Liberal Democratic Party (LDP)	New political party, unitary, secular
16. Organization of People's Congresses (OPCs)	Pro-Libya, supported by Gadafi (Green Book), advocates Arab socialism
17. The Alliance of the Working People (AWP)	Remnants of Numeiri's Sudan Socialist Union (SSU), ousted 1985
18. National Patriotic Coalition for South Sudan (NPCSS)	Unitary, pro-the military wing of the National Salvation Revolution, brought Bashir to power, Islamist
19. Development and Social Justice Party (DSJP)	New political party, social democratic

Source: Sudan Government (1999), *Directory of Registered Political Organisations*.

for the creation of people's congresses and grassroots democracy. The strength of the following of this latter group is not known, but given the large number of Sudanese immigrants in Libya (some 500,000), it could have some political impact, particularly among the urban poor.

The opposition forces and the National Democratic Alliance responded quite differently to the government's measures to democratise the Sudanese political establishment. Some prominent exiled politicians either returned (ex-President Nimeiri, Mubarak al-Fadil Al Mahdi, the Speaker of the Umma Party and Mohamed al-Hassan Abdalla Yassin, a former joint head of state and part of the leadership of the opposition Democratic Unionist Party) or contrived to return to the country, including ex-Prime Minister Al Sadig. The opposition was also allowed to resume political activities inside the Sudan.

Ironically, the National Congress Party, until recently the only party authorised by the government to operate in the Sudan, has hastened Al Turabi's political demise. The government announcement that it is committed to free and fair elections and its invitations to the European Union, the United Nations, the Arab League and the Organisation of African Unity to sponsor and observe the elections leave little reason for the opposition not to return to Sudan.

The Umma Party, led by Al Sadig, bid the National Democratic Alliance farewell and decided to return to operate within the new constitutional dispensations. At the end of March 2000, the Bashir government returned the confiscated Umma Party headquarters in Omdurman in anticipation of the imminent arrival of Sadig Al Mahdi back in Sudan. The Sudanese Communist Party (SCP) also began to look for accommodation and its leader Mohamed Mahjoub called on the government to return the Party's property confiscated by the government in 1989. The SCP demanded to be treated equally with the Umma Party, which received its confiscated property back.

The current struggle for the return to democracy in Sudan is shrouded with doubt and uncertainty. Lt.-Gen. Al Bashir's newly acquired political credentials fell short of luring the Sudanese opposition to join in a process that it is ill-equipped to control. The war of animosities and mistrust, characteristic of Sudanese politics, will do little to convince the opposition that Al Bashir is sufficiently serious to be trusted. Any *rapprochement* between the opposition and Al Bashir will assist the opposition to return to the peril of multi-party politics whose consequences are all too familiar to Sudanese. Any delay of this *rapprochement* may buy the Islamic movement some time to patch up its differences and consolidate its ranks. In effect, Sudan may return to the politics of the early years of post-1989, that is, dominated by Islamic die-hards. The

Islamists have cornered the sectarian parties (a) by drawing on their religious constituency and (b) by making it difficult for them to maintain any credible separation between state and religion, even if at the expense of democracy.

PROSPECTS FOR MULTI-PARTY DEMOCRACY

Although Sudan's prospects for a return to some sort of a democratic dispensation are real, the prospects for any success or long-term sustainable Westminster-style democracy are remote. Considering Sudan's miserable failure to uphold any democratic transition for more than five years at a time, the odds against a successful transition are mounting. Nothing has happened to suggest that the socioeconomic and political environment within which democracy was practised in the past has changed sufficiently to allow for any other outcome than the familiar pattern of a short and perilous democratic transition followed by a military coup.

The nature of the political culture expected to support democracy is such that affiliation to a political party is secondary to religious belief in the divinity of the leadership – the religious family, the mentors of the political party. Sudan's dominant political parties (Umma and DUP) are sectarian, religious-based and are not democratic in structure and content. Their followers constitute a horde of disciples, who have never been in a position to challenge the divine leadership from whom they seek religious blessing more than political or economic rewards. The leaders of these political parties (Al Sadig and Al Mirghani, respectively) bask in the homage bestowed upon them by their disciples, including an educated political elite that has betrayed its claims of modernity and Western education. The party faithful in this skewed political milieu are also religious faithful capable of conflating political, religious and ethnic loyalty. The elite is incapable of revolting against its masters, while the disciples accept a religious identity that defines all that is holy and spiritually absorbing.

However, between religion and ethnic faith, there is local politics and its internal determinants, predicated on ethnic solidarity and resistance to state designs, creating alliances with certain political parties on the hope of getting their share of the resources the state controls. Amid all this, the traditional leaders of these ethnic groups also foster ties with the educated elite, the mediators between the ethnic groups and the politico-religious establishment they support.

It is generally recognised that the religious families maintain great influence over an economically dependent political elite. The sectarian political parties are financed through the economic investments of the religious families that created them. While in government, party faithful are rewarded with high positions, and when ousted by military coup, those who flee the country and seek exile abroad live in part off their asylum-seeker positions and in part on the support offered by their political patrons. The outcome of this constellation of power is the creation of an educated political elite incapable of asserting itself *vis-à-vis* a politico-religious establishment premised on non-democratic values and contriving to rule through its ascribed religious authority rather than its political merits. A clientalism has fostered a vicious circle that has entrenched two powerful sectarian political parties, each assuming a God-given right to govern. Because the political elite and the party faithful were educated in Western or Western-style educational establishments, the general impression given to outsiders is that they are democrats presiding over modern democratic political parties. The reality on the ground points in a very different direction.

No thesis on transition to democracy in the Sudan is possible without reference to South–North conflict which culminated in one of Africa's bloodiest civil wars. The first civil war continued from 1955 to 1972. However, the war started again in 1983, when the Sudan People's Liberation Army and its political wing Sudan People's Liberation Movement (SPLA/SPLM) led the rebellion against the Sudan government. Among the factors which contributed the resumption of the second civil war were the lack of serious attempts to develop the South, the introduction of Islamic *sharia* law and the growing mistrust between southern and northern Sudanese politicians.

It is estimated that the war has claimed the lives of two million southern Sudanese and displaced over four million people, internally or living as refugees in the neighbouring countries. Southern Sudanese displaced by the war live on relief food provided by Operation Life Sudan (OLS), which was established by the United Nations in 1989 and supported by international Private Voluntary Organizations (PVOs) (see Mohamed Salih 1999a).

The discovery and subsequent development and export of oil found in the South as well as South Kordofan province bordering the South has added fuel to an already desperate situation. It is difficult for the North to contemplate its earlier pledges of granting the South the right to self-determination after the oil discovery. It is estimated that Sudan currently (2001) produces 200,000 barrels of oil per day, enough to sustain its ailing economy and boost its war effort.

The prospects of democracy while the war continues in the South are dim and it is near impossible to achieve political goals by using democratic means. In this complex political and social milieu, the meaning of history has become an indispensable ideological instrument in laying claims on the state. Furthermore, meaning construction is informed by Sudan's diverse cultures, ethnic groups and languages as well as the economic and political divide which caused the death of more than two million people since civil war began in 1983.

The prospects of a democratic breakthrough in the midst of an intensified North–South conflict are unthinkable.[1] The southern Sudan movement is fragmented and unruly and its prospects of using the collective memory of an oppressed nation to cement a sense of national identity are still remote. The defining elements of the South–North war of wills have been dominated by the prominence of a pseudo-Arabic speaking Muslim discourse versus other cultures and values. In reality that discourse, as the structure of the newly registered political parties illustrates, is no more than an ideological construct that feigns the essence of the daily struggles of the poor and the oppressed. Furthermore, it is clear that the Islamic elite has used the Islamic narrative as an instrument to transform religion into a political resource. The sectarian political parties (the Umma or Nation Party and the Democratic Unionist Party), with their religious credo, have done the same throughout the history of modern Sudan. As there is no future for multi-party democracy in the Sudan, the prospects of a peaceful coexistence between South and North in a unitary Sudanese state is even dimmer. The Sudanese military, and even civilian politicians, have used the civil war to overthrow democratically elected governments (the military coups of 1969 and 1989) or to jail their political opponents (the arrest of opposition leaders sympathetic to the SPLA/SPLM, known as fifth column, by Al Sadig's government or the arrest of Al Turabi in February 2001 for concluding an agreement with SPLA/SPLM).

Sudan's political parties combine the militancy of religion and the protection of ethnicity. In these circumstances, even the most rebellious modern political elite will find it hard to come up with alternative party structures and organisations. As Table 5.1 shows, even when new offshoots of these political parties emerge, they still cling to religion as a force for mobilising the faithful in their ethnic homelands. The promise of Western-style democracy would surely fall short of the requirements of even the remotest sense of quasi-polyarchy.

Amid the heightened expectations of a possible return to multi-party democracy, the odds against a Western-style democratic future in the Sudan are heavy. Sudan is politically tense, charged with regional, ethnic and religious animosities. These in themselves are not a challenge to democracy. The real challenge to democracy is the political leadership, the very political elite that Western political scientists hail as the guardians of democratic politics. In this highly charged political and social milieu, democracy can also be used as an instrument of oppression, as will be illustrated in Chapters 7 and 9. Instead of democratisation, good governance and respect for human rights, Sudan's authoritarian circus continued to play to the tune of democratic reversal in an age that prides itself with being concerned about the spread of global democratic values.

6
Sierra Leone: Democratising Anarchy

No event could have illustrated the grim fate of democracy in Sierra Leone better than the military coup of 25 May 1997 which overthrew the democratically elected government of President Ahmed Tejan Kabbah. The coup was masterminded by a coalition of the Armed Forces Revolutionary Council (AFRC) and the Revolutionary United Front (RUF). In October 1997, the rebel leader Major Johnny Paul Koromo and the AFRC/RUF allied forces were compelled to accept a cease-fire through the pressure exerted on them, first and foremost, by the Nigerian-led forces of the Economic Community of West Africa (known as ECOMOG). Although factors such as United Nations' sanctions, which included energy and weapons, and the role of the Organisation of African Unity (OAU), cannot be exaggerated, the fact that not a single country in the world had recognised the AFRC/RUF government must have contributed the junta's decision to relinquish power. Upon his return from exile (in Guinea) in March 1998, President Kabbah and his government were without a functioning national army. ECOMOG supported the remnants of the Civil Defence Force (CDF), also known as Kamajors, created by President Kabbah in his earlier period in power. The Kamajor forces remained loyal to President Kabbah, and had since worked together with the United Nations Observer Mission in Sierra Leone (UNOMSIL).

The departing AFRC/RUF forces wreaked havoc in Freetown, leaving about 5,000 people dead and more than 200,000 displaced, and destroying civilian houses and public amenities and offices. A semblance of normality was eventually brought to Freetown, but much of the countryside remained under rebel control. Despite reinstating the democratically elected government, Sierra Leone has been left in ruins, a collapsed state, which is in reality 'non-democratically governed' by scores of warlords, entrenched business interests and profiteers.

Some observers explain the military coup and the events that followed in terms of a military known for its lust for power, deprived of resources, and condemned to low salaries that could barely meet their basic needs. Although these explanations may all contain some elements of truth, the development of an anarchic situation in Sierra Leone cannot be isolated from the country's colonial and recent past, nor from the political culture of a military and business elite increasingly alienated from the populace. The events that occurred in Sierra Leone during the last three years coincided with the inception of the democratisation process. These were a by-product of democracy itself, which unleashed political voices that had been kept silent for centuries of colonisation and decades of authoritarian military rule in the post-independence era. In a sense, the freedoms that democracy brought along were detrimental to democracy and the political values it espoused. This chapter traces the specific nature of Sierra Leone's democratic reversal. It attempts to answer the question whether the anarchy that swept through the country along with the democratisation process is a symptom of much deeper social and economic problems rather than a sign of ethnic animosity. It also explores the issue of identity politics, often predicated on ethnicity, as a mode of political mobilisation, in order to delineate the ideological basis for recruitment to political party and/or insurgency group.

Colonial Sierra Leone had experienced relative freedom in establishing advanced forms of associations, including trade unions, professional and pressure groups. The freedom of organisation had, in early 1951, contributed to the emergence in Sierra Leone of political parties, including the SLPP (Sierra Leone People's Party). As the following sections of this chapter illustrate, the development of these parties and their inter- and intra-party rivalries played a major role in the disastrous events that took place in the late 1990s.

PRELUDE

Contemporary Sierra Leone is largely shaped by the historical events that led to its creation during the closing decades of the nineteenth century. Clapham (1976: 6–7) reminds us that 'Sierra Leone owes its origin to the position of "free persons of colour" in the United States and Britain', while according to Cartwright (1970: 15–7): 'the colonisation of Sierra Leone by these settlers began in 1787 when some 300 "Black Poor" from London were landed at the coast watering place called Freetown. By the 1850s new waves of African settlers from Britain and the United States as well as African slaves liberated by British Navy ships began to expand into the interior thus creating relations with the indigenous populations.' The Creoles were the product of this blend of liberated African slaves and local populations with their distinctive Krio language, the only language spoken by the twenty or so major ethnic groups. Owing to their Western education and their status as British subjects, the Creoles were able to leave their mark on trade and administration, a position taken over in later years by European and Lebanese traders and recently by 'indigenous' Sierra Leone peoples.

In 1808, the area of settlement governed by the Sierra Leone Company, which bought land from tribal chiefs, was transferred to British rule and became a Crown Colony. In 1896, an area of 27,669 square miles was declared a British Protectorate, a status which continued until the build-up to independence in the 1950s. In common with other British colonies, a Native Administration system was established in 1937 under the Tribal Authorities Ordinance. The chiefs became responsible for law and order, for the operation of the Chiefdom Treasury for keeping account of revenue and expenditure, and for maintaining inventories of Native Administration property. According to Kilson (1966: 22–3), 'the Native Administration ... weakened the bonds between chiefs and the masses and enabled the chiefs to modernise a fair part of their traditional sources of authority and power.'

The rise of a new Sierra Leone professional elite consciousness during the late nineteenth century was exemplified by the publication of African-owned newspapers such as *Sierra Leone Weekly News* and *Sierra Leone Times*, among others (Kilson 1966: 75). As mentioned in Chapter 2, the new African elite soon began to compete with the colonial administrators for higher-ranking positions, including the control of the state. The creation of the National African Congress of British West Africa, founded in Accra, Ghana (the Gold Coast) in March 1920, was a crystallisation of the aspirations of the West African elite: 'This development, as the new elite saw it, was basically a matter of the replacement of expatriate personnel at all levels of the colonial establishment. In Sierra Leone this policy of "Africanization" commenced in the late 1940s and by the end of the 1950s had no small achievement to its credit' (Kilson 1966: 90–1).

Due to the special relationship between the Creoles and the British, their representation in the colonial government came much earlier than in other British colonies in Africa. Kilson describes this as 'a process of political acculturation of educated Africans to the constitutional norms of the colonial oligarchy' (1966: 101).

During the period 1951 to 1961, government control in Sierra Leone began to shift gradually from British colonial officials to more independent national leaders, including some Sierra Leoneans taking ministerial positions. Milton Margai, a Sierra Leonean, became Chief Minister four years before independence in 1960 and Prime Minister in 1961 (for more details of this period see Cartwright 1978: 59–89).

The earliest exposure to interest group representation came in 1946 in the shape of informal chiefs' assemblies, formally constituted district councils, which provided the forum where the chiefs could meet, and the Protectorate Educational Progressive Union (PEPU). Three distinctive interest groups emerged: Creole intelligentsia, the Protectorate intelligentsia and the chiefs. None of these interest groups was strong enough to govern independently of the others and each brought specific qualities to the political process. The chiefs brought with them the loyalty of the majority of the population, the Creoles educational and administrative skills, and the Protectorate intelligentsia the flare of nationalism and a sense of embeddedness in traditional Sierra Leone society. The Constitutional reforms of 1947 were particularly instrumental in giving the Protectorate a stronger position than the Colony in the Legislative Council, and ensuring that Paramount Chiefs would control the elections to the Protectorate seats (Cartwright 1978: 44–5).

As Sierra Leone began the march towards independence, the chiefs were clearly well-placed to control election outcomes through their social and cultural proximity to their people. Education, modern lifestyles and the new professionalism of the Sierra Leone intelligentsia, on the other hand, had widened the gap between the rising modern political elite and their political base. In the words of Sesay (1999: 151): 'despite their inefficiency and authoritarian and extortionate tendencies, the chiefs became the channels for social development. Governance through chiefs superseded old forms of social control and survival strategies and enhanced the power of chiefs to the extent that they sometimes posed a threat to the stability of British colonial rule.' Although the Western-styled political parties were initially established as instruments for the control of state power independent of the chiefs, the political elite soon realised that they still needed the chiefs' support in order to obtain the majority that would advance their ascendance to power.

THE RISE AND FALL OF THE SLPP

As in other African countries, the youth of Sierra Leone were the first to create a pressure group against the colonial establishment. (The Sudanese Youth League and the Somali Youth League were other examples of the role of the youth in liberation struggles.) The Youth League was formed in 1948 by Wallace Johnson, a member of the Protectorate intelligentsia; it joined ranks with Bankole-Bright's National Council of the Colony of Sierra Leone, an exclusively Creole nationalist party. In response to this party, Siaka Stevens, an adviser, supported by the chiefs, launched the Sierra Leone People's Party (SLPP) in 1951. With the support of chiefs and many prominent figures, the SLPP secured an election victory in Sierra Leone's first national election, a year after its establishment. Cartwright explains:

> ... the SLPP's leaders could both isolate Creole-led opposition movements, and patch over both regional and class divisions within the Protectorate, by appealing to Protectorate solidarity, and identifying

theirs as 'the countryman's party'. Since the majority was automatically of the countryman's side, the more so as the franchise was extended, such an appeal had great attractions for the SLPP. [1978: 60–1]

The period after the Second World War and the build-up to independence did not go as smoothly as the constitutional reforms, the formation of political parties, or even the first election, which brought the SLPP to power. Riots in 1955–56, sparked by the artisan union's strike over pay, were followed by a series of riots, this time engineered by the transport and general workers, again over pay. The SLPP interpreted the riots as an attempt by the opposition parties to weaken its hold on power – a suspicion which proved correct when it was discovered that some of the riots' ring-leaders were headed by a Creole lawyer. This suspicion was reinforced by the fact that the riots were engineered by the United Sierra Leone Progressive Party (USLPP), established by Cyril Rogers-Wright in 1954. Following the 1957 elections, a caucus of SLPP MPs had, by a margin of one vote, replaced Milton Margai with Albert Margai his brother. (Actually, Milton Margai bowed to behind-the-scenes pressure and stepped down.) In September 1958, Albert Margai, joined by Siaka Stevens, launched a new party, the People's National Party (PNP) with the aim of pressing for more involvement of Africans in the colonial civil service in preparation for independence from British rule. The PNP had strong support among the young and educated elite, but was less popular than the SLPP among the chiefs and well-connected professionals, both Creole and indigenous Sierra Leoneans.

The resolutions of the London constitutional conference, held in order to prepare Sierra Leone for independence, were signed by all parties except Siaka Stevens who launched a new one, the All Peoples' Congress (APC), supported by northerners. During the early 1960s, relations between the opposition political parties (APC), the Sierra Leone Progressive Independence Movement (SLPIM) and the governing political party (SLPP) were acrimonious, opposition leaders being detained more frequently than during the colonial period. In my view this pattern of political intolerance, extended to today's Sierra Leone, is part of the colonial heritage of these political parties, as some of their leaders were part of the transition government which oversaw Sierra Leone's progression from colonial rule to independence

Sir Milton Margai died in April 1964 and was replaced by his brother Albert Margai as leader of the SLPP. However, after a short period of widespread popularity, Albert Margai was to face increasing discontent as a result of his attempts to centralise and strengthen the SLPP *vis-à-vis* the chiefs, who had traditionally formed the backbone of the party, and to suppress opposition political parties. The economic crisis of 1966 made life more difficult for Albert Margai, whose pledge to pursue a policy of affirmative action to give more resources to Mendeland, his homeland and main support base, was flouted. The prime minister's popularity reached an all-time low – he came under severe attack by the opposition for corruption, while the economic crisis and shortage of revenue was affecting all government departments (for more details, see Cartwright 1978: 77–8).

The idea of establishing a one-party system was born out of Albert Margai's fear that his own increasing unpopularity and that of the SLPP would contribute to his downfall. In February 1966, Albert Margai contemplated transforming Sierra Leone into a one-party state under the dominance of the Mende peoples, Albert Margai's ethnic group and chiefs – to the infuriation of the educated, professional and other progressive elements in society. Ghana's negative one-party state experience under Nkhrumah strengthened resistance to the idea, many claiming that a one-party state would exacerbate regional conflicts between North and South and would give regional and ethnic affiliation a more prominent role in the political life of Sierra Leone. However, the one-party state had failed and Sierra Leone was able to avert the general tendency among newly independent African states towards totalitarianism.

The army entered the political equation for the first time in 1967 when, afraid of losing power to the APC, Margai acted through the force commander, Brigadier Lansan, to stage a coup. The military came to power in a military coup in March 1967, four days after a new parliament was elected. The collapse of the SLPP was such a blow to the Mende-dominated polity that they decided to use the military in order to remain in power. Martial law was declared, the constitution suspended and all political activities and political parties banned. An eight-man National Reformation Council (NRC) was established to govern the country. It was rumoured during the chiefs' elections in February that the army had begun discussions to bring the ousted Prime Minister Albert Margai back to office.

When the junta's intention became an open secret, Brigadier Lansan was himself ousted in a counter-coup, this time led by Major Blake. By April 1967, Major Blake had succeeded in creating the National Reformation Advisory Council (NRAC) to prepare the country for the return to civilian rule. However, the presence of the NRAC did not prevent the junta from jailing many opponents and restricting the movement of many others. The pressure against the military began to build up, particularly from the banned All People's Congress (APC) party, trade unions and university students. The junta caved in and Siaka Stevens was sworn in as president. A number of failed military coups between 1970 and 1972 necessitated the intervention of troops from Guinea to strengthen the weakened security organs which themselves became part of the political turmoil.

The collapse of the SLPP in 1967 has been attributed in large part to its failure to handle the problem of mobilisation and tribal divergence. The electoral system did intensify regional differences: once the All Peoples' Congress established a base in the North, it was identified as the voice for that area. The SLPP was a coalition of local interests representing the chiefs and the middle class which had lost in terms of political and economic advantages. They were supported initially by the Temne people, enemies of the Mende who had dominated the state since independence; over time, the Temnes' apparent exclusion from government became more significant. As the northern membership of the SLPP fell, the influence of its southern membership increased, as did its identification with the Mende ethnic group. The inevitable result was an increasing polarisation along tribal lines, which ultimately led to a state of high tension preceding the 1967 election coup (Cartwright 1970: 280–1). However, in ethnic terms, although it is difficult to ascertain the ethnic nature of the dominant political parties, by 1967 it was evident that a Mende political elite was at the helm of political power in Sierra Leone.

In essence, the Sierra Leone elite's appetite for power exhibits a similar pattern to that of their Sudanese counterparts. Because they failed to live up to the expectations of Western-style democracy, they gradually drifted towards traditional political structures, relying on chiefs to promote their election chances. Although, on the one hand, their strategy was to keep chiefs out of the echelons of modern political power, they found themselves compelled by the realities of tradition to pay homage to the chiefs for securing the votes needed to access power. When the chiefs began to assert their authority, and when the educated elite realised that their chances of governing even within their own ethnic homelands were determined by the majority in government, they began to look for other ways into politics. In a situation where the bullet carried more weight than the ballot box or the logic and rationality of majoritarian democracy, the army was a natural ally. The extension of civilian into military politics and ambitions became the only viable choice for those excluded by the tyranny of an unwieldy majority.

THE MILITARY EXTENSION OF CIVILIAN POLITICS

Between 1967 and 1977, Sierra Leone was blighted by 15 coups, mostly carried out by army officers who felt that their ethnic groups were being marginalised. Regional divisions were subsumed under much deeper ethnic tensions. Civilian politicians and military officers from minority ethnic groups who felt that they could not rise to power through democratic elections began to use the army as an extension of civilian politics, thus thwarting the democratic process itself.

Due to the heavy-handedness with which they were suppressed by both military and civilian governments, Sierra Leone's opposition forces began to leave the country *en masse*. In 1978, Stevens proclaimed a new constitution that declared Sierra Leone a one-party state with the APC operating as the state party. Ethnically, the one-party state was dominated by the Limba and Temne, with some SLPP renegades joining the APC in order to protect Mende interests.

A second round of coups and counter-coups began in 1981, including the failed coups of 1982, 1983, 1987 and 1989, with the Limba ethnic group gaining prominence as the main operators of the notorious state security system. Most of these coups were staged by disgruntled army officers, often in alliance with, or at least with the blessing of, the ousted leaders of other political parties.

Sierra Leone was ruled by the military, in collaboration with the APC, from 1985 until the reinstatement of multi-party democracy in 1991. During this time, it became clear that the influence of the army in politics was increasing markedly. This can be seen, for instance, in Stevens' voluntary relinquishing of power to Major Joseph Saidu Momoh, who was subsequently elected president in 1988.

With the return of Sierra Leone to multi-party democracy in 1991, the United Front of Political Movements (UNIFORM) was formed. UNIFORM comprised six political parties: the National Action Party (NAP), the SLPP, the Democratic People's Party (DPP), the National Democratic Alliance (NDA), the National Democratic Party (NDP) and the Civic Development Education Movement (CDM). The Revolutionary United Front (RUF) was also formed in 1991, as an opposition force to UNIFORM and as a radical organisation with historical roots in youth vigilantism. Abdullah and Muana (1998) trace the RUF's roots to radical anti-establishment student politics in the 1970s and the revolutionary training in Libya of its leader Alfred Saybana Sankoh, following his deportation from Sierra Leone in connection with the 1971 coup against the government of Siaka Stevens. The contentions of Paul Richards (1996) that the RUF entered Sierra Leone from Liberia, that its young recruits received their military training there, and that the civil war was fought for the riches of Sierra Leone, have now been vindicated. Abdullah and Muana (1998: 235) elaborated some of his earlier views and noted, like Richards: 'their [the RUF's] failure to win the sympathy of the very people they claimed to be fighting for is understandable. They compelled them to recruit their army from lumpens and juveniles, two vulnerable groups to whom their push path to destruction appeared more appealing.' This view has also recently been echoed by Zack-Williams (1999), who goes on to identify children and women as the categories of people most affected by the Sierra Leonean civil war and its aftermath. The case was so not only because of the psychological trauma they have suffered, but also because their future prospects for building a tolerant democratic society have been greatly weakened.

Joseph Saidu Momoh was ousted from office in April 1992; one of the reasons for his downfall was his reliance on ethnic politics to maintain his grip on power. Zack-Williams (1999: 373–4) reports that 'Momoh resorted to ethnic corporatism, as he continued to rule with the help of the *Ekutay*, an association of ethnic elite based around Momoh's home town of Binkolo in the Bombali District. Indeed he (Momoh) argued the people of Sierra Leone should organize themselves into ethnic cabals in order to ensure that "no group was left out".'

The military seized power through Captain Valentine E.M. Strasser, who established the National Provisional Ruling Council (NPRC). As leader of the coup, Strasser was appointed chairman of the NPRC, Head of State and Minister of Defence. Political parties were banned, including the APC, which had been the sole political party during the prevous regime. NPRC was Mende-dominated and as such began to replace non-Mende with Mende in the government, the army and the police. The Limba-operated security apparatus was particularly targeted, with many of its rank and file forced to retire.

Strasser's period in power was dominated by the civil war, and particularly the strong resistance put up by the RUF. In January 1996, after five years in power, Strasser was ousted in a palace coup led by his deputy, Julius Maada Bio. Bio proceeded with elections which, in March of the same year, brought the SLPP of Ahmed Tejan Kabbah 59.5 per cent of the vote, while John Karefa-Smart of the United National People's Party received 40.5 per cent of the vote.

The issue of returning the country to civilian democratic rule had been on the agenda of the NPRC right from the beginning. The NPRC declared that its objectives in seizing power were to restore state capacity, end the rebel war and democratise the political system (Kandeh 1996: 398). The clearest indication that some members of the NPRC were rethinking their commitment to democratic civilian rule came 'in January 1996, when Strasser was replaced in a palace coup by his deputy Julius Mada Bio' (Kandeh 1996: 399). Once he had tasted power, Bio began to use various excuses in order to retain it.

One of the complaints of the military against the Kabbah regime was that the army lost supremacy to the Kamajors, considered to be Kabbah's personal military force, made up of members of his own ethnic group, the Mende. It is hardly surprising that the RUF rebellion, led mainly by Temne, was most vocal in its opposition to the perceived Mende domination of the country.

The deterioration of the economic situation and the lack of security prompted a military coup in May 1997 led by Johnny Paul Koromo. The country was ruled by the Armed Forces Revolutionary Council (AFRC), who were later joined by the RUF, a move that created a formidable Temne force against the Mende. The two main militia groups were the Kapras, who operated from the North, and Kamajors, who operated from the South and were mainly composed of Mende. Kamajor fighting was fiercest against the inhabitants of the diamond-mining region, who are predominantly Temne, Limbas and other northern ethnic groups – an RUF/APC stronghold. Although the exact number of the militia members are not known, it was estimated that the Kamajors numbered some 37,000 – about two-and-a-half times the size of the army, which was only about 15,000 strong, and which had already begun to disintegrate into tribal militias or armed forces offering allegiance to powerful warlords capable of supplying them with means of sustenance and arms. During this period, Sierra Leone was the scene of summary executions, looting, demolition of houses, burning of villages and brutal recruitment of child soldiers.

Although President Kabbah initially cooperated with the Kamajors, the peace deal struck with the RUF leader Sankoh turned them against the government troops and, by 1998, a protracted civil war between the three factions became inevitable. Several army defections and the increasing tribal polarisation within the army aggravated the situation. Richards (1996), Reno (1998), Zack-Williams (1999) describe in detail the events that contributed to ECOMOG intervention to liberate Freetown from the mayhem inflicted on the civilian populations by the retreating AFRC and Kamajor forces.

DEMOCRACY, ETHNICITY AND GREED

It is thus not difficult to explain the connections between ethnicity and the failure of democracy in Sierra Leone. Ethnicity played a central role here as an instrument of political mobilisation. However, an ethnicity-driven case, no matter how clear, should be qualified against the backdrop of the political events that contributed to the gradual ethnicisation of politics in Sierra Leone. More importantly, the transformation of Sierra Leone from an elite and region-based polity to an ethnically based political mobilisation requires a clear understanding of the economic circumstances that facilitated such a transition. Reno (1996, 1998), focusing on the political economy of the Sierra Leone crisis, has gone a long way to explaining the economic dimensions of the civil war. Any answer to the question of what went wrong with Sierra Leone's democracy is ultimately linked to the relationship between political modernisation and the rise of ethnicity. The contradictions between Western-style democratic models and ethnicity, both of which represent a host of institutional arrangements based on distinctive forms of political mobilisation, are probably less important than the capacity of the elite to reconcile them.

The modernisation of Sierra Leonean society by the Creole settler communities was premised on the interdependence of the Freetown peninsula and the interior as complementary rather than opposing poles. The external social and economic ties of the Creoles had encouraged Western education and urbanisation among the indigenous populations. However, the Creoles remained a privileged minority, representing only 2 per cent of the total population (over 4 million in 1996). This meant that, under democratic conditions, the Creole population could not hold the reins of power without allying themselves to one of the larger ethnic groups: the Mende (32 per cent), Temne (31 per cent), or Limba (9 per cent). In addition to the overwhelming distinction between settlers, mainly Creole and Lebanese, and indigenous groups, Sierra Leoneans are also divided by region and religion.

Distinctions by ethnic origin, or as settler or indigenous, are also asso-ciated with economic inequalities. Externally driven economic restructuring, such as structural adjustment programmes (SAPs), further aggravated these inequalities. Most studies describe how the economic crisis contributed to the political crisis and stress that the two cannot be isolated (see, for instance, Reno 1996, Zack-Williams 1990 and 1999). The consequences of structural adjustment are summed up by Zack-Williams (1999: 374): 'one of the major effects of SAP was to further reduce the legitimacy of the state, as more and more citizens turned to the informal economy for sustenance.' However, not all citizens have the necessary capital to enter the informal sector: many were left behind fending for themselves. The consequences of economic inequalities have been the subject of several publications and there is no need to elaborate further here. For the purposes of this chapter, it is sufficient to emphasise that there is an ethnic dimension to economic inequality and to patterns of regional geopolitics that ignite economic competition and gradually transform this competition into ethnic conflicts.

During the intensification of the civil war, Sierra Leone was controlled by warlord politics (Reno 1998). This politics has several linkages to global economic interests, in this case, the diamond riches of Sierra Leone. Reno laments that international foreign mining and military procurement firms 'used elections in Sierra Leone as a powerful marketing tool to appeal both to future clients and international organisations that still play a major role in the financial affairs of very weak states'. Because of the economic interest of civilian politicians and their reliance on the military for wealth extraction, 'the essentially private nature of the new political accommodation combined with the exigencies of economic austerity programmes meant the benefits of even civilian rule were primarily private and were limited to members of the accommodation' (Reno 1998: 138).

In so far as the relationship between ethnicity and primitive accumulation also offers opportunities to bare-handed scavengers for diamonds and the timber of the rainforest (Richards 1996), it generates a more diffused conflict than elite-centred accumulation. The North–South regional divide of the dominant ethnic groups (Temne and Mende) sheds light on this point. The Temne ethnic group dominates the North, with strong ties to the Muslim populations of Senegal and Mali. Although Temne are demographically dominant, they have little cultural and linguistic influence over their neighbours (Limba, Koranko, Loko, Yalunka and Susu) who continue to speak their own vernacular languages and practise their traditional beliefs and rituals.

The Mende inhabit the South; as a result of nineteenth-century and subsequent missionary activities, they are mainly Christian. With their close ethnic ties to the border populations of Liberia and Côte d'Ivoire, the Mende used their traditional rituals, particularly male secret societies (*poro, wunder*) for the control of the state. The secret societies are also bonding institutions that create loyalty to a collective identity and an ethnic faith. Mende dominance over the smaller ethnic groups surrounding their territory (Kissi, Gola, Kono, Sherboro, Krim Vai, Gola and others) is demonstrated by the fact that their neighbours gradually accepted Mende language and culture.

Ethnic divisions and tensions have traditionally been associated with access to state power and the use of that power to control material resources under the jurisdiction of the state. American and British missionaries spread Christianity in Mendeland from the nineteenth century onwards and, as a result, a strong political bond was created between some of the Mende and some Creoles. However, it must be stressed that, unlike in Sudan and Nigeria, the civil war in Sierra Leone did not exhibit any strong Muslim–Christian divide. The Mende elites who dominated the state were very secular in their political orientation. Their adherence to traditional secret societies as an instrument for controlling state functions, despite centuries of Christian missions, is still a puzzle to many observers. The social life of the Temne, with their

Muslim connections, is equally dominated by tradition and custom rather than by the practice of their Islamic faith.

During the colonial period, Mende chiefs used to send their children to be raised by Creole families from whom they acquired elements of Western culture and tradition. The Creole–Mende alliance was largely maintained through these relations. The SLPP has historically benefited from this alliance with Creole wealth and education and Mende elite ties with the chiefs. This could also be said for the APC and PNP, which were based on the same principle, illustrating the ethnic divisions of past and present Sierra Leonean political parties. (Also see Clapham's 1976 prediction of what he calls the 'politics of failure', dealing mainly with the negative consequences of clientelism on political instability and national disintegration.)

A somewhat simplified depiction of the constellation of the current power structure and the relationships between ethnic groups, political parties and the main guerrilla groups is very difficult to substantiate. The civil war has created its own dynamics, often denied or misrepresented by outsiders who are misinformed about the reality in the ground. However, this should not be treated as a sufficient reason to realise that at the instance of state collapse, local organisations, including ethnically based ones, remain among the main sources from which both victims and victors seek support.

Seen from a Western democratic perspective, it is obvious that Sierra Leone's long democratic tradition began to wane as a result of several factors, including the dependence of the Mende and Temne elites on the chiefs who were not fully integrated into the modern political process. The elites had, on more than one occasion, tried to reduce the powers of the chiefs by opting for more centralisation. The more the educated elite recognised that they were helpless without the support of the chiefs, the more they used the ethnic card to try to make the chiefs depend on them. Episodes such as the SLPP's 1961 Mendeland Policy, and subsequent elite tinkering with the democratic process by inviting the military to take power, illustrate how a combination of ethnic–military alliances have dominated Sierra Leone's political landscape.

Multi-party democracy has strengthened the role of the educated political elite and weakened the position of the chiefs. The gradual militarisation of society and frequent military coups have transformed chieftainship into an instrument for political mobilisation exploited by the elite to advance their own personal political agendas. In the circumstances, the chiefs no longer represent a form of local governance concerned with peace and order, or a collection of tributes and tribal representation at subregional and regional levels, but rather a contingency for mobilising fighters or facilitating the exploitation of local resources by private, state or international business interests.

What is of direct relevance to the Sierra Leone crisis is that ethnicity alone cannot provide a comprehensive explanation for the country's political crisis. Although several authors have offered convincing depictions of the political economy of the civil war in Sierra Leone, the relationship between this and the ethnic factor is yet to be fully understood. Although the remaining pages of this chapter are far too few to explain the complexity involved, I will offer some conclusions, drawing on the material presented here, in order to suggest a partial explanation for the regional geopolitics of the civil war in Sierra Leone and its implications for democracy.

DEMOCRATISATION IN COLLAPSED STATES

In a chapter entitled 'Democratisation in Collapsed States', Ottaway (1995: 235) argues that 'the collapse or threatened collapse of many African states at the present time has its ultimate cause in the mismanagement, pillage of resources, and abuses by authoritarian regimes that left the majority of the population without a stake in the existing system.' Although this statement seems correct at face value, the near-total collapse of the state in Sierra Leone was largely caused by the democratically elected elite who behaved in a fashion not much different from that of authoritarian regimes.

One of the reasons why democratic states in Africa are almost as prone to collapse as authoritarian regimes lies in the narrow definition of democracy used in the African context. Political democracy is often treated in isolation from issues of economic well-being, basic needs and what is nowadays referred to as human security concerns. In this vein, Thomas (1999: 8) argues that 'satisfying human needs depends in part on the political and economic institutions that serve as mechanisms for attaining such a goal. Simply put, democracy has different meanings and it remains an open question as to which model of democracy is most appropriate for satisfying needs and constructing secure societies.'

As Sierra Leone is still engaged in civil war, the question is how to re-democratise a democratic state that has collapsed, in part as a result of power abuse and in part as a result of its inability to create an enabling environment in which democratic culture could flourish. The question then is how to reconstruct the pluralistic fragmentation without leading to the collapse of the state or, in the case of Sierra Leone, the recurring temporary collapse of the state.

The current process of transforming anarchy into democracy in Sierra Leone has taken three distinctive routes. The first is international and regional pressure applied by multilateral international and regional institutions such as the UN, OAU and ECOWAS (the Economic Community of West African States). This route is similar to other experiences in war-stricken societies, with three common features – peacekeeping, disarmament, and relief and rehabilitation. The second route has been interest negotiation and agreements by the dominant political entities in Sierra Leone, including political parties, civil society organisations, insurgency groups and the military. The third involves collective action and civil society initiatives, reconciliation and anti-insurgency movements mediated by strong regional tendencies *vis-à-vis* the ethnicisation of politics by the infiltration of elite interests. We will look at these in turn in an attempt to explain their potential consequences in the quest for the democratisation process in Sierra Leone.

First, the current framework for the role of international and regional organisations in Sierra Leone was spelt out in the Lome Agreement of 7 July 1999 between the Republic of Sierra Leone and the Revolutionary United Front of Sierra Leone (RUF/SL) under the guidance of the Chairman of ECOWAS, President Gnassingbe Eyadema. The Lome Agreement was informed by two earlier agreements aimed at a negotiated settlement of the conflict in Sierra Leone – the Abidjan Peace Agreement of 30 November 1996 and the ECOWAS Peace Plan of 23 October 1997. This role is specified in Article Two on cease-fire monitoring as follows:

1. A Cease-fire Monitoring Committee (hereinafter termed the CMC) to be chaired by the United Nations Observer Mission in Sierra Leone (hereinafter termed UNOMSIL) with representatives of the Government of Sierra Leone, RUF/SL, the Civil Defence Forces (hereinafter termed the CDF) and ECOMOG shall be established at provincial and district levels with immediate effect to monitor, verify and report all violations of the cease-fire.

2. A Joint Monitoring Commission (hereinafter termed the JMC) shall be established at the national level to be chaired by UNOMSIL with representatives of the Government of Sierra Leone, RUF/SL, CDF, and ECOMOG. The JMC shall receive, investigate and take appropriate action on reports of violations of the cease-fire from the CMC. The parties agree to the definition of cease-fire violations as an integral part of the present Agreement.

3. The parties shall seek the assistance of the International Community in providing funds and other logistics to enable the JMC to carry out its mandate.

Although not without difficulties, Article Two of the Lome Agreement has been fully implemented, and a UN peace-keeping force has been

Box 6.1
Mercenaries in Sierra Leone

While ECOMOG forces devote themselves to peace-keeping in Freetown, Sandline International employees advise the Government as it plans the creation of a new army with no links to those involved in the coup d'etat. Efforts are also being made to organise the population in civil defence or self-defence forces. Hinga Norman, a chief of the Mende tribe, and educated in the United Kingdom, has set up a 20,000-strong paramilitary force called Kamajor with the aim of stamping out the rebellion. The paramilitary force is also reported to be committing gross violations of human rights with the acquiescence of the Government and after training and advice from Sandline International mercenaries. The UN Special Rapporteur has been informed of appalling acts of cruelty committed by mercenaries on captured rebels and on civilians suspected of collaborating with the insurgents. During the week of 30 November 1998, 70 rebels were killed in battle in Gberay, a rebel base 100 kilometres north of the capital. Many of the bodies were mutilated and incinerated. [United Nations 1998: 10–11]

invoked, although the peace achieved there is still very fragile. The role currently being played by the international and regional organisations is no doubt extremely useful, but their capacity to internalise the democratic ethos which the Agreement preaches is unrealistic. International and regional multilateral institutions operate at the state level and are ill-prepared to facilitate local-level negotiation. Moreover, even if multilateral institutions can assume some of these responsibilities, they lack the knowledge, skills and capacity to articulate local political stakes from a global perspective. In an article published in the *New York Times* (8 September 1998), Elizabeth Rubin wrote that in 1995 Sierra Leone hired Executive Outcomes (a South African private military services firm) only after the United Nations, the OAU and the international community had failed to help restore the democratically elected government in that country. In Rubin's words: 'The company was willing to do what the United Nations cannot: take sides, take casualties, deploy an overwhelming force and fire pre-emptively.' Another firm that hired mercenaries and trained the Kamajor paramilitary force loyal to President Kabbah was the British Sandline International. With the involvement of foreign mercenaries, the level of atrocities committed against civilians reached new heights (see Box 6.1). (On the role of mercenaries in current African and other civil wars, see Musah and Fayemi 2000.)

Such is the extent of UN and OAU complacency, that their claims to bring democracy to Sierra Leone should not be taken seriously. However, their potential capacity to pressurise Sierra Leone through international governance institutions is credible and could well be very useful. Even after securing a return to democracy, Reno (1998: 138) rightly observes that 'although all *counter-insurgency and cease-fire* activities sustained the outward image of a Sierra Leone state and permitted mining to continue, it did virtually nothing to address the needs of the people in Sierra Leone who had gone to the polls expecting a civilian government would mark a decisive change in the way the country was governed' (emphasis added). The most viable route for creating sustainable democratic institutions in Sierra Leone thus lies with the Sierra Leonean peoples and their political institutions, which are amongst the oldest and most experienced in the African continent.

The second route mentioned above is interest negotiation and agreements by the dominant political entities. The preamble to Article Three of the Lome Agreement which deals with governance issues stipulates:

the Government of Sierra Leone and the RUF/SL, recognizing the right of the people of Sierra Leone to live in peace, and desirous of finding a transitional mechanism to incorporate the RUF/SL into governance within the spirit and letter of the Constitution, agree to the following formulas for structuring the government for the duration of the period before the next elections, as Prescribed by the Constitution, managing scarce public resources for the benefit of the development of the People of Sierra Leone and sharing the responsibility of implementing the peace. Each of these formulas (not in priority order) is contained in a separate Article of this Part of the present Agreement; and may be further detailed in protocols annexed to it.

Article Three elaborates the main provision which calls for the transformation of the RUF/SL into a political party:

1. The Government of Sierra Leone shall accord every facility to the RUF/SL to transform itself into a political party and enter the mainstream of the democratic process. To that end:
2. Immediately upon the signing of the present Agreement, the RUF/SL shall commence to organise itself to function as a political movement, with the rights, privileges and duties accorded to all political parties in Sierra Leone. These include the freedom to publish, unhindered access to the media, freedom of association, freedom of expression, freedom of assembly, and the right to mobilise and associate freely.
3. Within a period of thirty days, following the signing of the present Agreement, the necessary legal steps shall be taken by the Government of Sierra Leone to enable The RUF/SL to register as a political party.
4. The Parties shall approach the International Community with a view to mobilising resources for the purposes of enabling the RUF/SL to

function as a political party. These resources may include but shall not be limited to: (i) Setting up a trust fund; (ii) Training for RUF/SL membership in party organisation and functions; and iii) Providing any other assistance necessary for achieving the goals of this section.

A Commission for the Consolidation of Peace (CCP) was established according to the provisions of the Agreement, with nine subcommittees: (1) Commission for the Management of Strategic Resources, National Reconstruction and Development; (2) Joint Monitoring Commission; (3) Provincial and District Cease-fire Monitoring Committees; (4) Committee for the Release of Prisoners of War and Non-Combatants; (5) Committee for Humanitarian Assistance; (6) National Commission on Disarmament, Demobilization and Reintegration; (7) National Commission for Resettlement, Rehabilitation and Reconstruction; (8) Human Rights Commission; and (9) Truth and Reconciliation Commission.

Although the work of all these committees has started, with varying degrees of momentum, it is too early to pass judgement on their success or failure. However, it is safe to argue that the very existence of these committees illustrates the complexity brought about by the civil war and the groundwork that is needed before any tangible results can be achieved.

None the less, the committees provided for in the Lome Agreement can by no means compensate for interest negotiations among the political institutions that were directly or indirectly party to the war. Recent reports show that the various political parties are engaged, with great difficulty, in confidence-building measures through the subcommittees of the Commission for the Consolidation of Peace, but given the economic crisis in Sierra Leone an aggregate elite interest may emerge as a dominant factor in these negotiations.

The third route was via collective action and civil society initiatives, reconciliation and anti-insurgency movements. These movements are currently led by youth, women and the chiefs, very weary of war and its politics. Trade unions and professional associations at anything but the highest level have always been pluralistic in their membership, and the informal sector now predominates in what is left of the modern economic sector, the number of those employed by state and private enterprises being very small. Those employed in ethnically plural sectors of the economy also constitute a minority, found mainly in relatively large urban and administrative centres. However, due to their exposure to education, a stable income (although steadily declining, even before the civil war) and connections within the state apparatus, those who joined politics from the ranks of this small elite have always played an intermediary role between their local communities and the state.

The Lome Agreement emphasises the role of elders and chiefs in the peace process, a compelling admission that traditional loyalties to religion, to locality and to *ethnie* matter considerably. There is a chance that collective action for peace and democracy on the part of the elders and religious leaders may take an unlikely turn and expose the militancy of ethnic politics and its nationalistic potential or religious credo.

The case of Sierra Leone demonstrates that democratising anarchy cannot be entrusted to the elite, although several Africans have proposed this. The leaders (or rather, as Reno suggests, the warlords) constitute the majority of the political elite who, in conventional democratisation approaches, should be the main stakeholders in the return to democracy. Unfortunately, their interest in self-enrichment and alliances with powerful outside parties with vested interest in Sierra Leone's diamond and timber riches makes this elite the most unlikely aide to democracy and the rule of law. Does this bleak assessment imply that Sierra Leone's political crisis is insurmountable? A number of possible scenarios can be contemplated here.

First, Sierra Leone may maintain a prolonged political stalemate, similar to that in Somalia, but with a strong semblance of normality at the centre. It may be possible to maintain the status quo as long as Alfred Saybana Sankoh, the leader of RUF, is assured of the continuation of his position as Minister of Minerals as stipulated in the Lome Agreement. Still there is no guarantee that the diamond-rich regions of Sierra Leone, currently held by several armed groups, will be handed over to the government. The latter's record in redistributing the revenues accrued from mining make a voluntary return of these resources to government most unlikely. According to this scenario, it is therefore doubtful whether Sierra Leone will become stable in the near future, given that diamonds are the main source of income for thousands of workers, local warlords and illegal diamond smuggling firms.

A second scenario involves the successful transformation of RUF into a political party, as stipulated in the Lome Agreement, and the integration of its fighting force into the Sierra Leone Defence Forces. The main problem here is that Sierra Leone does not have the resources to integrate a 37,000-strong guerrilla army with completely different command lines, hierarchy and adherence to discipline. Although disarmament, demobilisation and reintegration are the most detailed and well-articulated provisions of the Lome Agreement, their implementation depends on whether sufficient resources can be found. Experiences in other countries (Rwanda, Angola and Liberia) illustrate that financial resources could (although not without difficulty) be made available for expensive military intervention, which would be likely to worsen rather than improve the situation. The international community's record in responding to recon-struction and peace-building, including disarmament, demobilisation and reintegration, is rather discouraging.

Third, there is the possibility that the governing elite will aggregate its interests and create an oppressive state apparatus capable of quelling the warlords. This is, however, an almost impossible scenario. Confidence building may take decades to yield such a result, which is neither desir-able nor conducive to sustainable peace. There is at present no sign that a nationalist figure with a commanding appeal to the majority of the people of Sierra Leone – regardless of religion, ethnicity or aggressive past polit-ical ambitions – is likely to emerge. Even if such a figure were to exist, the willingness of the Sierra Leone elite to relinquish to the state the power that it has commanded through bitter fighting seems unlikely in the extreme. One also wonders whether the people of Sierra Leone would allow such an oppressive elite-dominated state, an elite that has, in the eyes of many, betrayed all that they have struggled to achieve since inde-pendence, that is, peace and liberty.

A fourth scenario would involve the reconstruction of the Sierra Leone state through a popular/social movement that would ally itself with the nationalist-traditionalist or conservative forces in society led by the chiefs. By and large, the chiefs have shown themselves to be much closer to the people than the educated political elite, although they lack the polit-ical skills needed to manage the state. They could expect to be confronted by a formidable resistance from the political elite, including the military, which has constantly undermined the authority of the chiefs throughout the history of Sierra Leone.

The fifth, and in my mind the most likely scenario, would entail Sierra Leone being decentralised, and a workable federal system of government being introduced. This system would give greater autonomy to the federal governments, thus reducing the centre's control over resources generated at the local level. This would have at least three positive outcomes: (1) it would bring government closer to the people, enhance participation and accommodate the aspirations of minority groups that do not see them-selves being represented at the national level; (2) it would allow the federal states greater control over a substantial proportion of the resources that are generated at the regional level, therefore promoting local development; and (3) it would ensure financial decentralisation, thus curbing the ability of the political elite operating at the central level to expropriate state resources. The central-level political elite would be entrusted with only a fraction of the national wealth, making central-level politics less attractive.

However, despite its tangible merits, the last scenario could only be implemented if the chiefs and regional/local-level political elite were to prove trustworthy and truly closer to the people than the elite operating at the national level. It would also be an expensive system, since it creates parallel administrative structures at the federal-state level. Another potential problem would be accountability and the possibility of replicating the corruption and mismanagement at the central level.

These five scenarios indicate that external forces, including mercenaries, externally driven democratisation and the conditionality accompanying it, are not likely to have any positive influence on the events and their potential outcomes. In the circumstances, making peace on terms that are workable within the context and complexity prevalent in Sierra Leone is probably more important. The major external players (UN, OAU, ECOWAS) can be useful facilitators to peace and democratic consolidation, but they cannot politically engineer the democratisation of anarchy. After all, the political processes unleashed by Sierra Leone's civil war are a result of political upheavals that were in part created by these very external forces. Not surprisingly, even the best of their intentions will be doubted by some of the domestic elements involved in the civil war and those responsible for making the peace.

7

Nigeria: Democracy, Ethnicity and Religious Faith

This chapter is concerned with the role of ethnicity and religion in Nigeria. Although this has been the subject of many publications, I intend to concentrate on the events leading to Nigeria's return to multi-party democracy and the root causes of the subsequent waves of ethnic and religious violence, with particular reference to recent events. However, in order to do this, a brief background to Nigeria's political development is necessary to delineate the historical events behind these political developments.

No explanation of military ascendance and democratic success or failure in Nigeria is complete without reference to ethnic and religious factors. Rather than treating them as distinct entry points to political instability in Nigeria, however, I attempt to illustrate how the three are in fact inseparable. This is not to imply that, given Nigeria's overall ethnic, religious and resource diversity, problems of ethnicity, religion or wealth distribution are evenly spread across all regions. The prominence of the North–South divide may lead one to underestimate inequalities within the North and the South. I introduce the case of the Ogoni people to show that South and North are not the only regional divisions in Nigeria and that larger synthesis often yields only partial explanation.

The triple discourse of ethnicity and faith, Islamic militancy, and democracy and Western-style secular elite-driven democratisation has produced an anomalous situation. None of the three is new; all originated in a struggle for supremacy that preceded the colonial legacy. However, post-independence politics and economic mismanagement have contributed to the reconfiguration of these ancient issues and wrapped them in new complexities and tribulations. Of particular relevance to Nigeria's political crisis are the role of the military in politics and civilian–military relations *vis-à-vis* the intricate relationship between region, religion and ethnicity.

The main premise of this chapter is that religious violence is used as an extension of civilian political activity: it is used to put onto the political establishment's agenda issues which would not normally be heeded. Further, this practice is more prevalent under democratic than authoritarian regimes. Democratic transition and the contestation of power in democratic elections challenge the status quo and leave the door open for new actors to join the race for political office. Political aspirants and power-mongers alike cannot afford to ignore the role of region, religion and ethnicity and their use and abuse in a country characterised by an uneven distribution of resources. Understandably, and given the political economy of Nigeria, ethnicity and religion have been more vocal, succeeding in overshadowing and even concealing the material basis of political discontent.

NIGERIA AND THE MILITARY

Nigeria was a British colony from the second half of the nineteenth century until it gained independence on 1 October 1960. Prior to colonisation, Nigeria was not a united country, but was made up of several ethnic groups speaking a number of languages. There has always been a clear South–North divide. In 1914, the British colonies of Northern and Southern Nigeria were merged into a single country. In 1947, the British divided the country into three regions, with a federal system: southern, eastern, and western regions. As in Sudan, socioeconomic transformation and the beginning of formal Western-style education, urbanisation, industrialisation and agrarian transformation marked the colonial era. Nigeria is one of Africa's richest oil-producing countries: oil exploration began during the colonial period and intensified during the 1960s and 1970s.

After independence, it took Nigeria only five years to descend into the dark ages of military rule, in a country dominated by a better-educated southern political elite. The military coup of 15 January 1966 was a desperate attempt by the southern politicians to secure a place in the political make-up of post-independence Nigeria. The difference between the southern Nigeria-led coup and that of Aboud in the Sudan (in 1958) is that the Nigerian coup was staged by the armed forces independent of civilian influences. The first Sudanese coup after independence was led by civilian politicians (the Umma Party) who, certain that power would slip out of their hands to the opposition DUP (Democratic Unionist Party), ordered the armed forces to take power. Since it was clear to the southern politicians that there was no way that they could achieve political power by the ballot box, they sought to achieve their ambitions through the bullet. The coup was meant to offer a military solution to their political ambitions.

For Nigeria, it was argued that:

... in September 1966, the Gowon regime set up the ad hoc Constitutional Conference to enable the country to chart a political agenda for the future. But by the time this took place, the foundation stones of Northern interests had already been well laid. The conference became the watershed for the nurturing of the seeds of the North/South dichotomy, a major test to the degree of their commitment to national unity. [Kukah 1993: 40]

It was at this conference that the northern political elite made an important concession pertaining to the creation of new federal states, to accommodate minority groups living under the shadow of oppressive northern Muslim emirates. Northern Nigeria's change of heart and call for unity instead of separation from the federation was put to the test by the outbreak of violence in the North where an Igbo massacre took place. The Biafra war, too, became another pretext for a new *jihad* premised on saving Nigeria from disintegration. The North sounded the trumpet of national unity against southern, particularly Igbo, separatism.

Kukah offers a plausible interpretation of how and why the military was able to conduct so many coups. He argues that, although the implications of military intervention in Nigeria have been well studied, the fact remains that each time the military intervenes, it alters the balance of power so decisively that reactions to military rule change among the ruling classes and the various communities in Nigeria (Kukah 1993: 259–60). A more hardened approach, from an advocate of military rule, claims that 'Nigerians owe a word of gratitude to the armed forces who showed such commitment to preserving the nation state without which there would have been no Nigeria or only parts of it to talk about today. It has proved that it is the only instrument capable of maintaining Nigeria's unity' (Ukpabi, quoted in Kukah 1993: 258). However, this unity is maintained by inflicting a heavy social and economic burden on the Nigerian peoples.

The government of Murtala is often associated with setting up the Constitution Drafting Committee in 1976. The process itself was considered part of the preparations for the return to civilian rule. When the Constitution Drafting Committee completed its work on 20 August 1976, the draft Constitution was subjected to open debate throughout the country. In my view the debate leading to the proclamation of the 1978 Constitution marked the beginning of the current *sharia* debate. It politicised the issue so that it became an important part of political mobilisation in Nigeria.

The civilian government of Shihu Shagari was elected in October 1979 and lasted for four years before being ousted by the military coup led by Mohammed Buhari in December 1983. Buhari's regime is remembered for measures that were considered repressive relative to Nigeria's previous military governments. It clamped down on the freedom of organisation, restricted the freedom of the press, prohibited public gatherings and speeches in what was known as the 'War Against Indiscipline' (see Nwokedi 1995). However, the economic situation was so desperate that many Nigerians associate Buhari's regime most strongly with the end of Nigeria's oil boom and the beginning of an unprecedented decline in standards of living. In fact, many attribute the military coup that brought General Babangida to power in August 1985, and his adherence to the World Bank-sponsored Structural Adjustment Programmes (SAPs), to the steep decline in the Nigerian economy (see also Olukoshi 1993 and Jega 2000). Ihonvbere sums up the association between the pains and cost of failed adjustment and political contradictions in Nigeria: 'economic underdevelopment, foreign domination and exploitation, rural decay and urban dislocation, unemployment, inflation, poverty, inequality, institutional fragility, and other manifestations of backwardness in oil-rich Nigeria are prerequisites of political contradictions and inequalities in the distribution of political power in the country' (1994: 212). The economic crisis created a sense of unity between democrats and human rights activists who felt that the non-democratic management of the country's affairs had denied them the right to participate in the making of their own destiny. As we will see in the following section, General Babangida responded by initiating a programme for transition to democratic rule in the face of an increasingly militant political activism that swept through Nigeria. Ironically, Babangida's programme for transition to democracy was so flawed with inconsistency and contradictions that it gave rise to the Abacha era (1993–97), which was brutally authoritarian.

Three aspects of military rule in Nigeria stand out as indicative of the country's unique but brutal experience of post-independence rule. First, it is difficult to separate Nigeria's military and civilian governments from any perspective other than their capacity to oppress the voices of their critics and their abuse of human rights. In all other negative attributes such as corruption, mismanagement of public funds and erosion of public trust, the civilian and the military governments were on a par with each other. Both negative attributes aroused discontent within a few years for failing to deliver on their promises of prosperity and the rule of law. However, civilian governments do have the advantage of being able to give the impression that they are chosen by the people as representatives of their sovereign will and are in some way 'accountable' to them.

Second, the fact that military coups were staged against incumbent military governments, and that civilian politicians were seen to side with one military leader against another are evidence of the fact that military rule had become the norm rather than the exception. Nigerian military governments often found a contingent of civilian politicians ready to serve in order to satisfy their lust for power and improve their economic fortunes. The involvement of a large number of civilian politicians in military government invites comparison with the case of Sierra Leone, where military rule became an extension of civilian politics. The main difference between the two cases is that the Nigerian Army has proved itself well-equipped to guard its monopoly over the use of force. It has been able to prevent the creation of civilian armies (or warlords) who might challenge its monopoly over the use of military force and to check the proliferation of renegade regional armies.

Third, although the military are often perceived as arbiters of different ethnic claims, using coercive measures to quell rebellion and consolidate national unity, in reality the Nigerian military has acted not merely to preserve the unity of the country, but to safeguard particular ethnic interests. The fact that military coups were staged to prevent members of a particular ethnic group from becoming president of Nigeria, or that political violence was used to make life difficult for an incumbent president because he came from the South were not coincidences.

DEMOCRATIC REVERSAL OR
CONSOLIDATION OF MILITARY RULE

Under considerable internal and external pressure, General Babangida embarked on an elaborate democratic transition programme, which was aimed at restructuring Nigeria's civilian political establishment and parties. The ultimate goal of the transition programme was a return to democracy under newly established political structures capable of cleansing the country of the political mismanagement and corruption that had characterised earlier civilian governments.

The first step towards realising such a programme was taken in 1987 when the military government established a Political Bureau responsible to the president. The Political Bureau's main task was to furnish the president with proposals delineating the future political development of the country, including a timetable for the end of military rule and the return to multi-party democracy.

After reviewing Nigeria's past experience with multi-party democracy, the Political Bureau recommended that the government should abolish all existing political parties and create instead a set of completely new ones. The new political parties were supposed to break the link with ethnic politics and with parties associated with the old political establishment, and to favour secular over religious or ethnic affiliation. The banning of individuals described as corrupt leaders of conventional political parties, opened the door for a 'new breed' of politicians. The government also banned organisations and individuals known for particular ideological positions ('leftists' critical of the Structural Adjustment Programme) and religious extremists (both Christian and Muslim).

The activities of the Political Bureau were supported by a number of institutions for research and political education, such as the Directorate for Mass Mobilisation for Social Justice and Recovery (MMSJR) and the Centre for Democratic Studies (CDS). Both these institutions received substantial government funding and were expected to support the work of the Political Bureau through research and political campaigns to explain the government's transition to democracy programme to the public.

The transition to democracy programme and the setting-up of the Constitutional Drafting Committee (CDC) in the same year (1987) were structurally connected. The Political Bureau was intended to work on the political front as an agent for political mobilisation, while the CDC was to create the legal framework within which the transition to democracy programme could be implemented. The CDC had completed its tasks by 1988, when the Constituent Assembly was created to debate and approve the new constitution. This assembly was supported by Transitional Tribunals and Monitoring Committees with the prime objective of ensuring that the transition programme was understood and adhered to at the federal and local government levels.

Among the most controversial recommendations of the Political Bureau was the establishment of two new government-funded political parties to replace the old ones. The first was the Social Democratic Party (SDP), ideologically committed to Western social democratic tradition. The second was the National Republican Convention (NRC), also in the Western, right-of-centre tradition. The Political Bureau had even drafted the constitutions that were supposed to govern the ideological and political commitments of the two parties. The modernisation antecedence of these policies is self-explanatory.

The Babangida government held the simplistic view that the establishment of two secular parties, with secular ideological orientation, would be a step forward towards political modernisation. Nigerians, the government thought, would support political parties that were neither religious nor ethnic, thus putting a lid on the complex problems that these two tendencies had generated since Nigerian independence.

The failure of the government's transition to democracy did not come as a surprise. It represented an attempt at political engineering whose fate could be anticipated well in advance. The old political establishment rallied its supporters and resisted every move towards legitimising the new system. Civil society organisations, trade unions, youth and women's organisations, and the religious establishment had not been consulted and hence felt alienated. The new parties were not the parties of the people and as such they became the parties of the rich and powerful, gradually falling under the control of the very wealthy politicians Babangida had pledged to remove from the political scene. Those whom Babangida labelled the 'new breed politicians' quickly learned the twists and turns of the 'old breed politicians' and even surpassed them in their corruption and disrespect for the ethics of political office.

During the 1993 elections, the South (Yoruba/Igbo) voted for the Social Democratic Party (SDP), while the North (Hausa/Fulani) voted for the National Republican Convention (NRC). The constellation of ethnic cooperation and rivalries was reflected in the Nigerian armed forces; most of the personnel recruited from the North came from the middle belt of the northern region and were opposed to the NPC (Northern People's Congress, mainly Hausa and Fulani) and to Hausa–Fulani dominance. Igbo from the eastern region formed the majority of the officer corps, which provoked intense distrust from other ethnic groups (Kalu 1996).

Mashood Abiola, a wealthy Yoruba Muslim, contested the presidency against Bashir Tofa, a wealthy Hausa from the North. Abiola's victory in the presidential election stunned the northern Muslim establishment and the army. General Babangida annulled the elections, in what was interpreted by most analysts as an example of northern Muslim intolerance to being ruled by a southern president – even a Muslim.

The contention that Babangida harboured some pro-northern Islamist tendencies cannot be ruled out, given the record of his top appointments. The commanders of the army, navy, and police were all northern Muslims; only the chief of the air staff was from the South. The ministries of external affairs, petroleum resources, internal affairs, and defence, considered the most powerful cabinet posts, were held by northern Muslims (the Minister of Defence being the President himself). These changes generated heated controversy and anti-government demonstrations by Christians in some northern cities, but Babangida emerged from the changes more powerful than before.

For many Nigerian Christians, Babangida's intervention to prevent Mashood Abiola from assuming the presidency of Nigeria fell into a pattern of pro-Muslim political nepotism. This flagrant intervention in the elections meant that Babangida had written the death certificate of his own transition to democracy programme. In less than six months (in November 1993), General Sani Abacha, a Muslim from the North, staged a military coup and seized power, beginning what turned out to be one of Nigeria's most repressive military regimes.

General Abacha took power on 17 November 1993 and proceeded to rule Nigeria with an iron fist: human rights activists were arrested and prominent opposition figures, like Nobel Prize winner Wole Soyinka, were accused of terrorist activities, forcing some to seek exile in Britain. On 31 October 1996, Ken Saro-Wiwa and eight other Ogoni activists were sentenced to death by a military tribunal. Abacha was an autocratic leader who earned the hate of democracy advocates and human rights activists. Mashood Abiola died in prison in 1998.

Civil society organisations campaigned in earnest against Abacha's military rule, culminating in the creation of the Campaign for Democracy (CD), a broad coalition of opposition political and civil associations. The creation of the Campaign for Democracy was followed by the establishment of the People's Committee for Liberty (PCL), the Association for Democracy (AC), the Association for Democracy and Good Governance (ADGG) and the Media Rights Agenda (MRA), among others. Resistance to Abacha's military rule continued unabated until he died of a heart attack on 9 June 1998, and was succeeded by Nigerian armed forces chief, General Abdulsalam Abubakar who was sworn in as the new head of state.

On 27 February 1999, Matthew Olusegun Fajinmi Aremu Obasango was elected President and Alhaji Abubakar Atiku Vice-President. Both are of the People's Democratic Party. In the presidential elections, Obasango won 62.8 per cent of the vote; his rival Samuel Oluyemisi Falae (AD/APP – see below) won 37.2 per cent of the vote. Elections were also held for the two chambers of the parliament: the House of Representatives with 360 members, elected for a four-year term in single-seat constituencies; and the Senate with 109 members, also elected for four-year terms, ending in 2004.

The distribution of votes and seats according to political party was as follows. The People's Democratic Party (PDP) won 57.1 per cent of the vote and 206 seats in the House of Representatives, and 56.4 per cent of the vote and 59 seats in the Senate. The conservative All Peoples' Party (APP) won 30.6 per cent of the vote and 74 House of Representatives seats, and 31.2 per cent of the vote and 29 of the Senate seats. The progressive Alliance for Democracy (AD) won 12.4 per cent of the vote and 68 seats in the House of Representatives, and 12.4 per cent of the vote and 20 seats in the Senate.

The inception of religious violence in Northern Nigeria less than six months after Obasango's election as President of Nigeria hardly came as a surprise. As the following section will show, it is part of a well-established pattern whereby Muslim presidents of southern origin (such as the late Abiola) would be subject to northern intimidation through religious violence. Such violence often questions the capacity of civilian governments to hold the country together and secure national unity. The fact that this violence is often exacted against southerners living in the predominantly Muslim North is a testimony to this North–South divide, which is essentially an expression of inequitable distribution of power and resources.

SHARIA MANIPULATION AND POLITICAL VIOLENCE

Nigeria has experienced three periods of Islamic agitation: pre-colonial, colonial and post-colonial. To that extent, the association between violence and *sharia* law is hardly a new phenomenon. In fact, the very emergence of Northern Nigeria as a distinctive political entity owes its existence to *sharia*. The Jihad of Osman Dan Fodio which began in 1804 aimed at creating a puritan Islamic society devoid of the practices of the corrupt emirs of the northern caliphates of Borno, Sokoto, Bauchi, Borgu (extending up to present-day Burkina Faso), Adamawa (present-day Cameroon), Nupe (including Auchi and Lokoja) and Koni (present-day Niger). In 1812, Osman Dan Fodio's two brothers divided the caliphate, which had by then become very large, between them. Bello ruled Zamfara, Kano, Daura, Katsina, Bauchi and Katugum, with Sokoto as his capital. Abdullahi ruled Nupe, Borgo, Dendi, Ilorin and Liptako, with Qwandu as his capital. Osman Dan Fodio, a learned scholar, retreated to prayers and the offering of *fatwa* on how to rule in accordance with the Koran, the teachings of Prophet Muhammad and the Islamic *sharia* law.

Northern Nigeria was born out of the forcible federation of its fragmented caliphates by the jihadists who called for a purer form of Islam against the backdrop of a decadent leadership which was considered more pagan than Islamic. Islamic *sharia* was reinforced and became law throughout the caliphates, until the incorporation of Northern Nigeria into the British Empire.

When Lord Lugard introduced the Native Administration in Northern Nigeria in 1906, the British Administration considered *sharia* law 'native' to the Fulani and the Hausa caliphates. In order to avoid confrontation with these two ethnic groups, which were known for their ability to mobilise their subjects to war, *sharia* law was kept intact and even reinforced by making it into civil law. Even non-Muslims in British colonial Northern Nigeria were governed under the Islamic *sharia* law. As will be shown later, the proliferation of states in post-independence Nigeria has largely been promoted by non-Muslims who support the idea of separate states in order to free themselves from their centuries-long ties to the Muslim legal system.

During the colonial period, Fulani and Hausa aristocracy 'chose a civil strategy to deal with the British, but refused to adopt their religion (Christianity)' (Kukah and Falola 1996: 3). In other words, the Fulani–Hausa aristocracy tolerated living under the secular constitutions introduced by the British.[1] This meant that the Islamic legal code was applied with the support of the British. In 1953, during the closing decade of British colonial rule and with the Nigerians preparing for independence, the United Muslim Party (UMP) was established in order to safeguard Muslim interests. Among its early demands was the improvement of Muslim access to the factors of development, including health and education. Militant Muslims who, in 1957, established the National Muslim League (NML) resented the modernist attitude of the UMP. Instead of settling for the material benefits of a Western-style way of life and opportunities, NML's demand was for respect for Muslims in a colonial system of government which they identified as Christian. The British answer to this militancy was to integrate more Muslims into the system of government and to allocate more favours to Muslim leaders. By buying Muslim leaders' loyalty to the system, the British colonial rulers managed to keep the lid on several complex issues, leaving them to be dealt with in the post-independence period. One of these complex issues was the role of Islamic *sharia* laws and their applicability in Nigeria, the populations of which profess not only Islam, but also Christianity and a multitude of traditional religions and systems of belief.

Non-Muslims had no right to appeal against the Islamic *sharia* laws (considered the law of God) until 1955, when the Native Courts of Appeal were introduced. One of the first post-independence confrontations between Muslims and Christians came in 1961, when the Sarduna of Sokoto formed Jamaatu Nasril Islam (JNI), an Islamic movement charged with the special responsibility of advancing the cause and message of Islam. JNI has very close associations with the Northern People's Congress (NPC). Likewise, the reformed Tijaniyya Islamic sect crossed the boundaries between the secular and the religious by associating itself with the Northern Elements Progressive Union (NEPU).

One of Nigeria's problems is its uneven wealth distribution; another is the insensitivity of its political elite to ethnic and geographical diversity. According to Bamishaiye (1976: 87): 'of the major ethnic groups in Nigerian polity, three occupy predominant positions in their various regions, that is, the Hausa, the Igbo and the Yoruba. The fourth largest ethnic group, the Fulani, are invariably lumped with the Hausa and together they form 28.1 per cent of the Nigerian population.' This situation has changed little in twenty years:

The final factor of major importance is the location of the ethnic groups, especially the majority groups, the Igbo, Hausa and Yoruba. They are located in the three geographical regions of the country created by the Niger and Benue rivers which join around the middle of the country before flowing together into the Atlantic Ocean. The Hausa are located in the North, the Igbo in the East and the Yoruba in the West. Minority ethnic groups of varying sizes cluster around them

... The regional concentration of these groups has given the nation a semblance of autonomous spheres in the geographical, political and sociological sense. [Nnoli 1995: 29]

Although the three regions were officially abolished during the First Republic, their ethnic character continued to inform the politics of both military and civilian governments in Nigeria. Even after the establishment of the Federal Republic of Nigeria in 1963, the political parties which dominated Nigerian political life were divided according to ethnic groups. The federal parliamentary election campaign in December 1964 – the first since independence – was contested by two political alliances incorporating all the major parties (Metz 1991). The Nigerian National Alliance (NNA) was composed of the NPC, Akintola's Western-based Nigerian National Democratic Party, and opposition parties representing ethnic minorities in the Midwestern and Eastern regions. It was opposed by the United Progressive Grand Alliance (UPGA), which joined the NCNC (National Council of Nigeria and Cameroons) and the remnants of the Action Group with two minority-based Northern allies, the Northern Elements Progressive Union and the United Middle Belt Congress. (For a more detailed analysis of the evolution of Nigeria's political organisations and parties, see Bamishaiye 1976, Nnoli 1995 and Dlakwa 1997.)

Concerns over *sharia* and its application in Northern Nigeria are thus a long-standing issue that have spanned the pre-colonial, colonial, and post-independence periods. The military coup of 15 January 1966 brought into power Major General Aguiyi-Ironsi, a Christian, who became head of state. Two prominent northern political figures, Al Haji Abubakar Tafawa Balewa and Al Haji Ahmadu Bello were killed, an act interpreted by Muslims as a Christian coup against Islam. The issue of whether a Christian could rule Muslims contributed to the eruption of the first major *sharia*-instigated violence in Nigeria in 1967. Because this period coincided with the Biafra war, Udoidem argues that:

The Christians in Biafra believed that they were fighting and resisting Muslim expansion. The Biafra warlords, in their bid to gain international support (at least from the Christian world), canvassed that the war was between the Muslim North and the Christian East. Even the Pope, the spiritual Head of the Catholic Church was caught in the crossfire when he was quoted as having made a public statement to the effect that 'his beloved people were suffering in Biafra'. This was interpreted and politicized to mean that those Christians who were not in Biafra enclave were not his beloved ... It was utterances like these, whether from Muslims or from Christians, that made people conclude that the civil war was not free of religious undertones. [Udoidem 1997: 159]

An immediate effect of the triumph of the Muslim North over Biafra was a display of arrogance on the part of the Muslim northerners and their use (or misuse) of the Nigerian state power and wealth to sway the balance in favour of the North. President Al Haji Shehu Shagari, a Fulani from Qwandu, which had been ruled during the pre-colonial period by the Fulani, headed the Second Republic. President Shagari was also known for his support to the traditional Muslim establishment in the North, with which he worked closely to undermine the authority of Shaikh Gummi. He also lost no opportunity to show his preference for Northern politicians in his top appointments, understandably interpreted by Christians as an anti-South bias. (For a more comprehensive historical coverage of events, see Kukah and Falola 1996.)

The Muslim–Christian conflicts became increasingly politicised, particularly during the debates of 1977 when Muslims began to insist on the extension of *sharia* from state courts in the North to the federal courts, thus making it the *de facto* law of the land. Another area of contention was the admission of Nigeria in 1986 into the Organisation of the Islamic Conference (OIC), an international association of Islamic states in which Nigeria had long held observer status. Christians treated this as a deliberate move by Babangida's Muslim-dominated government to Islamicise Nigeria.

Chronologies of religious crises and violence in Nigeria since the Biafra war have been compiled by Udoidem (1997: 159–79) and by Kukah and Falola (1996), covering the period from 1970 to 1992. Using these as a basis, I have updated the chronology to March 2000 and added commentaries. A complete picture of religious violence in Nigeria can therefore be summarised as follows:

- 1970–75: Muslim assertion and quest for dominance after the Biafra war; increased Christian resentment as a result of increased Muslim influence; state favouritism for and appointment of Muslims in high government positions, particularly during the reign of President Al Haji Shehu Shagari.
- 1976–79: *Sharia* crisis associated with the drafting of the 1979 Constitution which began in 1976, and the question of whether to declare Nigeria a Muslim state. A compromise was reached by making provisions for the establishment of both *sharia* courts and Customary Courts of Appeal at the state level for those states that desired them.

- 18–29 December 1980: Kano riots. The main cause of the riots was the creation by a militant Muslim figure, Alhaji Muhammadu Marwa, of an enclave in Kanu for his followers, and his declaration that anyone who read any book other than the Koran was a pagan. Alhaji Muhammadu Marwa mounted attacks under the name of *jihad* in which an estimated 4,179 people were killed and property worth millions of dollars was destroyed.
- October 1982: Burning of churches in Kano after the laying of foundations of a church near a mosque in Kano.
- 27 February 1984: Jimeta, an enclave in Adamawa state, was used by remnants of the disciples of Alhaji Muhammadu Marwa; they rampaged through the city, destroyed the local market and burnt houses, leaving 50,000 people homeless.
- 29 April 1985: Gombe riots, instigated by Alhaji Musa Makanaki, one of the defenders of Jimeta.
- March–May 1986: The Ilorin disturbances, inflamed by Christian marches during Palm Sunday through a Muslim residential area (similar to disturbances caused by the marches of the Protestant Orange Order through Catholic areas in Northern Ireland). Muslims attacked Christians throughout northern Nigeria, particularly at Usman dan Fodio University, Sokoto and Ibadan University.
- June 1988: Ahmadu Bello University crisis provoked by Christian students' call for an end to Muslim discrimination against Christians. During elections to the Students' Union, the Christian students' slogan was 'a vote for Stephen [a Christian student], is a vote for Christ'. Muslim reaction was swift, culminating in the burning of churches, and killing of priests and prominent Christian figures.
- 20–22 April 1991: It is reported that hundreds of people were hurt and millions of dollars' worth of property lost in Bauchi because of a misunderstanding whether the meat sold by Christians was dog or pork meat – prohibited for Muslims.
- 11 October 1991: Kano riots erupt when the state chapter of Christian Anglican Churches (CAC) was attacked by Muslim fundamentalist youths in protest at the presence of the German Christian preacher, Reinhardt Bonke. This was seen as a deliberate anti-Muslim act, because earlier in the year the state government had refused to grant permission to a Muslim fundamentalist preacher to visit Kano. The youths described their action as an attack against the religious crusade organised by the state chapter of CAC.
- October 1992: Katsina riots, caused by an article in the *Fun Times*, a publication of the Nigerian *Daily Times*, in which a Muslim claimed that Prophet Muhammad had had an affair with a woman of easy

virtue and later married her. This was in reply to an earlier news article in which the author claimed that a Christian could marry a prostitute if she is 'born again'. Mallam Yahaya Yakubu, a 35-year-old Islamic teacher who had political conflicts with the Christian governor of Katsina State, turned this incident into a call for an Islamic revolution. He was supported by El-Zak Zaky Shi'ite Muslim fundamentalist movement protests. The *Daily Times* office was vandalised, and the protest spread to other cities such as Sokoto and Kaduna.

- 2 April 1992: Further rioting in Bauchi, caused by a Muslim–Christian conflict over the leadership of Lere District. Despite the Christian majority in the area, they remain under the leadership of the Emir of Bauchi, who is also responsible for appointing the district leader. A further problem is the Christian butchers' practice of slaughtering and selling pigs' meat (prohibited for Muslims). The Tayiawa Christians used this conflict to vent their anger on the Fulani Muslims: several lives were lost and many churches and mosques were destroyed in this riot.
- May 1992: Zangon-Kataf Uprising, over the relocation of a market ordered by the Emir of Zaria and the Kataf Christian governor of Kaduna State. The riots, south of Kaduna, resulted in several deaths and the destruction of churches, mosques and houses.

I have traced the latest incidences of politico-religious violence in Nigeria and produced the following chronology which covers the period following the return of multi-party democracy:

- 29 May 1999: Riots in Odi, a small town in the southern state of Bayelsa; when the military was sent to the area, it virtually razed the town to the ground.
- 15 June 1999: Violent militiamen in Obasango's south-west region rioted, killing non-natives, many of them Northern Muslims.
- 8 October 1999: Two bills passed by the Zamfara State Assembly authorising *sharia* law were signed into law by Ahmed Sani Yerima. Reports indicate that no sooner had Yerima signed the bills than a number of Muslim zealots went on a rampage. Two churches were torched in Gusau – the Methodist Church and the Christian Evangelical Fellowship of Nigeria. The secretary-general of the Christian Association of Nigeria (CAN) in the state, B.A. Eguavon, alleged that one Christian accused of an offence bled to death when both his arms were amputated. *Sharia* law authorises amputation of the arm or leg of a convicted thief. Reports further indicate that it took the personal intervention of the governor to secure the release of

twenty people accused of operating beer parlours. Yerima said the accused, mostly Christians, should be compensated if any of their goods or property were destroyed in the course of the arrest.

Religious violence began to escalate again in December 1999 during the writing of this chapter. It was reported by *Marantha Christian Journal* (15 December 1999) that:

> [Eighteen] churches in Ilorin, the capital of Kwara State in north-central Nigeria, were vandalised or destroyed by Islamic extremists and Christian leaders are threatening to retaliate if the state government does not act to stop further violence. The attacks were orchestrated by militant Muslims who raided churches in the ancient city that links the southern part of the country to the north. Equipment ranging from fans and musical instruments to vehicles was stolen or damaged, and some of the buildings were set ablaze. Shola Kolapo, an assistant pastor of the United Missionary Church of Africa, said he was praying with two people inside their 50-year-old building when the church was attacked and before they knew what was happening, the attackers started breaking the gate with different weapons. The Rev. S.A. Ekundayo, senior pastor, was quoted as saying that Muslims and Christians in Kwara State have had a frosty relationship for decades. Ilorin has a history of yearly clashes between Christians and Muslims around Easter. Muslims usually refuse to permit processions by Christians through traditional Muslim areas. Christians recently protested a directive by the Emir of Ilorin that churches be relocated outside the town center. Islamic leaders in the state have disassociated themselves from the recent attacks. On the other hand, Chief Imam of Ilorin, Mohammed Bashir was also quoted as saying, 'we believe in peace, Islam is about peace'.

- 23 February 2000: Riots spread to Zaria and Kachia in the southern part of the state, where 210 people were killed. The riots followed the same pattern as in Kaduna, with houses destroyed and businesses burnt.
- 27 February 2000: Unrest following a march organised by the Christian Association of Nigeria (CAN) to protest against the proposed introduction of Islamic law in the state of Kaduna. Angry Muslims attacked Christian demonstrators. The result of the violent clashes was the destruction of lives and property. The violence left over 100 dead.
- 28 February 2000: Disturbances in Aba, started by a group of renegades who felt that they were taking due revenge for the murder of their kin in Kaduna, whose bodies were brought back on a trailer.

The religious violence of January–March 2000 was largely sparked by Ahmed Sani Yerima, the governor of Zamfara State; he declared Zamfara a Muslim state, proclaiming Islamic *sharia* laws as the guiding principles of socioeconomic and political life in the state. John Oloto of the *Vanguard* newspaper explained the factors that contributed to Ahmed Sani Yerima's decision:

> The first factor could be his faith in Islam, which has been his long dream of having a good opportunity to actualize it. This was clearly expressed in his address during the launching where he said the 'event will be marked in the annals of not only Zamfara State but throughout our beloved country, Nigeria as the culminating point in the actualization of the hopes, ideals and aspirations of majority of our citizens, the Muslims'. He went further to berate Muslims for their inactivity in the past saying that 'Muslims Ummah in this nation had for too long been dormant, inactive and indeed, in a state of slumber which had given the impression that we are the silent majority'. He reminded the Muslims of their partial victory with independence but regretted that their lack of planning robbed them of the fruits of their struggle.
>
> The second factor that could have influenced Yerima's decision could be internal, possibly from those powerful groups in the North to derail the administration of President Obasango and our fledging democracy. This group saw the success of Obasango as their success. Thus they believed he will protect their interests, but the reverse is now the case.
>
> The third factor is the external influence from Arab nations. Already Yerima had sent a five-man committee to Saudi Arabia to learn and under-study the system and how they would overcome the initial difficulties in the application of the *Sharia* in Zamfara State coupled with the N500m grant from five Muslim nations in support of the take-off of the *Sharia* legal system in the state. [2 March 2000]

The introduction of *sharia* laws in the Northern states has challenged Nigeria's 1999 Constitution. Although partially conceding that, President Obasango has declared:

> The council also reviewed the remote and immediate causes of the disturbances, and noted that the *Penal Code* currently in force in the Northern states is substantially based on *Sharia* Law, with the modifications that imprisonment is substituted in place of amputation of limbs, as punishment for stealing, and as punishment for adultery, instead of stoning to death. The council noted that these modifications are consis-

tent with the human rights principles enshrined in our constitution, and considered the punishments adequate in the circumstances ... The council unanimously agreed that all states that have recently adopted *Sharia* Law should in the meantime revert to the status quo ante. That is, *Sharia*, as practised in Penal Code, continues to be practised by all states concerned. The council urges all Nigerians to remain calm and law-abiding. Provocative and inciting utterances will not be tolerated. [President Obasango, House of Representatives, 24 February 2000]

In examining the association between religious violence, democracy and major political events in Nigeria, it is immediately clear that the vast majority of violent incidents occurred during 'democratic' civilian rule. While it is not appropriate to associate democracy with violence, it is valid to ask why violence intensifies during periods of democratic rule in Nigeria, particularly northern Nigeria. Since violence is associated with northern calls for the introduction of Islamic *sharia* laws, we might also ask why such calls are not voiced during military rule, given that the majority of Nigerian rulers since independence have been Muslims.

ETHNICITY, RELIGION AND DEMOCRATIC REVERSAL

The literatures on ethnicity, religious conflict and democratic reversal in Nigeria are mutually reinforcing. As in other ethnically divided societies, democracy is confronted with the formidable challenge of containing rather than augmenting ethnic conflicts. One of the potential areas of conflict between democracy on the one hand and ethnicity and religion on the other is that all three are institutions of inclusion and exclusion. In effect, inclusion in any one of these three institutions may contribute to the exclusion of one or two of the others. The Nigerian case is further complicated by the tendency to conflate ethnicity and religion, particularly the association between the northern states and Islam, in the collective historical memory. Horowitz (1994: 35) offers a succinct commentary on this: 'Democracy is about inclusion and exclusion, about access to power, about privileges that go with inclusion and the penalties that accompany exclusion. In severely divided societies, ethnic identity provides clear lines to determine who will be included and who will be excluded.'

If ethnicity, religion and democracy are institutional mechanisms for inclusion and exclusion, three questions can be asked: (a) what are the social forces that reinforce inclusion or exclusion? (b) who benefits from inclusion or exclusion? (c) in intra-ethnic, inter-religious group relations, do inclusion and exclusion mask the fact that such groups are highly internally differentiated? In other words, does the inclusion and exclusion principle also operate within those ethnic groups that strive to exclude or include others?

These are difficult and complex questions to answer within the space available in this chapter. However, it is possible to illustrate that various ethnic and religious groups interpret democracy, religion and ethnicity in the light of how much they can gain from each. While majority groups such as the Yoruba, Igbo, Hausa and Fulani may welcome the rewards of the democratic principle of majority rule, minorities may not. Democracy in this sense institutionalises inclusion and exclusion based on majority rule. In the same vein, democracy can institutionalise the rule of the ethnic groups that constitute the majority of the population, particularly when political mobilisation based on ethnic affiliation is feasible.

What are the social forces that reinforce exclusion through ethnicity and religion? The chronology of religious violence presented above illustrates that in Nigeria, religion and ethnicity have mutual connotations, although neither Islam nor Christianity is an ethnic faith. Islam has spread across the ethnic divide, even among the major ethnic groups, so that large Muslim communities exist among the Yoruba in South and North Nigeria. Likewise, there are a large number of minority non-Hausa–Fulani Muslim groups in the North who have historically been overwhelmed by the assertiveness of the Hausa–Fulani alliance and its Islamic orientation. The problem here is not Islam or Christianity *per se*, but the use of Islam or Christianity to advance other causes. Four major social forces are at play here.

The first is the historical Islamic establishment, which has ruled over the lives of northern Nigerians for over two centuries, and which has continued to dominate Nigerian national politics since independence. In the North, the National Party of Nigeria's election campaigns use chiefs and emirs to mobilise grassroots support under the slogan 'Vote for a northern Muslim' (Kukah and Falola 1996: 112). Islamic religious personalities such as the Sarduna of Sokoto and the Emir of Kanu still hold political sway, with thousands of chiefs and millions of followers behind them. One of the most renowned and militant Muslim activists and scholars was the late Shaikh Abubakar Gummi of Kaduna. He used *Jamaat Izalat al bidi' wa Iqamat al sunna*, a militant anti-Sufi movement dedicated to the eradication of innovations it perceived heretical and un-Islamic, by using the Federal Radio Corporation of Northern Nigeria (FRCN Kaduna), two newspapers (*New Nigerian* and *gaskiya ta fi kwabo*) and recorded cassettes of his teachings. Kukah (1993: 218) observed that, by 1978, 'some of his pupils had penetrated the main political institutions like the army, the media, the universities and the business world in the country, bolstering his base within and outside Nigeria.' With his contacts in high places including President Shagari, Shaikh Gummi had developed an aura of influence around himself which gave *Jamaat Izalat al bidi' wa Iqamat al sunna* legitimacy and acceptance. However, Shaikh Gummi found himself under immense pressure from Nigeria's traditional Muslim establishment such as Jamaatu Nasril Islam (JNI) and its relationship with the political parties in Northern Nigeria. The ferocity with which the politico-religious alliance of the northern establishment had attacked Shaikh Gummi caused scepticism among many Nigerians who understood that his teachings may go beyond religion to the advocacy of an alternative political order. No matter what Shaikh Gummi's political religious teaching and political manoeuvring might have entailed, it reveals that the Muslim movement in northern Nigeria is far from unified. It is divided and beset by ideological as well as material differences.

The second social force is the northern political elite, which found in Islam and ethnicity readily available and powerful institutions for political mobilisation. Islam and ethnicity are unifying factors that bring along with them a large number of voters, a political resource that transcends economic and social differentiation. The collective sentiments of an ethnic or religious group can also be mobilised through the creation of a real or imagined enemy, and the need for collective protection against this 'enemy' from a different ethnicity and a different religion. The northern elite also consciously aims to keep job opportunities in government and universities for northerners. A covert 'northernisation' policy has been at play since the 1970s, in which citizens from the South were hired into jobs that required higher qualifications, but only until a northerner was sufficiently trained to take over. The policy of keeping particular jobs within northern hands was also a way to create a basis of political support. Similar policies have also been adopted by the southern states, thus reinforcing the prejudice of each side against the other.

The third social force at play is the northern business class and its quest for the monopoly of trade, land and government contracts, to the exclusion of southerners. A common characteristic of religious violence in northern Nigeria is the burning and destruction of the property of southern traders, businesspeople and estate owners. In the February 2000 riots, it was estimated that $800 million worth of property, most of it belonging to southern Nigerians, was destroyed. The destruction of property is a form of ethnic cleansing: northern residents believe that southern Nigerians should return to their 'homelands'. President Obasango commented on this in his Address to the Nation at the beginning of March 2000: 'What I found most astounding was the discovery that a majority of those who died in the disturbances were Nigerians who had lived all their lives in Kaduna, and could not truthfully call anywhere else their home. All so suddenly, people who had been their neighbours for decades turned on them, and massacred them.'

The fourth and final social force consists of the militant Islamic sects, brotherhoods and fundamentalist groups, some of which have external connections to global Islamic revival movements. The main objective of these groups is to convert Nigeria into a Muslim state: short of that, their aim is to install Islamic rule in Northern Nigeria. Most important among these Islamic brotherhoods are the following: Jamaatu Nasril Islam, the El-Zak Zaky Shi'ite Muslim fundamentalist movement, the Ansarul Din, the Ahmadiyya, and the Jamatul Muslemeen Council. These Muslim brotherhoods and sects build their creed on the determination to advance Islam and ensure the application of *sharia* as a Muslim way of life. All the incidents of religious violence have involved one or more of these militant Islamic groups.

The Nigerian version of political Islam is unique in at least two respects. First, Islamic militancy in northern Nigeria has popular appeal associated with a collective memory of past glory (the nineteenth-century Jihadist) and the anguish of a troubled present marred with economic pressure and political bankruptcy. This militancy is pitched against the northern elite who use Islam as an instrument for political mobilisation, some of them with no commitment to the establishment of a Muslim state at the expense of the Nigerian Federation. The northern elite, living para-sitically off the southern oil wealth, is ill-prepared to part with these resources, and is therefore committed to protect the Federation. The exis-tence of a strong, professional and well-trained, northern-dominated military ready to step in to protect the unity of Nigeria is one of the main reasons why Nigerians often greet military coups with mixed feelings. On the one hand, military rule is autocratic; on the other, it maintains the status quo and consolidates the power structure which favours the northern elite. The northern elite's apparent indifference to religious violence bears the hallmark of an elite ready to use the military as an extension to civilian rule by employing the all-too-familiar argument of maintaining national unity.

Second, the militancy of some strands of northern Nigeria's Islamic movement and its struggle to establish a Muslim state is derived from a perceived golden age as custodians of Islamic purity and the return of the rule of the authentic *sharia* laws. The northern leaders of the militant Islamic movements also assume moral leadership through their claim to the status of charismatic learned men. While the economic and political fortunes of the secular 'modern' Western-educated elite depend on the Nigerian Federation, those of the 'neo-jihadists' depend on the mass of the northern poor who constitute the majority of the population.

Ideologically, the majority of the northern Muslims perceive the Christian South not only as the enemy of their faith, but also as an increasingly assertive entity in the struggle for Nigeria's wealth, a wealth that has hardly improved the socioeconomic conditions of the poor. Unfortunately, the inequitable distribution of wealth and inequitable distribution of power go hand in hand, allowing ethnicity and faith to inform a public consciousness susceptible to calls for redemption from poverty and need. Neither the militancy of the northern Nigeria version of political Islam nor the manipulation of ethnicity by the secular political elite is capable of offering a sustainable future. Political violence in Nigeria cannot be explained with reference to ethnicity and faith in isolation from the socioeconomic and political conditions prevailing in the country.

The issue of minorities and the nation state will be dealt with in more detail in Chapter 9 where the Nigerian case will resurface. However, the question that remains is that in severely divided societies the problem is less of managing diversity than of accommodating minorities in a fair system of power sharing. Obviously, minority representation in first-past-the-post democratic systems poses a serious challenge to the capacity of any such state to be genuinely democratic. Because numerical minorities lack sufficient votes to ensure effective representation, the capacity of democracy alone to ensure equitable and just representation is questionable. Where the disadvantages of numerical and social minorities are combined, they would certainly lose out in first-past-the-post systems because they command neither sufficient material resources nor votes to be fully represented in the legislature, and hence feel alienated by the very democratic process.

In the Nigeria case, the squabble between the dominant North and the South, which is endowed with huge resources, is obviously a source of contention between democracy (where the numerically dominant majority governs, while the South remains a subservient political majority), ethnicity and religious faith. In such circumstances, the struggle over the constituents of the state such as the dominant nation, religion, and region become part of the political struggle. As in other parts of the world, the centrality of the state is sufficient reason to make it a focus of bitter struggles between a political elite divided according to allegiances informed by symbols that fit the dominant political culture of the ethnic groups that make up the state.

8
Southern African Democracies and South Africa's Resilience

The countries of southern Africa, particularly Botswana, South Africa, Zambia and Zimbabwe, represent a special case in African democracies and politics. With the exception of Botswana, which is considered one of Africa's most stable democracies, these countries have, since the 1990s, pursued a transition to multi-party democracy. As elsewhere in Africa, the experiences of these countries with multi-party democracy vary considerably. While the ANC ascended to power in South Africa after a long drawn-out liberation struggle, the government of Zimbabwe has only recently, under considerable internal and external pressure, opened up the space for political contestation against the state party, ZANU-PF. In Zambia, the United National Independence Party (the ruling party under the leadership of Kaunda) lost power to the Movement of Multi-party Democracy (MMD) of Frederick Chiluba, the incumbent president of Zambia. Botswana's multi-party democracy is unique in the African continent; first, the political parties are of relatively recent origin, dating back to the early and late 1960s (the Botswana Democratic Party and the Botswana National Front, respectively). Second, Botswana is one of just a handful of African countries that have not experienced reversal to military rule. Third, since independence, Botswana has instituted a House of Chiefs, a largely advisory 15-member body consisting of chiefs of the eight principal tribes, four elected sub-chiefs, and three members selected by the other twelve.

In contrast to Botswana, Zambia and Zimbabwe are representative of a more typical African pattern, in which post-independence multi-party democracy immediately degenerated into authoritarian one-party states. The original one-party states were forced to democratise by external pressures typical of the post-Cold War good governance and democratisation projects. Zambia and Zimbabwe share with South Africa the existence of a white minority; these had a largely common colonial history but essentially different political outcomes, the introduction of apartheid by South Africa in 1948 distinguishing it from Zambia and Zimbabwe. Ironically, the political outcomes of the post-apartheid legacy seem less tenacious than the ultra-nationalistic policies of the current Zimbabwe government.

Economically, southern Africa is the fastest growing subregion in the continent. It is in this region, too, that one finds Africa's most prominent case of racial tolerance, following the end of the apartheid regime in South Africa, and an example of the most unequal land distribution, in the case of Zimbabwe. The sizeable white minority in the region has left its mark on the history of the continent, if not on the world's attitudes towards racial segregation. Yet despite its immense potential and rich resource endowment, the majority of the population of this subregion is poor, and pins much hope on democracy. The question is whether southern Africa's economic potential may be indicative of a sustainable democratic transition.

This chapter attempts to explain the substance of southern African democracies. Are they extensions of one-party regimes which failed to come to terms with multi-party democracy (Zambia and Zimbabwe)? Are the political parties in reality ethnic political parties denied maturation by a political elite divorced from people's aspirations? Attempting to answer these questions is important for delineating the scope and nature of the politics of democratisation, its promises and challenges. (For a comparative perspective on Zambia and Zimbabwe's elections and democratic transition in general, see Chan 1992).

ZAMBIA: COMPARING THE FIRST AND THE THIRD REPUBLICS

For the greater part of its independence, Zambia was ruled by President Kaunda. The political history of independent Zambia can be divided into three segments: the multi-party system that followed colonial rule, known as the First Republic (1964–72); the Second Republic (1972–90), which was dominated by a one-party system under the United National Independence Party (UNIP), and the Third Republic, which began in 1990. If the First and the Third Republics are characterised by multi-party democracy, how do they compare to each other? Do any of the factors that contributed to the first democratic reversal from multi-party to single-party state still pose a threat to the Third Republic?

Two parties with unequal access to power dominated the politics of the First Republic: the United National Independence Party (UNIP) and the African National Congress (ANC). Although ANC was organisationally weak and failed during the first years of independence to pose a credible threat to UNIP, it defied Kaunda's prediction of a natural death and began to grow. According to Chikulo (1988: 68), 'the challenge to UNIP came from within as its strength has invited intra-party rivalry and intense competition over its leadership. With the ANC gaining strength while UNIP is increasingly weakened … The factional conflict was exacerbated in 1967 when UNIP General Conference was dominated by ethnic and regional interests.' UNIP's internal divisions became apparent in the UNIP Central Committee's elections when two broadly ethnically based factions emerged – a Bemba- and Tonga-speaking faction, and a Lozi- and Nyanja-speaking faction. Molento (1972) summarised the ethnicisation and regionalisation tendencies within UNIP as follows: in the Central Province, there were reports of the formation of the Bantu Botatwe Association by the Illa-Lenje-Tonga group within the UNIP, with the main objective of removing Kapwepwe from the post of vice-president. In the Western Province, there were increasing rumours of secession. And in the Northwestern Province, there was dissatisfaction with the allegedly unfair distribution of parliamentary seats. In Luapula Province there was an assertion of Luapula identity *vis-à-vis* the Bemba in the call for the election of true 'Luapulans' to represent them in Parliament.

Intra-UNIP divisions strengthened the United Party (UP) which began to challenge UNIP in the Western Province. When violent clashes between UNIP and UP supporters in 1968 were used as a pretext to ban UP, followers of UP shifted their support to ANC, which began to challenge UNIP in its stronghold in the Southern Province. In an attempt to curb 'tribal divisions' within UNIP, Kaunda introduced new measures, according to which the number of votes cast in the elections to the UNIP Central Committee corresponded to the number of party regions it contained. This gave the northern politicians a clear electoral advantage (for more details, see Chikulo 1979). The factional divisions within UNIP resulted in the split of the party and the formation of a new political party, the United Progressive Party (UPP). President Kaunda was by then certain that UNIP was on the way to disintegration and his power base was beginning to erode. The UPP was outlawed, its leaders imprisoned and its property confiscated by the government. The establishment of a one-party system was declared on 4 February 1972, with the justification of safeguarding the country against political disintegration and violence in the name of democracy.

Although the literature on the one-party system in Zambia is very well documented (Molento 1972; Gertzel, Baylies and Szeftel 1984; Donge 1995; Sichone and Chikulo 1996), it suffices the purpose of this chapter to allude to the factors which contributed to its demise. Sichone laments that:

During the Second Republic, 1972–1991, UNIP exercising 'party supremacy' in all spheres of social life orchestrated political ritual from the village school to the national headquarters ... Alongside the extravagant waste of public funds on political ritual the Zambian economy continued to decline steadily from the mid-1970s through the

1980s. As the standards of living fell so did the alienation of the party from the people grow. [Sichone 1996: 113]

Sichone thus suggests that it was economic hardship that forced Zambians to rebel against UNIP after 27 years in government rather than agitation for multi-party democracy *per se*. Although the one-party participatory democracy could have prepared the populace for multi-party democracy, its populist policies had antagonised many important sectors, particularly the intelligentsia, the church, human rights activists and a large variety of civic organisations, including trade unions and women's and students' organisations (see Mills 1992).

However, by the time of the October presidential and legislative elections, seven political parties were banned because, according to the government, they failed to meet the requirements of a political party stipulated in the Constitution. A third important difference is UNIP's attempt to abide by the separation of power principle, with President Kaunda separating party and state. This act meant, at least officially, UNIP no longer had the resources of the state at its disposal. More importantly, it signalled a major difference with the First Republic where UNIP's dominance and monopoly over power presented it as the 'party of the state', operated by using the resources of the state. The formation of political parties and organisations, enshrined in the Constitution, made it possible for new political parties to be registered. Furthermore, in May 1992 UNIP not only lost power to MMD, but it also split and a new splinter party known as the United Democratic Party (UDP) was formed (see Burnell 1997 for more details on the intricacies of the democratic politics in Zambia).

One of the most interesting features of the politics of the Third Republic is the frequency of inter-party alliances and intra-party splits. Many examples of this process of interest aggregation can be highlighted, such as the July 1993 informal alliance between UNIP, the UDP and the Labour Party, in a campaign of civil disobedience in protest against the economic austerity measures; and the formation of the Zambia Opposition Front (ZOFRO) in June 1994, consisting of seven parties, including UNIP, the UDP, the LP and other smaller political parties. In January 1996, ZOFRO resisted the Chiluba government's attempt to amend the Constitution in order to bar some of its opponents (such as President Kaunda) from politics. Another case of interest aggregation occurred in March 1999, when the Zambia Alliance for Progress (ZAP) was formed by the Zambia Democratic Congress (ZADECO) and the Agenda-for-Zambia Party (AZ), in collaboration with other opposition parties. The government refused ZAP's application to register as a political party until all the opposition parties that formed it were dissolved. In August 1999, ZADECO and other parties joined ZAP thus repudiating their parliamentary seats.

The democratic politics of the Third Republic has also shown a great deal of interest negotiation and elite interest aggregation, such as the discussions between President Chiluba and opposition parties, including Kaunda, in August 1996 in preparation for presidential and National Assembly elections in November of that year. However, interest negotiation had little effect in softening the coercive methods adopted by President Chiluba: accusations levelled against the government include the arrest and killing of political opponents, heavy-handed treatment of trade union and student strikes (which took place in March 1996), and police brutality (Human Rights Watch 1996).

The Third Republic had also inherited the hallmark of the First Republic's ethnic politics, particularly the elitist nature of politics and the ethnic orientation of political leadership. Two examples illustrate the elitist nature of Zambian politics. In the 1996 elections, traditional chiefs and rulers were banned from involvement in public office. One casualty of this ruling was ex-President Kaunda's deputy, Chief Inyambo Yeta, who was prevented from contesting the elections. Second, in October 1996, President Chiluba announced the nomination of a junior minister, Paul Tembo, to stand in Kabwe constituency instead of a popular local businessman, Austin Chewe. President Chiluba was thus seen to exercise direct control over who should stand in the elections on behalf of the MMD, and in what constituency, in a manner very similar to Kaunda's one-party system nominations of eligible candidates. The whole furore about ex-President Kaunda's nationality and his exclusion from contesting the 1996 presidential elections on this ground provides another illustration of the political manipulation of democracy and the presence of strong civilian dictatorship tendencies.

As the case of Zimbabwe will reveal, even the transformation of Zimbabwe into a multi-party democracy under mounting internal and external pressures has not prevented Zimbabwe African National Union-Patriotic Front (ZANU-PF) from ruling the country as a one-party state, hardly heeding popular demands for change. The question that persists in both cases is why a multi-party democracy that came about through the defeat of the single ruling party through democratic elections has equally failed to bring about a semblance of quasi-polyarchy. The elite-dominated nature of democratic transition has failed not only to accommodate popular demands for change, but also facilitated the circulation of the old militant socialist guards who operated like democrats camouflaged under the new democratic façade of multi-party democracy.

ZIMBABWE: LAND AND DEMOCRACY

While the recent violence over the land question in Zimbabwe is clearly part of President Mugabe's cynical ploy to hang on to power at any cost, it is equally true that the land question must be solved democratically if Zimbabwe is to live in peace with itself. The political ramifications of the violence exacted on white farmers by the National Liberation War Veterans Association may be felt far beyond southern Africa, particularly in countries where land alienation is a major concern. The agrarian nature of African economies means that land continues to play a significant role in the lives of the majority of African peoples. Despite the historical specificity of the situation in Zimbabwe, here as in the rest of Africa it is power relations rather than race that mediate the land question. (For a concise summary of the constitutional issues of the land question in Zimbabwe, see Van-Horn 1994.)

The history of the land question in Zimbabwe is well documented, and will be discussed here only in order to show how land entered into the democratic debate and to clarify the role of the war veterans in the current political fray. On the eve of Zimbabwe's independence from Britain in 1980, 97 per cent of the population owned 45 million acres of land. The rest of the land, some 42 million acres, was owned by just 3 per cent of the population under the watchful eye of the Lancaster House Constitution, which gave total protection to private land ownership. Since independence, five major pieces of legislation dealing with land acquisition, reform and resettlement have been promulgated:

1) Communal Land Act (1981)
2) First Phase of Land Reform and Settlement Programme 1980–1990
3) Land Acquisition Act (1992)
4) Second Phase of Land Reform and Resettlement Programme (LRRP) (1998)
5) Constitutional Amendment (May 2000).

All these measures are aimed at transferring land away from large-scale commercial farmers. Three categories of farmers are eligible for resettlement: the landless, those living on congested farms, and those settled on poor agricultural land. Land reform and resettlement is clearly a strategy with developmental as well as poverty alleviation objectives. This aim was emphasised in the 1980 Zimbabwe Conference of Reconstruction and Development (ZCRD) supported by three major donors – Britain, the US and, at the time, West Germany.

The 1992 Land Acquisition Act was more explicit on the criteria for acquisition. Five categories of land were considered eligible for acquisition: derelict land, under-utilised land, land owned by absentee landlords, land owned by farmers with more than one farm considered suitable under given ecological conditions, and farms adjacent to communal areas. The second donor conference of September 1998 was attended by 48 countries which pledged support under a land reform and resettlement programme similar to the first donor conference of 1980. The general objective was to reduce poverty, increase the contribution of agriculture to the country's GDP, promote environmentally sustainable land utilisation and improve the conditions for peace and social stability by removing imbalances in land distribution.

According to Zimbabwe government statistics, 524,890 families are still awaiting resettlement. The financial requirements to resettle these families are well in excess of one billion US dollars. The land reform and resettlement programme favours the politically vocal ex-farm workers, ex-mine workers, graduates of agricultural training institutes and colleges, and women and indigenous peoples intending to make a living from commercial farming. Of the latter two groups, indigenous peoples with commercial farming interests are beneficiaries as part of government policy to increase cash-crop production, while women have been given preference in order to satisfy explicit donor conditionality.

From 1990 onwards, land acquisition policies became more politicised. The introduction of a multi-party system and the struggle for political pluralism have gradually transformed the land issue from a socioeconomic necessity to a profitable political resource. More than ever before, land acquired a vote-winning status and President Mugabe was quick to capitalise on this new resource. The 1992 Land Acquisition Act gave the government legal grounds for compulsory land acquisition and the right to purchase about 50 per cent (5.5 million ha) of the land owned by white farmers. In a more proactive attempt to protect the interests of land-hungry farmers, Zimbabwe introduced an investment act in 1996 which barred foreigners from purchasing land without government approval, except in marginal lands. In November 1997, Mugabe's government announced that 1,471 commercial farms were designated for compulsory acquisition with compensation for land improvement, but no compensation for the land. The IMF entered the land fray in January 1998 when it demanded a land compensation conditionality before releasing any further financial assistance to Zimbabwe.

The House of Assembly elections of 2000 and the presidential election of 2002 almost certainly put additional pressure on the government of President Mugabe to be seen to be doing something on the land front. In November 1998, the government announced the compulsory acquisition of 841 farms covering 2.2 million ha, with the full involvement of the

Commercial Farmers Union.[1] In May 1999, the Cabinet approved an Inception Phase Framework Plan (IPFP) calling for the resettlement of 77,700 families by 2001.

However, in early 2000, militants of the National Liberation War Veterans Association, many of whom fought under Mugabe's command in Zimbabwe's war of independence, took matters into their own hands and led the illegal occupation of more than 1,700 white-owned commercial farms. Many admitted receiving money and transport from ZANU-PF, the ruling party. It was reported that President Mugabe had described farm invasion as 'a minor trespass', protesting unfair ownership of land by whites, and ordered police not to intervene. In the build-up to the legislative elections of 22–25 June, farm occupations and political violence intensified, with 31 people killed in the clashes.

In the debate over constitutional amendments to allow the government to seize land owned by white farmers without compensating them, Mugabe described a guarantee in the constitution that landowners should receive compensation for farms nationalised by the government as a 'stupid clause'. One of the main areas of contention between opposition and the ZANU-PF in the debate over the new constitution was a clause calling for the seizure of white farms and their redistribution without compensation. The debate was so uncompromising that the National Constitutional Assembly (NCA) boycotted the government's constitutional reform process for favouring ZANU-PF.

The ZANU-PF government appointed a 400-member commission to draft a new constitution to replace the one which had been negotiated before Zimbabwe's independence in 1980, and extensively amended since. Approval of the new draft constitution – which would consolidate the powers of the president, allowing Mugabe to stand for an additional two terms, and allow the government to acquire privately owned land without paying compensation – was to be by referendum, held on 12–13 February. The referendum was won by the opposition forces, with 54.68 per cent (697,754) voting against the new Mugabe/ZANU-PF Constitution.

The Movement for Democratic Change (MDC) led the protests, supported by the Zimbabwe Congress of Trade Unions (ZCTU), the National Constitutional Assembly, churches, NGOs, women's groups and human rights activists. The state-controlled media described the MDC as a puppet of foreign powers party financed by 'Rhodesians' based in South Africa. The MDC's secretary-general, Morgan Tvsangirai, and its president, Gibson Sibanda, describe the government media accusations as familiar tactics used by ZANU-PF to discredit their opponents. In the same vein, Ms Margaret Dongo, the member of parliament for Harare South and the president of the Zimbabwe Union of Democrats (ZUD), issued a communiqué on 4 March 2000, to her constituency and the public in general with respect to land invasions, stating that 'The farm invasions are politically inspired acts of wanton destruction and intimidation, and are totally condemned by myself in my person and political capacity as the president of ZUD, and the country-wide ZUD membership. Our future food security and future foreign currency reserves are being endangered to the extreme by a government who has nothing to lose.' Ms Dongo adds:

> As the independent MP for Harare South, I raised the issue of farm allocations in parliament and brought to the nation's attention the fact that land was being allocated in a corrupt way: people with farming experience and capital were not receiving much of the land. Instead the land was given, at often bargain price, to Ministers, senior civil servants and to ZANU-PF supporters (the last two are usually interchangeable)'. [See Alexander 1994]

The question was not race, or about ideological purity. Some white farmers negotiated a settlement with the government, some supported the opposition, while others even negotiated with the militants who occupied their lands. The interest gap between commercial farmers who opted for profit and quick exit and opposition activists who are striving for a long-term strategy, including the change of government, is understandable.

The Movement for Democratic Change (MDC) is an offshoot of the National Working People's Convention which was held in Harare on 26–28 February 2000. It is a broad mass organisation aimed at ensuring political change that serves the interest of the working people, promoting employment and the advancement of the rural peoples. The main objectives of MDC are as follows:

1) To unite organisations of working people, as currently set out in the working people's Agenda Declarations.
2) To ensure that there is a government which makes decisions on national policies that are in the interest of the people who are the source of sovereignty.
3) To ensure the conditions for and from the base/foundation upon which a political party can be built that is able to contest the (year) 2000 elections. To create, mandate and own the political party formed and monitor its performance in relation to the aims of working people.
4) To build national integration so that all Zimbabweans work together without barriers of race, colour, tribe, ethnicity, status, political or religious affiliation.

5) To embark on voter education for change.
6) To democratise all political processes in the country.

Two of the principles guiding the activities of the MDC are of particular significance for this chapter: the first principle is that the MDC stands for social democratic, human-centred development policies, pursued in an environment of political pluralism, participatory democracy, accountable and transparent governance. This development is to take place in a manner that recognises equality of opportunity and treatment of all people in the building of a united, non-racial, non-ethnic democratic society. The second principle derives from the first and demonstrates the MDC's orientation towards advancing the participation of citizens and civil society in nation building through organs of participatory democracy that complement the existing forms of representative democracy – parliament and executive.

Since its establishment, the MDC has made an impact on Zimbabwe's political make-up. In the elections of April 1995, President Robert Mugabe (ZANU-PF) was elected unopposed for a six-year term, with 117 seats out of 120. Zimbabwe African National Union (ZANU-Ndonga), led by Ndabaningi Sithole, won two seats. In the June 2000 elections, however, ZANU-PF won 62 of the 120 seats of the National Assembly. The MDC won 57 seats and ZANU-N won one seat. ZANU-PF is able to hold on to power only because the president is allowed to appoint twelve non-constituency members, eight ex-officio members, and ten ex-officio chiefs, making a total of 30 of the 150 members of the House of Assembly.

The political violence, intimidation and seizure of commercial farms has continued, and will probably extend well beyond the presidential elections due in 2002. All the indications are that the days of ZANU-PF in power are gradually coming to a close. The question is whether Zimbabweans will be able to handle their political future with justice and reconciliation, and take the opportunity to show political maturity in order to preserve the unity and relative economic development they have so far achieved. Recent African history provides vivid reminders in the shapes of Somalia, Liberia, Sierra Leone, Angola and the Lake Region that statelessness and anarchy can be the outcome of irresponsible leadership. President Mugabe's unwillingness to use the state's legitimate authority to stop the illegal occupation of farms until a just solution is found by the government he has headed for the last 20 years gives little cause for optimism. (For more informed analysis of the politics of opposition, see Makumbe 1998, Sylvester 1995 and Schiphorst 2001.)

Moyo concludes his excellent contribution to the debate on land reform under structural adjustment in Zimbabwe by arguing that

... the state has continued to successfully trade off the interests of indigenous elites against white elites *vis-à-vis* those of the rural poor. The government strategy has been to offer a little bit of land and related resources to the black interest groups, and continually threaten to implement large-scale radical land transfer albeit doing this in practice only on a small scale and at a gradual pace. The higher commodity-specific financial returns at the micro level from new land uses have, indeed, simply increased the appetite of larger segments of the population for access to land since only a few white and black elites have been visible beneficiaries of this Economic Structural Adjustment Programme (ESAP) export oriented development strategy. [Moyo 2000: 166]

The land crisis in Zimbabwe is more a crisis of leadership than a racial attack on farmers because of the colour of their skin. For example, the build-up to the elections witnessed the revival of the Zimbabwe African People's Union (ZAPU) of Deputy President Joshua Nkomo, who in 1987 joined the ruling ZANU-PF, with a keen interest in resolving impending resource redistribution crises. The party's social base is among the Ndebele people of Matabeleland who make up 20 per cent of Zimbabwe's population. ZAPU 2000 members are intellectuals, businesspeople, the young and disenfranchised, and middle-class, middle-aged and former ZAPU members who never joined the ruling party. Despite huge tourist incomes generated by Victoria Falls and Hwange National Park, Matabeleland is poor and frequently drought-stricken. The Ndebele peoples feel discriminated against due to ethnic rivalry between them and the Shona who form the majority of ZANU-PF supporters. According to the Ndebele, this explains why most hotel managers and workers are Shona. Bulawayo – Zimbabwe's industrial powerhouse on the eve of independence – is now one of the poorest regions in the country. Industries there either collapsed or relocated closer to Harare, which is Shona heartland, following the 1981 genocide of the Ndebele peoples by the Zimbabwean armed forces.

If Zimbabwe's land question is, for historical reasons, seen in the light of racial divide, the struggle against land alienation and authoritarian development in other African countries – often described as ethnic – is no less racial. I have argued in Chapter 3 of this volume and elsewhere (Mohamed Salih 1987, 1992, 1998, 1999b) that race and ethnicity are instruments of political mobilisation in most of Africa. Under the kind of 'democratic' conditions in which the political elite considers elections and votes as ends in themselves, rather than the means to true participation, both ethnicity and race can be brutally used to achieve narrow political gains. Unfortunately, such short-sighted gains often discount the future and lay a heavy burden on the very people who vote for them. What is taking place in Zimbabwe could have far-reaching implications for the rest of Africa, where land alienation amongst Africans is the norm rather than the exception.

BOTSWANA: THE STABLE DEMOCRACY

The history of Botswana, formerly known as Bechuanaland, is long and complex. For the purpose of this chapter, the establishment of Bechuanaland as a British Protectorate in 1885 will be used as a reference point in discussing the events which influenced the country's development into one of Africa's oldest modern democracies. The visit of three Tswana chiefs to London in 1895, and their petitioning of the British government for protection against the Boers, was to a large extent responsible for securing Bechuanaland's political existence. The establishment of the Protectorate was not accidental. It was meant to provide access to the missionary road, a potentially vital link with Rhodes' scheme of a Cape-to-Cairo railway, and to act as a buffer against the encroachment of other imperial powers, particularly Germany. The Protectorate gathered more significance from a British point of view as the South Africa Act of Union provided for the establishment of the Union of South Africa, initially to include the Cape, Natal, the Orange Free State and the Transvaal, with the eventual incorporation of Bechuanaland, Basutuland, Swaziland and Rhodesia. The Protectorate status shielded Bechuanaland from annexation by South Africa; in this it was supported by two important factors. First, the country's huge mineral resources, particularly gold and diamonds, remained untapped until independence had been assured; second, the low level of mobilisation among the populace meant a very limited threat to the authority of South Africa and the Tswana chiefs who ruled it, with a minimum British administrative involvement.

The period between the two world wars saw many administrative developments, including the creation of the Native Advisory Council, which consisted of representatives of six southern tribes and their paramount chief, and a maximum of four others from each reserve. The Native Advisory Council became the African Advisory Council in 1940, and by 1950 each tribal reserve and district was represented, roughly in proportion to its population (for more details, see Vengroff 1977: 25–31).[2] A European Advisory Council was established to represent the views of the 2,379 Europeans who lived in Bechuanaland at the time, but the African Advisory Council demanded the establishment of a joint council. Recognising that their interests might be better served under such an arrangement, the members of the European Advisory Council accepted the proposal and a 20-member Joint Advisory Council was established. This was followed in 1959 by a Legislative Council, empowered with the responsibility of establishing a Constitutional Committee. Demands that the African representatives to the Legislative Council should be elected rather than appointed were heeded, and became a reality for the first time in the history of Botswana. On the making of the modern system under which independent Botswana has thrived:

> The continued hold on the people by the chiefs made it essential that the powers of the chiefs be limited ... The British administration under increasing pressure both internally and from the United Nations, agreed to a constitutional review in 1963, which upheld the one-man-one-vote principle, with all major groups in Bechuanaland permitted to send representatives. A unanimous agreement was reached that no legislative seats will be reserved for Europeans and that minority interests were to be safeguarded by a bill of rights ... The Constitutional consultations completed in November 1963 provided for the establishment of a parliamentary government on the Westminster model. [Vengroff 1977: 37–9]

Party formation in Botswana began with the establishment of Botswana People's Party (BPP) in December 1960 as Bechuanaland People's Party (BPP). Two of the three founders, Vice-President Philip Manate and Secretary General Motsamai Mopho were former active members of the Pan African Congress and African National Congress.[3] The third founder, who was not a member of either political organisation, was President Kgeleman Motsete. In 1964 BPP split into two factions, one led by Mopho, who attempted a communist take-over of the party, the other led by Motsete and renamed the Botswana Independence Party (BIP).

Seretse Khama and some members of the Legislative Council created the Botswana Democratic Party (BDP) in 1961 in order to counteract the radical activism of the BPP. Khama's royal origin, his marriage to a white British woman, his close association with the administration and the fact that he was awarded an MBE (Member of the Order of the British Empire), assured the party support from the administration (Vengroff 1977: 83). In the 1965 elections, the BDP won 28 seats (84.4 per cent of the vote) and the BPP won three seats (14.2 per cent of the votes). The BIP did not win any seats although it did gain considerable support among the San (Bushmen) to whom Mopho belonged.

In recent elections, however, the BDP has suffered some decrease in popularity. In the October 1994 general election, the BDP lost four seats to the main opposition party, the Botswana National Front (BNF). The BNF increased its share of the vote to 37 per cent and saw its representation in parliament increase from three to thirteen seats, winning all six of the new urban seats which had been created since the previous election to accommodate the large increase in urban population.

Unlike other African countries, Botswana has not experienced any major constitutional crises or army coups. The constitution vests legislative power in a parliament comprising a unicameral National Assembly, now with 40 elected members, the president (ex-officio), speaker, attorney-general and four members nominated by the president and subject to confirmation by the elected members. One of the main features of Botswana's system of political representation is the 15-member House of Chiefs which has advisory powers only and is not involved in the regular scrutiny of bills passed by the National Assembly. The president is elected by parliament, in practice by the party commanding a majority. Both the assembly and the president are elected for five-year terms, on the basis of universal adult suffrage with full freedom to organise political parties (see Charlton 1993).

The question of why Botswana has been able to maintain such an impressive record of democratic stability can be answered with reference to at least four points. First is the economic factor: Botswana's mineral wealth has generated considerable resources which enabled the state to undertake major social development programmes in health, education, housing, clean water supply and various employment and income generating programmes.[4]

Second is the dominance of the Botswana Democratic Party, derived from the legacy of the late Seretse Khama the first president after independence. The social democratic ideological orientation of the party, its concern with poverty alleviation and proactive support to improve housing and the infrastructure must have struck a resonant chord with the population. These notions of social care and welfare, integrated with Botswana's people's traditional values, have also been incorporated, thanks to its mineral riches, into government policy. Tordoff (1989: 284) sees this as a positive tendency where 'as a society, and system of government, Botswana has blended the modern and the traditional, combining elements of continuity with elements of change.' This view is also reflected in the next point which emphasises the role traditional political culture played in cementing Botswana's democratic tradition (see Van Binsbergen 1995 on political culture in Botswana and Zambia).

Third, the late President Seretse Khama recognised the need for African countries to develop their own guiding ideologies, political structures rooted in their own experiences and needs. In fact, the incorporation of the chiefs into the parliament meant that an effective communication channel has been developed between the central and local communities. The existence of two traditional institutions, such as the Dikgotla and Dikgosi (go-between chieftaincy institutions even led by Cabinet ministers) subsumed under the chiefs, also represented in parliament is also unique in contemporary African democratic experiences where all that is traditional is considered archaic and should therefore be relegated to oblivion (see Holm and Molutsi 1989). Although those who pay visits to Botswana's parliament may get the impression that the chiefs are doing nothing or very little; in actual fact they play a significant role in bringing pressure to bear on the government. The fact that the government would seek renewal through democratic elections means that the chiefs can use their power to sway voters to withdraw their support from the government in aggrieved constituencies. This alone could explain why, although Botswana was governed by the BDP during the last 35 years, the popularity of the party fluctuated from one election to another (see Picard 1987, Holm et al. 1996, Wiseman 1998 and Molomo 1998).

Fourth, Botswana's mineral wealth meant that the national cake is big enough to satisfy the needs of all, including rent-seeking officials, corrupt politicians, power-hungry army generals and disenchanted unemployed poor, urban migrants and drought-stricken traditional farming communities. In the view of this author, political stability in Botswana can first and foremost be attributed to its relative wealth which has so far been shared (although not without resentment by some groups) more equitably than any other African country, despite the increasing gap between poor and rich (see Tsie 1996).

At its face value, there is not much difference between Botswana's legislative and executive structure, constitution, election rules, etc., and other southern African countries. The difference could be in whether the president is elected directly by the people (South Africa, Zambia and Zimbabwe) or by the parliament (Botswana). The second difference lies in the powers of the president and whether the constitutional power is vested in the president or the parliament. However, these differences do not in themselves speak for or against the democratic or non-democratic nature of the political system. In the rest of this section I attempt to offer some explanations of political stability in Botswana *vis-à-vis* the other African states that I have alluded to in the earlier chapters of this book.

However, I have not alluded to the critique of the Botswana system since such material is directly related to minority representation, particularly the San (or Bushmen) and their precarious position in Botswana's polity (see Hitchcock and Holm 1993, Carrol and Carrol 1997, Danevad 1995, Good 1996 and Solway 1994, among others). The issue of minorities in first-past-the-post democratic systems is taken up in Chapter 9.

The case of South Africa with its equally huge economic resources and shameful inequality and uneven distribution of wealth provides a sobering argument as to why differences in democratic experiences matter. Ironically, Botswana, which parted with the Union of South Africa in 1948, is now leading the way by becoming an exemplar of blending traditional and modernity in order to create a unique African experience in self-government.

SOUTH AFRICAN RESILIENCE: A REGIONAL PERSPECTIVE

The end of apartheid – the rigid racial segregation policy that divided the governing white minority population and the non-white, mainly black majority population – is one of the most radical political transformations seen by the African continent during the last several decades. The relinquishing of this extreme system of political and economic oppression and its gradual transformation into an all-race, multi-party democracy is undoubtedly a major triumph for anti-apartheid activists and supporters the world over. The message of hope ushered in by this political transformation is predicated not on the subtleties of abstract notions of democracy, no matter how compelling these may be, but on the capacity of South Africans to share their economic resources more equitably.

South Africa offers a classic case of negotiated transition in a complex political environment marred by an authoritarianism that combined racial segregation and political oppression. An important factor in democratising the South African state was the possibility of negotiating a common future that involved a balancing act of competing political and economic interests. The need for compromise and magnanimity succeeded in subverting the gruesome urge for the use of force and subdued the militant temptation of the 'winner takes it all' principle. It was compromise and realism that made a negotiated settlement possible and was amicably enhanced by Nelson Mandela's visionary leadership and the pragmatism espoused by F.W. de Klerk. The partnership of the African National Congress (ANC) and the National Party (NP), the two major players in the negotiations, was not a mere marriage of convenience but a reality based by structural factors inherent in South Africa's complex economy, polity and society.

The negotiated settlement involved the National Party, the African National Congress, the Concerned South Africa Group (later renamed the Freedom Front), the Democracy Party, the Pan African Congress (PAC) and the Azania People's Organisation. The collapse of the first round of negotiations which were held under the Convention for a Democratic South Africa (CODESA) can be explained by the strong presence of apartheid institutions and their ability to infect the Convention with an undercurrent of ethnic sentiments (Kiloh 1997: 314). The stalemate was resolved when the ANC and NP signed a Record of Understanding which contributed to reducing the mass actions, riots and strikes organised by the powerful Congress of South Africa Trade Unions (COSATU). The trade unions' interest in an orderly transition to multi-party democracy was motivated by economic rather than political considerations. The multi-party Negotiation Forum which began in March 1993 concluded its deliberations by creating a Transitional Executive Council (TEC) to oversee South Africa's progress towards racially inclusive elections. As stipulated in the Transitional Executive Council negotiations, all parties winning 20 per cent of the total votes would share executive power during an interim period of five years.

No matter how the world may view the Truth and Reconciliation Commission (TRC), established by Nelson Mandela in 1995 and headed by Bishop Desmond Tutu to look into the South African past, I believe it represented a unique instance of African tolerance. That the Commission conducted public hearings, that victims of human rights abuses including apartheid gave evidence, that amnesty was considered and given to perpetrators – this is testimony, not only to procedural success, but also to the potential realisation of what Jaffe (1993) calls the need for 'healing the body politic'. Those on both sides of the struggle over apartheid and from both sides of the racial divide were confronted with their past deeds in public hearings, in front of the whole country. The greatest portion of the blame was justifiably reserved for the practices of the South African government from the introduction of apartheid to the approval of the non-racial Constitution on 8 May 1996. The Truth and Reconciliation Report states that 'The state, in the form of the South African government, the civil service and its security forces, was, in the period 1960–94 the primary perpetrator of gross violations of human rights in South Africa and, from 1974, in southern Africa.' The report has this to say about the ANC and the PAC: 'The ANC and its organs as well as the PAC and its armed formations … committed gross violations of human rights in the course of their political activities and armed struggles, for which they are morally and politically accountable.' The collaborators in apartheid, including 'big business', the Afrikaans media, Mangosuthu Buthelezi, leader of the KwaZulu-Natal based Inkatha Freedom Party (IFP) and others bore the brunt of the report's condemnation. The TRC Report insisted that:

- Evidence gathered by the commission that could be used in prosecution will be made available to prosecutors.

- In order to avoid a culture of impunity and to entrench the rule of law, the granting of general amnesty in whatever guise should be resisted as a glaring example to seriousness of this undertaking.
- Where there is evidence that an individual has committed a gross violation of human rights, and where amnesty has not been sought or has been denied, then prosecution will be considered.

I am aware of the criticisms levelled against the Truth and Reconciliation Commission, and the view that it was an institution of appeasement. I am also aware of the claim that the TRC Report has achieved little in terms of sending perpetrators to jail. None the less, I believe that the elements of confronting the past and seeking redemption from within are the most precious contributions to South African polity. History will judge South Africa not from what its political elite can offer, but by how much its populace can tolerate the elite, both black and white.

Processes currently under way indicate that the higher echelons of South African society have begun to find ways of accommodating each other, to the neglect of the very masses that sustained the anti-apartheid struggle. In short, the problem in South Africa is not so much one of racial, political or administrative integration, but rather of economic integration, and that is where South Africa's resilience will be tested in the not too distant future. Harbeson sees another challenge to South Africa's resilience in the socialisation of its civil society to oppositional politics during the struggle against apartheid:

> The ANC and other political parties that collaborated with it to end apartheid were impeded by the nature of the struggle itself from nurturing polyarchical practices within their own ranks. However, in comparison with the situation elsewhere in Africa, threats to the viability of the South African polity have been somewhat subdued ... Nevertheless, one can argue that both immediate and long-term crisis-generating issues have been addressed within the newly minted democratic framework precisely because broadly constituted rules of the game have been established and recognised as legitimate. [Harbeson 1999: 45]

In my view, the broadness of the pact that brought about the transition from apartheid to multi-racial political dispensation is far less important than the economic potential of South Africa, which promises a future in which even the poor seem to have a stake in political pluralism:

> Beyond merely levelling the political field for a fair and equitable political settlement, the formation of the Transnational Executive

Council sent a signal to the multilateral institutions, developed countries and development agencies to support the political transition. There was consensus that an unmanaged collapse of apartheid could result in the loss of confidence on the part of these international institutions and governments about South Africa as a potential source for investment. Maintaining a degree of political and economic stability in order to attract desperately needed foreign capital, investment and development aid was a major preoccupation during the transition. [Shezi 1995: 195]

South Africa has adopted a system of proportional representation with a two-chamber parliament, whereby the seats of the National Council of Provinces and the National Assembly are distributed according the total votes obtained by each political party. In this system, the National Council of Provinces forms the upper house of Parliament and ensures that provincial interests are taken into account in the national government. It replaces the former Senate as the upper house. The Council consists of ten-member delegations from each of the nine provinces, each delegation comprising four special members, including the provincial premier, and six permanent members. Each delegation casts a single ballot on most votes. The National Assembly is the lower house of Parliament. It consists of no fewer than 350 and no more than 400 members who are elected for a five-year term through proportional representation.

The 1994 all-race, multi-party election was won by the ANC, followed by the National Party which gained 20 per cent of the vote, giving former party leader F.W. de Klerk one of two deputy presidential posts. The Inkatha Freedom Party, supported by about 8 million Zulus, won 10 per cent of the vote, and Buthelezi served in President Nelson Mandela's cabinet as Minister of Home Affairs. The Democratic Party, a liberal political party supported by middle-income whites, won less than 2 per cent of the votes.

The 1999 elections were again dominated by the ANC which won 66.5 per cent of the vote, earning 266 of the 400 seats in the National Assembly. Deputy President Thabo Mbeki was appointed president, replacing Nelson Mandela. The newly established Democratic Party became the leader of the opposition in the National Assembly with 38 seats. The Inkatha Freedom Party held its third place with 34 seats. The New National Party drooped from second to fourth, with 28 seats.

The increase in the ANC majority led to opposition fears that the ANC may change the Constitution to consolidate its power or turn South Africa into a one-party state. In a typically South African defiance of doomsday scenarios, neither of the two fears has materialised thus far. While apartheid has disappeared at the surface, South Africa is still a racially divided society. This racial divide is reflected in the government–opposition trajectory, with the ANC having proportionally few whites amongst its ranks, and the Democratic Party and the New National Party counting even fewer blacks among their numbers.

DEMOCRATIC TRANSITION RECONSIDERED

The Institute for a Democratic Alternative in South Africa conducted surveys in Namibia, Zimbabwe, Botswana, Malawi and Zambia in 1999 and in Lesotho in 2000, on democratic conditions in Southern Africa. Nevertheless, the fact that the writing of this chapter coincided with the publication of these reports by the Institute for Democracy in South Africa affords us the opportunity to glimpse into its findings.

These two reports are important on at least three grounds:

1) They are based on field surveys rather than speculations about citizens' views in democracy.
2) They have developed a very detailed and comprehensive methodology dealing with democracy not as an ideal normative dispensation, but as a political activity with socioeconomic consequences for the well-being of societies.
3) They apply a rigorous comparative method, the privilege of institutions with wider regional networks of committed and well-placed researchers capable of conducting such delicate surveys. These reports will undoubtedly improve our understanding of the state of democratic development within the democratisation process which has swept Southern Africa during the last decade or so.

The first survey's findings on the democratic characteristics of the countries of concern to this chapter are as follows:

- Multi-party governments were responsible for significant increases in political freedom, but did not bring greater personal or economic security compared to the regimes they replaced.
- State and government institutions received very mixed ratings in the four criteria of trust, responsiveness, corruption, and overall performance. Of these four criteria, the performance of present governments is no better, and is sometimes actually worse, than the former authoritarian governments.
- Based on a profile of the attitudes of its citizens, Botswana appears to be a maturing democracy. Several decades of sustained democratic practices have brought about, or have been accompanied by, the

development of a healthy democratic culture. The people of Botswana rank far ahead of South Africans in terms of their attitudes toward democracy.

- In Zambia there are relatively high levels of perceived supply of democracy. Zambians are apparently unconcerned about the significant flaws of the 1996 elections. There is little desire to return to the past regime of one-party rule, and little interest in other non-democratic alternatives.

- Zimbabweans express a high level of 'demand' for democracy, yet display a very low degree of perceived 'supply' of democracy in their political system. There is a widespread sense of disillusionment and cynicism about the political system. It is important to note that the public mood is not just anti-Mugabe, but expresses a generalised discontent with the system of one-party, ZANU-PF dominant rule. There are severe problems of legitimacy, very low levels of trust, little sense that government is concerned with public opinion, and widespread perceptions of extensive corruption in government. Government institutions also receive very low levels of job approval. In terms of citizenship, Zimbabweans feel especially unable to influence the political system, and are the least likely of all southern Africans to feel they can improve things through voting and elections. [Mattes, Davids, Africa and Bratton 2000]

The second survey (Mattes, Davids and Africa 2000) revealed that in common with other South African countries, the South Africa survey also showed that the level of citizen satisfaction with democracy is also rather low. However, the survey has also shown that dissatisfaction with democracy is declining, which gives some room for optimism. Understandably, the concerns among the black population are still largely to do with housing, education, health issues, jobs and predictable income, all of which are essential for democratic consolidation (see Mattes, Davids, Africa and Bratton 2000).

The results of the surveys support three of the major points made in this chapter. First, political democracy is not a guarantee for economic security as poverty has increased and disenchantment with democracy is growing, particularly among the poor and those who felt themselves powerless in the face of coercive authoritarian rulers in the guise of democracy. Second, the performances of democratic and authoritarian governments in Africa vary only slightly, particularly in the realm of polyarchy and social justice. Democracy has done almost nothing to promote the redistribution of wealth or to provide for the poor and underprivileged. Third, the last point could be explained against the elite-dominated nature of the political parties and the political elite who operate these parties. These three points lead to the conclusion that, with the exception of South Africa, the southern African sub-region cannot develop sustainable democratic institutions within the current socio-economic and political realities. With the exception of Botswana and South Africa, both of which are relatively wealthier than the other countries in the sub-region, a democratic crisis is unfolding, with increasing tensions and social conflicts. In the circumstances, short of a social revolution, the regions' corrupt political elite will continue to act and behave like virtual democrats presiding on virtual democracies.

9
Minorities in 'First-Past-the-Post'

In democratic systems based on first-past-the-post voting practice, the question of minority representation becomes a problem because the minority is numerically small and lacks sufficient votes to secure effective representation. Minorities could also lose out in democratic regimes because often they do not command sufficient material and human resources to participate fully in the democratic process. However, the minority/majority issue is not only about an assemblage of votes. More than that, minorities have 'ethnic, religious or linguistic characteristics different from those of the majority of the population, bound up with one another, animated, if only by a collective will to survive and aiming at *de facto* and *de jure* equity with the majority' (Chaliand 1989: 7).

Not all minorities are oppressed; in some states, a numerical minority might resort to the army and hence oppress the majority, as in the case of South Africa during the apartheid regime and the current situation of the Tutsi in Rwanda and Burundi. Even if the Hutu–Tutsi question is resolved by adherence to the principles of political accommodation and perhaps proportional representation, the socially stigmatised 'Pygmoid' Batwa would not fare well in any such political dispensation (see Box 9.1). Furthermore, the majority might stall progress towards reforming the political system, since the status quo serves its interest.[1]

The debate on democracy in Africa has devoted much attention to how to ensure majority rule in what is sometimes tantamount to the neglect of minority problems in Westminster-style democracies premised on first-past-the-post or 'the winner takes all' majoritarian tradition. The issue of majority rule as prescribed in Western democracies has often clashed with the conduct of democracy in countries that are severely divided by ethnicity, religion, class and region. These differences are not intrinsic sources of conflict, although they have the potential to become problems when ethnicity, religion, class and region become instruments of political domination or the justification for supremacy over others.

In severely divided societies the problem is less of managing diversity than of accommodating minorities in a fair system of power sharing. Obviously, minority representation in first-past-the-post democratic systems poses a serious challenge to the capacity of the system to be genuinely democratic. Because numerical minorities lack sufficient votes to ensure effective representation, the capacity of democracy alone to ensure equitable and just representation is questionable. Where the disadvantages of numerical and social minorities are combined, they would certainly lose out in first-past-the-post systems because they command neither sufficient material resources nor votes to be fully represented in the legislature, and hence feel alienated by the very democratic process (see Dahl 1989, Mohamed Salih 2000).

However, the minority–majority question is not only a quantitative one about assembling votes. The difficulties occur in three problematic areas. First, in cases where people vote for candidates from their own ethnic groups, the largest ethnic group also produces the largest number of members of parliament and may therefore control the state indefinitely. The predictability of the ethnic vote may make a mockery of the elections, infuriating and frustrating the minority ethnic groups. Second, minorities living under a dominant 'supermajority' may resort to non-democratic means, such as the military, to control the state. Third, interest aggregation through minority group coalitions could provide a possible answer to the tyranny of the majority. However, such an option depends on the minorities being large enough in number to tilt the political process in their favour.[2] Minorities are disadvantaged not only because they are small in size, although this is an important factor in rising to power in a parliamentary democracy. In some instances, it is also because they are consciously excluded and as such unable to influence the political process on an equal footing with the majority.[3] While the majoritarian tradition has its merits (such as maximising utility and self-determination), majority rule without legislative safeguards and long democratic experience can be used as an instrument of domination. Minority groups that feel they have no hope of accessing state power and influencing decisions that they may perceive as detrimental to their well-being (or survival) may take extra-jurisdictional steps (such as military coups, election rigging, fraud, etc.) to control the state.

However, the minority position in the democratic state and how it may fare in majoritarian democracy cannot be isolated from the wider political and economic environment within which democracy operates (see also Dahl 1985). Because the state consists of a set of organisations judicially located in a particular territory, invested with the authority to make binding decisions and to implement these decisions using force if necessary, it is also an arena where different social forces compete for power. Power – the ability to make policy decisions, influence and even change policies through legitimate means – is neither neutral, as liberals make out, or without anchorage in the social forces that make up society. In developing countries, the state assumes an even greater significance in the pattern of power that determines access to social and material

Box 9.1
The Batwa of Rwanda

Studies of democracy and minority politics in Rwanda have concentrated on explaining the dominance of the Hutu majority over the Tutsi minority during the civil war, and the turn-around after the 1994 genocide to Tutsi minority domination. The Batwa minority position in Rwandan politics, its important place in the discourse of the dominant majority and its search for ways to return an enlightened Hutu majority to power, have barely featured. The Hutu majority is still bent on recapturing the Rwandan state by waging a war of attrition against the Tutsi-dominated government.

The fate of the Batwa minority was either not reported at all or was subsumed under the general rubric of genocide victims. Many readers might wonder who the Batwa are, and why they should (or shouldn't) be accorded any attention in reporting a genocide as inhuman as that which took place in Rwanda in the early 1990s.

The Batwa comprise some 20,000 to 30,000 people, and inhabit an area of about 26,338 km^2 on the Rwandan side of Burundi, Uganda, Democratic Republic of Congo, and Tanzania. Batwa constitute 0.4 per cent of Rwanda's 7.3 million inhabitants, a tiny minority compared to the Hutu (85 per cent) and the Tutsi (14 per cent). In common with the Hutu and the Tutsi, all Batwa speak Kinyarwanda, the main language in Burundi and Rwanda. According to Sebalinda (1993: 163), 44.63 per cent of Batwa are Catholics, 14.88 are Protestants, 8.86 are Muslims and 31.81 per cent belong to other religions.

The Batwa have historically been a minor and neglected player in the Hutu–Tutsi competition to control the state. Sebalinda, the Deputy Legal Representative of the Association for the Global Development of the Batwa of Rwanda (ADBR), sums up the sentiments of an excluded minority and the manner in which they have been treated by the Tutsi–Hutu dominated state apparatus: 'From time immemorial, the Batwa were considered by their neighbours as mentally backward, as buffoons, as executioners, as imbeciles, as villains, as deprived of intelligence, indeed as next to wild beasts and fit to be marginalised. They were discriminated against and marginalised. That is the reason why since early days no Mutwa (or Batwa) acceded to primary or secondary education. They were clearly their masters during the Monarcho-colonial period as well as after independence … During the first republic regime that lasted twelve years, nothing was done for the welfare of the Batwa. They were always kept away from the country's wealth. Even though a bit was done to improve their situation during the Second Republic era, such as allowing access to secondary school education and even to University for a small number of Batwa, it was too little to be significant. Thus no Mutwa (or Batwa) is to be found among ministers, director-generals, prefects (province governance), Burgomasters (district chiefs), local councillors, heads of parastatal bodies or private enterprises' (Sebalinda 1993: 164).

resources. The centrality of the state becomes more significant in the field of development, where the combined effects of resource distribution and conflict over resources are apparent. The social forces that control the state are also capable of using the state organisations to pursue their interests in an arena characterised by domination and opposition.

The formation of political parties and institutions identical to those in the West would strengthen rather than weaken the very forces that

Western observers hold responsible for conflict and political instability. The majority of the political institutions are often ethnically, culturally, religiously and linguistically based and represent distinct nations. In the democratic game, however, the elite considers them modern political institutions with no connection to traditional values. In other words, the political parties the elite creates out of the womb of traditional values are expected to behave like their Western counterparts, a responsibility these prototype institutions are ill-prepared to undertake in form or content. Second, instead of integration, democracy opens the door to political participation, but often not on terms originally anticipated by its architects. Although this should be viewed as a positive outcome, minorities tend to overreact to expansion of their interests, including the possibility of realizing their own independent state. Third, the majority may use the power of the vote or the fist of the security forces to stall political decisions necessary for undertaking significant reforms.

Obviously, majoritarian democracy ensures the political dominance of the demographic majority. Furthermore, it denies minority groups the possibility to secure political representation in two ways: first, minority strength lies not in aggregated individual preferences, but in its ability to use the collective will of its membership. Second, by assigning individual preferences a legal entity, majoritarian democracies attack the very basis of minority strength by laying the political ground rules that stifle their collective strength (Mohamed Salih 2000).

The case of the Tutsi-controlled military government in Burundi, where the Hutu form the majority of the population, is an example of this. Third, interest aggregation through minority group coalitions could provide a possible answer to the tyranny of the majority. However, such an option depends on the minorities being large enough in number to influence the political process in their favour. An example of this type of scenario is provided by the aggregation of minority ethnic groups which voted Daniel Arap Moi into power in Kenya's 1996 presidential election, beating FORD (Forum for Restoration of Democracy), which was supported by Kenya's two largest ethnic groups, the Lou and Kikuyu.

Minorities are disadvantaged not only because they are small in size (which is an important factor in rising to power) but also, in some instances, because they are consciously excluded by the majority from acquiring wealth, education and other endowments essential for entering the political process on an equal footing with the majority. The case of the Creole minority in Sierra Leone – with their material wealth and education – can be contrasted with that of the Hutu majority in Burundi. The first is a demographic minority, while the second is a political minority despite its demographic dominance. While the majoritarian tradition has its merits (such as maximising utility and self-determination), majority rule without legislative safeguards and long democratic experience can be used as an instrument of domination. Minority groups that feel they have no hope of accessing state power and influencing decisions that they may perceive as detrimental to their well-being (or survival) may take extra-jurisdictional steps (such as military coups, election rigging, fraud, etc.) to control the state.

PASTORAL MINORITIES AND DEMOCRACY

Pastoral societies have not featured prominently in the debate about democracy and socialism in Africa. This omission can be attributed to the fact that African states, whether colonial, neo-colonial, or independent, have concentrated their attentions on the political processes taking place among urban dwellers and peasants. Several objective factors can explain this emphasis. First, peasants and urban dwellers represent the majority of the population in Africa. Second, they are major contributors to the economic activities that constitute the main source of national wealth in the form of revenue and foreign exchange earnings. Third, most African states have forged alliances with the educated urban elites, business-people, and wealthy farmers, and see in the poorer classes a potential challenge to their economic interests and political whims. (For a more elaborate account for pastoralism and democracy in Sudan in particular and Africa in general see Mohamed Salih 1992.)

Ruling elites, therefore, have shown little interest in remote pastoral societies whose homage to tribal leaders is seen as vitiating their support of urban-based political parties. Whereas the peasant vote is decisive in national elections, the pastoralists are in the minority and, perhaps more important, contribute less to the national economy than urban dwellers or farmers. Furthermore, the pastoralists tend not to make politically conscious voters when it comes to modern political ideology and practice.

The pastoralists' marginalisation and poor representation in the centres of power can also be attributed to the nature of pastoral production which, because it must respond to seasonal variations in rainfall and pasture, is based on continuous movement from one ecological zone to another. Without the confines of regional administrative boundaries, the pastoral-ists' mode of livelihood connects them only loosely to national policies. Pastoral communities in frontier regions have little regard for national boundaries and often drift into other states, having roamed these territo-ries centuries before modern African state boundaries were created. This quest for freedom and aloofness from the administrative controls of the modern African state provokes conflicting reactions – outrage from the politicians and administrators who have taken responsibility for guarding the territories they inherited from the colonial legacy, and support from conservationists who feel that subjecting pastoralists to modern administrative controls may destroy their culture and traditional way of life. These two reactions have produced two contradictory responses. The first has been to put into effect settlement programmes designed to facilitate the provision of health, water, education, veterinary services and other social amenities, the integration of pastoralists into the market economy through taxation, livestock marketing boards and higher rates of 'off-take', and political modernisation through pastoralist representation in mainstream political institutions such as political parties, cooperatives, and youth and women's organisations.

The conservationists, by contrast, point to the staggering failure of development programmes, which have caused a deterioration rather than an improvement in pastoralist living standards. In pursuit of their goal of conserving the pastoral way of life, they claim that the political institutions of the modern African state are an evil through which the pastoralists will eventually lose their freedom and future destiny – even apparently beneficial policies are regarded as means of inducing 'uncaptured' pastoralists to enter the realm of the state. They argue that pastoralists should be given the freedom to practise their traditional way of life, that the state should not impose its vision of development and disrupt the rhythm of their delicate system of production, and that pastoralists should be allowed to develop unfettered, with few or no economic and political controls.

The polemic between these two approaches is significant to any discussion about pastoralism and democracy in that neither may represent the pastoralists' perception of their own political reality. Socialism and liberal democracy, as they have developed in the Western political tradition, are alien to pastoralists; any attempt to integrate them into mainstream political values and institutions is a major undertaking requiring serious political mobilisation.

Although the pastoralists have maintained some independence from the might of the African state, they have already been subsumed under modern administrative structures. They have long been integrated into the market economy and, as producers of primary products, their economic well-being and standard of living are closely related to fluctuations in the national and international market economy. Furthermore, most of the people involved in armed conflict in the Sudano-Sahelian zone, for example, are pastoralists fighting for forms of political expression that are different to those of their states. They are fighting to create new political systems that would cater to their rights, give them liberation and greater autonomy from the state. Consider, for example, the Dinka, the Nuer, and the Shuluk, who constitute the bulk of the Sudan People's Liberation Army (SPLA), or their Baggara rivals who fight alongside government troops in Sudan. Similarly, we might take as examples the Beni Amir, the Afar, and the Ogadens in Ethiopia, and the Ogadens and the Ishaaq pastoralists in Somalia (Markakis 1998). The main grievances of these groups stem partly from the inadequacy of present systems of political expression.

In this section of the chapter, I do not intend to question whether pastoral and modern notions of democracy are reconcilable. This question is posed in relation to the wider debate on democracy and majority representation and the consequences of that on power relations and the position of the minority in the polity of a given state. The underlying premise of this chapter is whether the conflict between pastoral and modern notions of democracy emanate from the state to superimpose the supremacy of one value system over the other. This conflict, I argue, can be attributed to the manner in which the state accords a prominent position to modern notions of democracy while denouncing pastoral political culture. The outcome of this mismatch between these two political cultures is the demise of modern democracy and its subversion by the traditional pastoral elite.

PASTORALISTS AND THE SUDANESE STATE

Numerous pre-colonial and colonial sources reveal that pastoralist relations with sedentary people were more peaceful in Sudan than in other parts of Africa and the Middle East. In most cases, the pastoralists forged alliances with the old kingdoms of the Sudan and paid tribute to the ruling classes (Hasan 1971). There are also a few reports of centralised states being governed by pastoralists – the Shuluk and the Anuak of southern Sudan and, to some extent, the Beja of the Red Sea hills – but these were not strong pastoralist states in the sense of the Fulani in West Africa (see Chapter 7 for more on the Fulani *jihad*).

The advent of Turco-Egyptian rule (1821–81) was met with fierce battles, but the advanced military technology used in the conquest overcame the resistance. Heavy taxes were levied mainly on the sedentary population and to a lesser degree on the pastoralists. According to Holt and Daly (1988: 54), until the 1820s 'Taxes were to be paid by owners of slaves and animals at the rate of 15 dollars per slave, 10 dollars per cow and 5 dollars per sheep or donkey. The burden fell on the settled people of the riverine villages, not on the nomads (there was no mention of camel-tax) who were still virtually outside the control of the state.'

Box 9.2
Tuareg pastoralists and democracy in Mali

The Tuareg pastoralists of Northern Mali represent over half a million people, out of a population of around 8.2 million inhabitants. Since independence in 1960, a succession of national governments has deprived the Tuareg of their social, economic and political rights, leading to rebellion in 1963. The Malian armed forces used heavy-handed tactics, including house burning, summary executions and detention of those associated with the rebellion. The rebels surrendered their weapons as a result of the mediation of the clan chiefs between the rebels and the government. During the Sahelian droughts of 1973 and 1983, the military government used international food aid as a weapon against the Tuareg, hundreds of thousands of whom died. For many Tuareg, the drought has not only brought death en masse, it has also weakened their resolve to withstand pressure. Many sought refuge in Algeria, and lived in abject poverty and destitution. Those who lost their wealth also lost their positions of authority in the government and were treated with disrespect and humiliated.

In June 1990, the Tuareg's second revolt was ignited when youth leaders were arrested upon their return from refuge in Algeria. The Malian government seemed bent on a military solution based on mass killing, destruction of Tuareg property and confiscation of cattle. In 1991, Niger and Algeria mediated an agreement with the Popular Movement of the Aawad, better known as the Tamanrasset Agreement of 5 January 1991. By April 1992, the Tamanrasset Agreement had paved the way for the Bamako Agreement which contained several provisions designed to provide the Tuareg with more autonomy and better dispensations for self-government (compiled from Gunvor Berge 1993: 233–5). However, subsequent elections have shown that due to the small size of the Tuareg population, they did not fare well during multi-party democracy and continue to be dominated by the Hausa and other major ethnic goups.

Through punitive expeditions, such as those directed against the Shukriya and the Beja (Paul 1954, Holt and Daly 1988), the pastoralists were gradually subdued. The pastoral Nilotes of southern Sudan became the main source of slaves and were raided by Northern Sudanese, European slave traders and Turco-Egyptian troops.

The demise of the pastoralists continued unabated throughout the Mahdist state (1881–98). Both the Mahdi and his successor, Khalifa Abdullahi, relied on an army recruited from the Baggara of western Sudan to defend their regimes against the riverine Ashraf of northern Sudan (Holt and Daly 1988). At a later stage, the majority of the Mahdiya troops were formed by pastoralists from western Sudan and the Beja tribes. Reliance on military support from some pastoralist groups did not mean, however, that the Mahdists enjoyed a peaceful relationship with all pastoralists; indeed, pastoralists were forced to pay heavy taxes prescribed by the Islamic *zakat* (Islamic alms) system.

The Battle of Omdurman (1898) marked the collapse of the Mahdist state and the advent of Anglo-Egyptian condominium rule. Major political and economic changes were introduced that had a profound impact on the whole of Sudan. Early administrative measures to integrate the pastoralists into the colonial state came in 1921 when indirect rule was enacted, and the powers of the Nomad Sheikhs Ordinance were introduced in the following year. According to this policy, traditional courts composed of about three hundred sheikhs were organised, the native administration system was reinforced and village courts were inaugurated for the settled population (Howell 1972). These various ordinances and regulations formed the structure of local administration in the rural areas and were based on a hierarchy of local chiefs corresponding to their tribal structures – the whole tribe is ruled by a paramount chief (*nazir*) and subtribal chiefs (*omda*) supported by sheikhs at the lower level of the administrative hierarchy.

Pastoral societies enjoyed greater autonomy from the colonial state, although they were subject to regular inspections by colonial officers. The whole system rested on the colonial state overseeing the rural population through chiefs, whose only merits were their loyalty to the colonial administration, their ability to collect taxes and their readiness to report any signs of revolt against the colonial government.

With the imposition of these positions of power among the pastoralists, differentiation and inequality in terms of access to power and resources began to emerge. The existence of an egalitarian ideology amid social and economic differentiation provided the powerless in pastoral societies with a resource with which to develop considerable resilience in dealing with the oppression and exploitation of the colonial state and their own leaders. Neither during the colonial period nor after independence were rules, regulations, or policies introduced or implemented among pastoralists in a democratic manner. Often the very nature of leadership was not territorially based. According to Cunnison (1966: 147), because the leaders controlled a lineage or alliance of people wherever they might be, rather than just a stretch of land with people in it, leadership among the Baggara of western Sudan was independent of local geographical and political considerations. Colonial policy also created a class of tribal elite from a few favoured chiefly families, from which others were excluded. Among the Kababish of northern Kordofan:

> ... historically, the course of the dominant power of the Awlad Fadllalah (the chiefly family) was achieved by the gradual elimination of the autonomous power which section sheikhs held in the early years ... the maintenance of the monopoly of power has rested largely on the de facto control of the basic means of political administration over the tribe as a whole in which physical coercion or direct persuasion have played little part'. [Asad 1970: 238]

A similar situation was depicted among the Rufa'a El Hoi about whom Ahmed (1972: 47) asserted: 'power to make decisions, settle disputes and the control and distribution of new economic resources by hiring the support of the followers and the government officials, are the most important factors in the dominance of the tribal elites.' It is thus clear that after the colonial experience, the pastoralists were no longer independent of the centres of state power. Asad (1970) concurred with this view, adding that the extension of state power included the use of coercion and persuasion in many other pastoral societies in Sudan.

When the Sudanese nationalist movement began to mature during the early 1950s, contacts were made between the emerging political parties and the pastoralists' leaders. By 1953, the major political parties had succeeded in creating alliances and centres of support among pastoralists. For example, the *Ashiqqa* (Brothers) later split into *Al-Shapp Al-Dimograti* (People's Democratic Party) and *Al-Watani Al-Itihadi* (Nationalist Unionists). By 1966 the Democratic Unionist Party (DUP) had emerged as an offshoot of the Nationalist Unionist Party that gained tremendous support among the Beja and the Shukriya pastoralists. The Umma (Nation) Party was supported by the Baggara pastoralists of western Sudan (Abdel Rahim 1969, Woodward 1979, see also Chapter 5 above for more details).

National elections since independence in 1956 have revealed an intimate relationship between voter behaviour, tribal origin and party affiliation. Pastoralists have voted for neither modern political ideologies nor well-debated and accepted political programmes in the conventional sense. Because the main political parties in the Sudan tend to have been sectarian, Sudanese voting has followed the lines of tribal sentiments and religious faith. For example, the DUP is the political expression of the Khatmyia Muslim religious sect and the Umma that of the followers of the Mahdiya religious sect, which was founded during the Mahdiya period (1881–98). The National Islamic Front (NIF) is also based on Islamic ideology but has more support among the educated elite than among the peasants and pastoralists. The only major political party not to appeal to sectarian or religious sentiments is the Sudanese Communist Party (SCP), although, like the NIF, it has failed to capture the peasant or pastoralist vote.

In recent decades, education, migration to towns and centres of employment, and the spread of modern political concepts have all challenged the authority of the tribal leaders. Democratic forces in Sudan came to recognise that the Provincial Administrative Act, passed by the military government (1958–64), reinforced the powers of the tribal leaders whom the military governors had appointed to the Provincial Council. The elite's demand for the abolition of the Native Administration System became a major political issue among progressive forces. Many educated elites felt their political role threatened by the existence of a tribally inspired system of local administration based on neither education nor personal qualities. One of the main demands of the October 1964 revolution, which overthrew the military junta, was the abolition of the Native Administration System and the hegemony of the tribal leaders over their followers (Howell 1972, Holt and Daly 1988: 181–94). The wish to abolish the Native Administration System was not fulfilled because it was inconceivable that the sectarian conservative political parties would dismantle their own power base as represented by the tribal leaders. Pastoral societies voted their tribal leaders to the Constituent Assembly, but the latter were under the sway of the politico-religious leadership of the sectarian parties. As religious and political followers, the pastoralist leaders received diktats and were not in a position to discuss democratically issues of regional or national interest. This posture of non-democratic decision making in the sectarian political parties contributed to the social, political and economic bankruptcy that again propelled the military to the centre of the political stage in 1969, this time under the banner of socialism.

NIMEIRI'S SOCIALIST REFORMS

A debate on whether or not any socialist system in Africa is truly socialist is bound to be inconclusive. Most socialist states in Africa came to power through military coups, and it is therefore difficult to associate their political practices with either socialism or liberal democracy. What occurred in most of these countries were short-lived political agitations that failed to reach the populace or to ensure their full political participation. Furthermore, political institutions in African 'socialist' states were tailored to suit the political aspirations and perceptions of educated political elites and little attention was paid to those of peasants or pastoralists. Centrally devised policies were often deployed for implementation without proper political mobilisation or appeals to the people who were expected to execute them and to ensure their success. Nimeiri's early socialist agitation (1969–76) was no exception, and he soon fell out with the Communist Party (see Warburg 1978). In common with other African socialist regimes that had usurped power through military coups, Nimeiri suspended the constitution and banned political parties and trade unions. His regime correctly criticised liberal democracy in Sudan for serving the privileged few to the exclusion of the illiterate peasants, pastoralists and workers. Part of his socialist programme involved nationalising foreign banks and major economic enterprises and placing them in the hands of the public sector. The country's economic, political and educational orientation shifted from that of the Western capitalist countries to that of the East European socialist countries. These measures were, however, no different from the socialist blueprints that were prevalent in other African experiences. More innovatively, the Sudanese Socialist Union (SSU), consisting of an alliance of working people – workers, peasants, the armed forces, intellectuals and national capitalists – was established in 1971. As is common in such cases, the pastoralists were placed in the 'peasant' category.

Nimeiri's socialist policies towards the pastoralists are particularly relevant to this chapter. To ensure that his policies reached the rural areas, a new system of people's local government was introduced in 1971. Its political structure corresponded to that of the SSU: both included a basic unit (village, animal camp), an area council (rural or town), a district council, and provincial and national representation. At this juncture, two objectives of the new local government system were important: to provide a new leadership capable of mobilising the masses behind the May Revolution, and to promote the SSU's political programme in the rural areas.

These measures were followed by the abolition of the Native Administration System, with a view to breaking the monopoly of power by the tribal leaders who were still loyal to the conservative sectarian parties. However, when they realised that the new socialist programme threatened their power and privileges, the traditional leaders joined the opposition and rallied behind the sectarian parties:

> the traditional elites and the native authorities ... tended to have their own attitude towards the new system. They realized that the objective behind the whole administrative reform was a desire on the part of the government to establish and sponsor a new modernized local leadership. It was not surprising, then, that the traditional elite expressed opposition, mistrust and suspicion towards the new system right from the beginning. [Idris 1987: 68]

The *nazir* and *omda* – the backbone of the Native Administration System – were abolished and their holders banned from political participation. Elections for new political and administrative positions were held regularly in the hope that a non-tribal, modernised leadership would emerge. This did not happen. As Zaki (1987: 214) pointed out: 'no two or more candidates from the same tribe competed for the seat of their constituency in order to avoid the disintegration of the tribe and the division of the votes, for that would increase the chances of success of candidates from other tribes.' In other words, the pastoralists had succeeded in transforming the socialist programme's objective of popular participation into a function of tribal politics. In so doing, the pastoralists may have rendered themselves captive to a new breed of educated tribal elites who fulfilled functions similar to those of the ousted traditional leaders.

As these contradictions between different value systems began to emerge, the rising educated elites became increasingly unpopular. These new elites promoted policies handed over to them by the state and were expected to address local issues according to rules and regulations unknown to the people, and to pronounce a political ideology alien to the pastoralists. This is not to argue that a socialist programme is irrelevant, rather that there are conflicting value systems that seek different means of political expression. One value system is close to the hearts of the pastoralists; another represents the dominant political ideology, which supports the conveyance of power to the modern educated elites. No wonder certain contradictions in government policy began to emerge if, to settle tribal conflicts and major disputes, it depended on the same traditional leaders it had ousted.

Nimeiri's attempt to solve disputes between pastoralists was the Mobile Administrative Officers Scheme, established to collect taxes and observe animal vaccination. By 1978, however, this scheme had collapsed for lack of acceptance by the pastoralists. Tax collection was at an all-time low and intertribal conflict flourished (Ahmed 1972, Geili 1987). Some of the educated elites who had struggled for new positions of power found nomadic life harsh, especially the university graduates who had been socialised in the towns and urban centres into expecting a more comfortable lifestyle.

Critics of Nimeiri's regime maintained that the SSU and the people's local government scheme were empty political structures. The provincial commissioners held the balance of both political and executive power and could overrule any decisions that were not in line with stated policy. Real power, however, was vested in the politburo, which was headed by the president, who was also chairman of the SSU. Concentration of power in the hands of the president jeopardised any possibility of popular participation and social mobilisation (Khalid 1985).

In 1980, the new decentralisation policies were implemented and nine regional government authorities were established in various parts of the country. The reconciliation policies of 1977 brought back to politics the Muslim Brothers and the sectarian political parties that shared power, albeit in a disguised form, with the remaining veterans of the SSU. This period witnessed the gradual return of the tribal leaders, who could by then be seen in the corridors of the SSU, since some *omdas* or tribal leaders had already been reinstated. The reconciliation policies marked the end of the socialist programme, the acceptance of IMF and World

Bank policies (see Ali 1995), a shift from socialism to Islam, the imposition of the Islamic *sharia* laws, and the beginning of the downfall of Nimeiri's regime, which collapsed in April 1985.

Liberal democracy was given a third chance in 1985, and in 1986, old and new political parties contested the national elections. It is unfortunate that the same tribal leaders were resurrected. The National Islamic Front gained ground, especially in graduate constituencies, while the communists lost ground in some of their old strongholds after almost two decades of persecution during Nimeiri's regime. As the old corrupt practices of the sectarian parties continued and the war situation in the south deteriorated, the military again took power in June 1989. It again suspended the constitution, banned political parties, and embarked on formulating its own vision of a new form of political organisation.

We can draw three main conclusions about the status of the pastoralists and about Nimeiri's socialist policies, from the above discussion:

1. While the policy devised by the SSU was intended to extend a new vision of democratic expression to pastoralists, the traditional leaders of the pastoralists and their followers greeted the policies with stiff resistance.
2. The rejection of these policies by the pastoralists does not mean that the policies were not devised with good intentions. Pastoralists benefited greatly from the reforms and gained access to education, health, water and veterinary services. The question here is of political consciousness and whether the pastoral mode of production is capable of sustaining a socialist ideology and a democracy other than its own.
3. The strength of the traditional political leadership is derived from its appeal to tribal sentiments, a sectarian politico-religious ideology, and the dominance of tribal political values that perceive of the traditional elite as having the sole legitimate right to rule.

These three interrelated points suggest that a prerequisite for the pastoralists' acceptance of any notion of political 'modernisation', socialist or otherwise, is the development of their material base.

FROM SOCIALISM TO ISLAM

No discussion on pastoral democracy would be complete without reference to Lewis's widely read book on the theme. Lewis identified two basic principles in Somali pastoral democracy: '[The first] lies in kinship. The second and one that is complementary to kinship is a form of social contract.' However, Lewis argued that he did 'not claim that the Somali political contract corresponds in all respects to any one of the many doctrines of the social contract of the political philosophers. But ... [he does] hold that it includes essentially contractual elements having closet affinities with these political theories which saw the origins of political union in an egalitarian society' (1961: 3).

Contractual relations are obviously important to political life in many tribal groups. But unless democracy is redefined, the associations made between contractual relations and democracy are likely to be inadequate. Among the Baggara (Cunnison 1966) and the Kababish (Asad 1970) in Sudan, traditional contractual relations provided the basis for administrative structures that gave the tribal leaders dominance over their followers. The persistence of *dia* (blood compensation) paying groups during both liberal and socialist democracies indicates that factors related to the maintenance of peace and order are important to any society regardless of its level of political and economic development.

The majority of fighters in the SPLA and Sudan People's Liberation Movement (SPLM) are Dinka, Nuer and Shuluk pastoralists, none of whom articulate the SPLA/SDLM socialist programmes. While proclaiming its own socialism, the Sudanese government has since 1985 been arming the Baggara tribal militia to confront SPLA/SPLM forces (Mohamed Salih 1989). Unlike the *anaya nya* Southern Movement that fought the first civil war (1955–72),[4] the SPLA/SPLM is fighting to create a new democratic Sudan. According to its manifesto (1983), the SPLA/SPLM is fighting to 'transform the Southern Movement from a reactionary movement led by reactionaries and concerned only with the south, jobs and self interest to a progressive movement led by revolutionaries and dedicated to the socialist transformation of the whole country'. Reports suggest that the SPLA/SPLM is already making inroads into the liberated areas. Political consciousness raising is said to be one of the main objectives of its fighters. It remains to be seen whether, given the upsurge of conservatism and Islamic fundamentalism in northern and central Sudan, the SPLA/SPLM will be able to transcend the African socialist experience.

As I have argued in Chapter 5, the fall of the Nimeiri regime (1969–85) was followed by a four-year multi-party democracy which lasted until 1989. The democratically elected government of Prime Minister Al Sadig Al Mahdi was ousted before it completed the administrative and political reforms, as it was pre-occupied by the war in southern Sudan and did little to assure the Sudanese people that the end of the war was in sight. The Islamic National Front Government (1989) supported by the Sudanese Armed Forces has introduced several changes to the pastoral sector, unfortunately, most of them are closely linked to the Islamisation programme it espoused. Ironically, the pastoralists' leaders, who were seen more than a decade ago in the corridors of the Sudanese

Socialist Union were again seen strolling in the corridors of the National Congress Party, which was dominated by National Islamic Front supporters. However, the pastoralists are still loyal to the religious families and the political parties that have just begun to re-enter the political arena, as described in Chapter 5.

The case of Sudan raises important questions about the choice among pastoralists between pastoral and liberal democracy. Attempts by these states to extend their visions of democracy were unsuccessful and in all three instances illustrated how conflicting systems of political expression could result in violence and warfare. To maintain a degree of autonomy from the state, pastoralists have shown their readiness to go as far as taking up arms against their central governments, irrespective of whether or not those governments are socialist. African leaders were wrong to assume that socialism could prevail without wide societal acceptance. This constraint on the simultaneous implementation of socialism and democracy was further reinforced when it appeared – and not only to pastoralists – that some African statesmen were using socialist rhetoric largely to justify their monopoly of power, rather than to serve the interests of 'the people'.

THE OGONI AND THE NIGERIAN STATE

It must be stressed from the outset that the Ogoni represent only one case in the spectrum of Nigeria's overcharged minority politics. However, the complexity of this case overshadowed other similar instances of minority rights abuse (see Box 9.3 below). The importance of the Ogoni of Nigeria's Niger Delta illustrates vividly how a majority can impose its will on the minority using democratic as well as authoritarian methods under the pretext of 'national development' and its counterpart 'national security'. Furthermore, it illustrates that the majority can also abdicate the majority right to self-determination, if the minority happens to occupy parts of the country endowed with internationally valued natural resources, such as oil in the Ogoni case. In fact, because of the existence of oil in Ogoniland, neither the democratically elected nor the military governments have heeded the Ogoni plea for social justice, let alone their struggle for self-determination.

In Chapter 7, I introduced the role played by ethnicity and religion in the political crises which have engulfed the Nigerian state since independence. This chapter complements Chapter 7 by exposing how ethnic politics contribute to the fate of democracy. Rivalries and frictions in the Nigerian political establishment contributed to the declaration in May 1967 of the secession of the Eastern Region and the establishment of an independent Igbo state, the Republic of Biafra. A naval blockade was imposed by the

Box 9.3
Nigeria: authoritarian development exposed

Nigeria is a multi-ethnic and multi-cultural society, with an estimated 250 ethno-linguistic groups. Some of these ethno-linguistic groups are larger than some neighbouring countries in the West African subregion, while others are as small as a few thousand.

The major ethnic groups consist of the Hausa-Fulani in the north, the Yoruba in the west, and the Igbo in the east. Other lesser but prominent ethnic groups include the Tiv in the Middle Belt, the Edo in the middle-west, and the Efik, Ibibo and Ijaws in the east.

The immediate post-independence era therefore had four regions which formed the principal nucleus of distribution in Nigeria. The major ethnic groups in control of these regions seemed fairly satisfied over distributional issues as they got the 'lion's share' of everything within their areas of authority. This was in sharp contrast to smaller and less prominent ethnic groups, generally referred to as ethnic minorities, who bitterly complained of domination and marginalisation by the major ethnic groups as a whole and in their regions in particular. [Igbo 1992: 202]

---

federal government (McCaskie 1999); civil war broke out, and continued unabated until January 1970, when the Biafran forces surrendered. McCaskie reports that 'during the civil war casualties reached an esti-mated 100,000, but between 500,000 and 2 million Biafran civilians died, mainly from starvation as a result of the federal blockade' (1999: 782).

The Ogoni (Babbe, Gokana, Ken-Khana, Nyo-Khana and Tai) number about half a million people; they inhabit an area of some 650 square kilo-metres in Rivers State at the southernmost tip of the Niger Delta. They are subsistence farmers and fisherfolk. They grow a variety of tropical crops such as maize, banana, yam, beans and palm oil; fishing is their second most important subsistence activity and provides their major source of protein intake.

The first oil wells in Ogoniland were discovered in Ebubu and Bomu, where exploration began in 1958. In 1965, Nigeria's first oil refinery was established at Alesa Eleme, also in Ogoniland. Today there are about 56 oil wells in Ogoniland, making it the fifth largest oil-producing commu-nity in Rivers State (Osaghae 1995). Despite the fact that Ogoniland is blessed with huge oil reserves, the Ogoni people are poor. According to many studies (for example, Osaghae 1995, Ondadipe 1996), the problems of the Ogoni people stem from political concentration and ethnic domi-nation by the large ethnic groups, notably Igbo, Yoruba and the Hausa–Fulani alliance. The Ogoni themselves also see their plight as resulting from the expropriation of oil resources by commercial oil companies and the Nigerian state. This situation has contributed to the emergence of strong Ogoni activism seeking greater autonomy from the

Nigerian state and access to more resources for social and economic development (Naanen 1995). The Ogoni people's 'Bill of Rights' (quoted in Saro-Wiwa 1995: 6) includes the following set of statements which are important for understanding Ogoni grievances:

1. That the Ogoni people, before the advent of British colonization, were not conquered by any other ethnic group in present-day Nigeria.
2. That British colonization forced us into the administrative division of Opobo from 1908 to 1947.
3. That in 1951 we were forcibly included in the Eastern Region of Nigeria, where we suffered under neglect.
4. That we protest against the neglect by voting against the party in power in the region in 1957, and against the forced union by testimony, before the Willink Commission of Inquiry into Minority Fears 1958.
5. That this protest led to the inclusion of our nationality in Rivers State in 1967, which state consists of several ethnic nationalities with differing cultures, languages and aspirations.
6. That oil was struck and produced in commercial quantities on our land in 1958 at K. Dere (Bomu oilfield).
7. That oil has been mined on our land since 1958 to this day from the following oilfields: (i) Bomu (ii) Bodo West (iii) Tai (iv) Korokoro (v) Yorla (vi) Lubaara Creek and (vii) Afam by Shell Petroleum Development Company (Nigeria) Limited.

Confrontations between the Ogoni people, the oil company Shell, and the Nigerian state are thus the result of what the Ogoni perceive to be injustices committed against them by these powerful interests. Oil – which has developed Nigeria's economy and created its wealth – has done little to improve the lives and environment of the Ogoni people. In highlighting the suffering of his people, the late Ken Saro-Wiwa not only pointed to the Nigerian state's denial of human rights and rights to compensation for the lands lost to oil exploitation, but also to the history of post-independence Nigeria. The Biafran civil war (1967–70) can be seen as a reference point; it informed subsequent military action, brutality being used to deal with peaceful demonstrations in the fear that they may develop into separatist movements. However, separation has never been a factor in the Ogoni resistance to injustice: according to Saro-Wiwa (1995: 75), 'Ogoni have a moral claim over Nigeria as 30,000 Ogoni were murdered during the civil war by Ojukwu's followers.' Osaghae argues that:

Demands for more equitable and privileged treatment by oil-producing minority communities, as well as struggles by them and other minorities, to redress power imbalances in the federation which make them subordinate to the majority groups are not new. Beginning from the agitation for separate states in the 1950s and 1960s which led to the setting up of the Minorities Commission in 1956, right down to attempts by politicians from the minority groups in the Second Republic to organise to wrest political power from the majority elements, the minorities have been in the forefront focusing on the national question as a problem. [Osaghae 1995: 325]

Although the confrontation between the Ogoni and the oil companies has been presented as an Ogoni/Shell issue, the Ogoni Bill of Rights claims that:

... the multinational oil companies, namely Shell (Dutch/British) and Chevron (American), have severely and jointly devastated the environment and ecology, having flared gas in our villages for thirty years and caused oil spillage, blow outs, etc., and have dehumanized our people, denying them employment and those benefits which industrial organisations in Europe and America routinely contribute to their areas of operation. [quoted in Saro-Wiwa 1995: 91]

Oil operations in Nigeria have the capacity to produce one million barrels a day. An estimated 14 per cent of Chevron's production outside the US comes from Nigeria. It is estimated that between 1970 and 1988, the Federal Government of Nigeria received a total of US$183.1 billion in revenue from oil extracted from the Niger Delta. Shell is estimated to have extracted over US$30 billion worth of oil from the Ogoni region. Thirty years of oil production in Ogoniland, involving environmentally damaging production techniques and transport methods, gas flaring, oil waste and oil spills, has resulted in Ogoni land and water courses being heavily polluted by oil. According to a Greenpeace report (1995) and Fentiman (1998), the multinational oil companies have destroyed the Ogoni's way of life, and with it their ability to maintain a livelihood in a healthy environment. Greenpeace has elaborated several of the negative health, economic and social impacts of oil operations in Ogoniland. The operation of gas flares close to Ogoni villages (Yorla, Korokoro, Dere and others) for 24 hours a day over 30 years has resulted in air pollution and acid rain, causing a high incidence of respiratory infections, and poisoning the agricultural land and water courses. Oil pipelines, meanwhile, take land from poor communities in one of Nigeria's most densely populated states; fractures of high-pressure pipelines destroy property, while oil spills and leakage contaminate water and pollute soil. Reports suggest that it often takes weeks before oil spills are contained or fractured pipelines repaired. The longer oil is allowed to escape, the more lasting the damage it inflicts on the vital resources of water and land. Furthermore, although the Nigerian government is supposed to direct 3 per cent of its oil revenue back to the communities where the oil is produced, minimal assistance has been provided to Ogoni villages affected by oil spillages and flares. Over 25 years, only US$200,000 are estimated to have been spent on community assistance programmes – far less than 0.5 per cent of the value of the oil extracted (Greenpeace 1995).

Although oil extraction operations began in the 1960s, the Ogoni people were never compensated adequately for the land appropriated by the government for oil production. While Shell claims that it paid adequate compensation for land, crops, trees and so on, successive Nigerian governments have failed to channel that compensation through to the Ogoni people. Even where some compensation payments were made, they were so inadequate that they could not sustain those who had lost their means of survival beyond a very limited period of time. A few months after receiving compensation, most Ogoni found themselves suffering impoverishment and deprivation.

There are three activist organisations operating in Ogoniland: the Movement for the Survival of the Ogoni People (MOSOP), the Ethnic Minorities Rights Organisation for Africa (EMIROAF), and the National Youth Council of Ogoni People (NYCOP). I focus most attention on MOSOP, because it is the best known internationally (particularly after Saro-Wiwa's death at the hands of General Abacha's military regime), and because there has been better coverage of its activities than those of the other Ogoni activist organisations.

In October 1990, during the military government of Babangida, the Ogoni people formed the Movement for the Survival of the Ogoni People to resist oil exploitation by Shell Petroleum Development Company, and to seek compensation and better environmental management from Shell and the Nigerian government, in order to protect their sources of sustenance. These events have been described by several environmental NGOs, such as Greenpeace and Friends of the Earth, as well as by Ken Saro-Wiwa and other NGO activists. On 4 January 1993, for instance, a peaceful Ogoni protest was met with brute force, beatings and the detention of the protest leaders, including Ken Saro-Wiwa. When MOSOP boycotted the 1993 elections, in protest at the Nigerian government's disrespect for minority rights, Ogoniland was sealed off by federal government security forces and people were prevented from taking part in demonstrations or any form of peaceful protest. Ogoni villages were burnt several times between 1990 and 1995, many people losing their homes and property. A catalogue of human rights abuses and injustices have been committed against the Ogoni and other communities (such as Ogbia, Igbide, Ijaw, Etche, Izon, Irri, Uzere) in the Niger Delta.

Oil companies have always sided with the Nigerian federal government. For instance, during the civil war (1967–70), Shell-BP refused a demand by the lawyers of General Ojukwu (the Biafran leader) that it should pay taxes to the government of Biafra. This was reinforced by the federal government's capture of the Bonny oil fields followed by the eviction of Biafran forces from Port Harcourt and the surrounding drilling fields of the Rivers State, which convinced the British government and Shell-BP of where their true interests lay (Stremlau 1977: 76). According to Osaghae:

> The discovery of oil and subsequent exploration activities in Ogoniland changed the circumstances of intra-Ogoni relations as well as those of its relations with other groups and the Nigerian state. For one thing, environmental degradation and in particular destruction of farmlands and fishing, the main occupations of the Ogoni peoples, which came with oil explorations provided a new basis for forging closer ties to deal with common problems ... For another, the continued social and economic underdevelopment of Ogoniland and the group's marginalization from state power in spite of its new status as a centre of wealth for the country led to the closing of ranks to fight what was commonly seen as injustice. [Osaghae 1995: 325]

The Ogoni suffered at least two predicaments: the systematic appropriation of their land and natural resources by the state and by private national and/or transnational corporations; and the denial of human rights, by means of political persecution, ethnocide and genocide, which continued after independence from the colonial powers. The emerging post-colonial African states have unwittingly reinforced the political values inherited from the colonial state apparatus. The gulf between the Nigerian ruling elite and minorities such as the Ogoni peoples is a result of power structures devoid of legitimacy or popular engagement. The genocide and ethnocide committed by the Nigerian states support the suggestion that their forced annexation policies are designed to complete an unfinished colonial legacy.

The Ogoni case illustrates that the deployment of coercive measures by authoritarian and democratic governments against minorities says more about the nature of the state and the limited possibilities that democracy can deliver to minorities. However, democratic rule is in a better position to impose limits on the levels of coercion applied by a state security apparatus against minorities struggling for self-determination.

In the Ogoni case, state repression cannot be explained away against the lack of financial and other resources that often impose serious limitations on the state's ability to address the immediate Ogoni concerns. This has resulted in increased state coercion, brutality and the use of non-democratic means to solve what is essentially a political problem. In the circumstances, oppression is often perceived as a form of formal political engagement by the state.

The twin oppressions of authoritarian development and state coercion against minority groups are symptoms of an undesirable democratic practice where the majority uses democracy as an instrument of political subjugation. It is common practice for Ogoni and other such groups that, even under democratic conditions, the minority continues to live under the tyranny of the majority, justified by adherence to majoritarian principles. In the Ogoni case, and others across the African continent, strong vested ethnic, class and regional interests found in democracy an ally of the strong, and used it to curtail people's collective property rights. Those capable of manipulating the state are, not surprisingly, also capable of manipulating democracy to serve their own interests – sometimes even against the majority, let alone the minority.

ETHIOPIA: IN SEARCH OF ALTERNATIVES

The reader may get the impression that the position presented so far constitutes an argument against democracy as a political arrangement superior to authoritarianism. Another misunderstanding could emerge from my contention that the majority will maintain the status quo, even if minority pleas for justice, equity and participation are credible. In fact, I am arguing that the potential to frustrate such legitimate demands transforms democracy into an authoritative instrument of domination, legally vested in the hands of the representatives of the majority. The question is whether there is any workable alternative that has been tried out in Africa and whether this alternative conforms to liberal democratic theory.

The following case study introduces an example which is the closest I have come across to an alternative political system within the African experience. This is what is known as ethnic federalism in Ethiopia, which has generated a heated debate. I will focus mainly on the case of the southern peoples of Ethiopia and how they have figured in the federal democratic structures which have been developed since the collapse of the Mengistu regime (1974–91).

The territories south of Shoa were annexed by Emperor Menelik, who by the late nineteenth century had brought under his control the southern territories including Oromia, Bali, Arsi and Sidama. By the turn of the century, the Ethiopian Empire had taken shape, including the present regions. The settlement was comparable to settler colonialism, with the invading nations becoming a distinct class. The settlers were called *neftenga-gabbar* (an Amharic term for gunowner) – those who controlled people and land by the barrel of the gun.

The reign of Emperor Haile Selassie was known to many historians as the era of consolidation and modernisation of the Ethiopian Empire. Although Emperor Haile Selassie retained intact, and in some ways consolidated, the privileged positions and symbols of the Ethiopian Empire (church, military and land-based aristocracy), the southern peoples were left out of Haile Selassie's modernisation programme and the southern territories remained closed to social developments such as modern education and health services. Despite the existence of traditional political systems and customary laws, the Empire imposed legal codes according to which taxes on land were used as declarations of property rights or *gabbar*. Under this system, the populations of the southern regions lived under an oppressive regime which legalised virtual slavery until the end of the Second World War.

The Mengistu regime introduced profound transformations among the southern regions and peoples. These included the spread of education, and land reform, by which land was seized from landlords previously sanctioned by the Imperial government and reallocated to the local populations. Accumulated grievances from the past contributed to the flare-up of a relatively ineffective military resistance by the Sidama Liberation Front, which formed the only liberation front active among what are today referred to as the Southern Nations, Nationalities and Peoples (SNNP).

The Southern Nations, Nationalities and Peoples Regional State was created in 1992 from a confederation of five former *waredas* (provinces). According to the 1994 Population Census, the Southern Nations, Nationalities and Peoples Region is inhabited by over 11 million people. According to the current federal structure, they are organised into nine zones (subregions), five special *waredas* and 77 *waredas* (provinces), with 3,804 rural *kabeles* (councils), 234 urban *kabeles* (neighbourhood councils) and 149 towns. Ethnically, the region is inhabited by 13 ethnic groups – Walaita (24 per cent), Sidama (17.5 per cent), Gurage (15.9 per cent), Agwa (8.9 per cent), Hadiya (8.8 per cent), Kembatta (6.5 per cent), Kaffa (5.8 per cent), Gedeo (4.4 per cent), Amhara (2 per cent), Oromo (2 per cent), Bench (1.8 per cent), Konso (1.4 per cent) and Korya (1 per cent).

The struggle against the Mengistu regime culminated in the creation of a coalition called the Ethiopian People's Revolutionary Democratic Forces (EPRDF). The EPRDF was organised by the Tigray People's Liberation Front (TPLF) and included the Ethiopian People's Democratic

Table 9.1

Representation of Ethiopian ethnic groups in the Transitional Government (TGE) and the House of People's Representatives (HPR)

Political Organisation and Coalition Membership	1991 TGE Council	1995 HPR
Afar Liberation Front (ALF)	3	3
Afar National Democratic Movement (ANDM)	–	–
Afar National Liberation Front	–	1
Afar People's Democratic Organisation		3
Agaw People's Democratic Movement (APDM), CAFPDE member	1	
All-Amhara People's Organisation (AAPO)	–	–
All-Ethiopian Socialist Movement (Meison), COEDF member	–	–
Amhara National Democratic Movement (ANDM), EPRDF member	10	143
Argoba People's Democratic Movement (APDM)	–	1
Benishangul and South West Ethiopian People's Democratic Unity Party (BSWEDUP)	–	5
Benishangul and Western Ethiopian People's Democratic Party (BWEPDP)	–	2
Benishangul People's Liberation Movement (BPLM)	2	–
Burji People's Democratic Organisation (BPDO)	1	
Democratic Movement of Arguba (DMA)	–	1
Ethiopian Somali Democratic League (ESDL)		15
Forum 84 (faction of EPRP)	–	–
Gambella People's Democratic Unity Party (GPDUP)		1
Gambella People's Liberation Movement (GPLM)	2	–
Gambella People's Liberation Party (GPLP)		2
Gedeo People's Democratic Organisation (GPDO), SEPDU member	1	
Gurage People's Democratic Front (GPDF), former SEPDU member	2	
Hadiya National Democratic Organisation (HNDO), SEPDU member	2	
Harari National League (HNL)	1	1
Horiale (Ogaden Liberation Front)	1	
Islamic Front of the Liberation of Oromia (ILFO)	3	
Issa and Gurgura	1	
Kaffa People's Democratic Union (KPDU), former SEPDU member	1	
Kembatta People's Congress (KPC), former SEPDU and now CAFPDE member	2	
Omatic People's Democratic Front (OPDF)	2	

Political Organisation and Coalition Membership	1991 TGE Council	1995 HPR
Oromo Abo Liberation Front (OALF)	1	
Oromo Liberation Front (OLF)	12	
Oromo Liberation United Front (OLUF)		4
Oromo National Liberation Front (ONLF)		3
Oromo People's Democratic Organisation (OPDO), EPRDF member	10	182
Sidama Liberation Movement (SLM), SEPDU member	2	
Southern Ethiopian People's Democratic Organisation (SEPDU), EPRDF member		111
Tigray People's Liberation Front (TPLF), EPRDF member	10	40
United Oromo People's Liberation Front (UOPLF)	1	
University Representative	1	
Western Somali Liberation Front (WSLF), now Western Somali Democratic Party (WSDP)	2	2
Workers' Representatives	2	
Yem Nationality Democratic Front (YNDF), SEPDU member	1	

Movement (EPDM), Oromo People's Democratic Organisation (OPDO), and the Ethiopian Democratic Officers' Revolutionary Movement (ERODM). In addition, there was also the historical alliance between TPLF and Eritrean People's Liberation Front (EPLF) (for more on the rise of EPRDF, see Markakis 1998, Mohamed Salih 1999b).

The triumphant arrival of the TPLF-led Ethiopian People's Revolutionary Democratic Front (EPRDF) forces in Addis Ababa in 1991 was the start of a new era in Ethiopian history. The 1991 Charter, which granted the right of self-determination to nations, nationalities and peoples of Ethiopia, acted as a precursor to the 1994 Constitution. Following the collapse of the Mengistu regime in 1991, representatives of the above-named ethnic groups were invited to participate in the Transitional Government (see Table 9.1). The EPRDF also began to establish People's Democratic Organisations (PDOs) throughout the country.

The 1994 Constitution established the Federal Democratic Republic of Ethiopia and adopted a federal system of government. The ethnically based states decreed by the constitution are Tigray, Afar, Amhara, Oromia, Somali, Benishangul/Gumuz, Southern Nations, Nationalities and People, Gambilla and the State of Harari People. According to the Constitution, these ethnic groups must establish their own Regional Governments (as elaborated in Chapter Four, Article 3).

One major implication of ethnic federalism is that ethnic political organisations and not political parties in the strict Western sense contest elections for the Regional States Councils as well as the House of People's Representatives. When the constitution became law, many people thought that the days of a unitary Ethiopian state were numbered and that the country would break into several independent states. In effect, Ethiopia became the only country in Africa that gives ethnicity an explicit role in the democratisation process.

The Southern Nations, Nationalities and Peoples were organised under an umbrella organisation called the Southern Nations, Nationalities and People's Democratic Front (SNNPDF). SNNPDF became a member of the EPRDF as well as the representative of the SNNP at the regional state level. The Hadiya and Kembatta-dominated Southern People's Democratic Union (SEPDU) was formed in 1992 by ten organisations.[5]

In 1993, SEPDU split under pressure exerted upon it by the EPRDF because of its endorsement of the Ethiopian opposition's Paris Conference, which supported the idea of removing the EPRDF government by force.

The Kembatta People's Congress (KPC) was initially a member of SEPDU, but is now a member of the Council of Alternative Forces for Peace and Democracy in Ethiopia (CAFPDU). CAFPDU was formed in December 1993 following the opposition conference held in Addis Ababa, including the Southern People's Democratic Union. However, the rest of the political organisations of the Southern Nations, Nationalities and Peoples are SEPDU members and therefore members of the EPRDF ruling coalition.

The Southern Nations, Nationalities and Peoples Democratic Front (SNNPDF) dominates the Regional Council. In fact all the members of the Regional Council are SNNPDF representatives drawn from a coalition of ethnically based parties, and members of the EPRDF. The SEPDU is the main opposition party in the region, with representatives also being elected to the House of People's Representative (HPR). According to a government report:

> The policy of allocating resources on the basis of ethnically defined administrative units has encouraged some groups to attempt to assert their ethnic autonomy, in a bid for a separate slice of the regional 'cake'. The most advanced instance of this dynamic at work has been the application made to the HoF in early 1997 by Slite Gurage Party for recognition as a nationality separate from the Gurage Bet. The matter was referred back to the Regional Administration and resulted in a referendum that reaffirmed the status quo. Some observers view the lengthy intervening process of popular debate and mobilisation as

an example of democratic process at work. Others, however, dismissed its significance. [Federal Republic of Ethiopia 1998: 50]

As a result of this experience, representatives of ethnic groups that were kept invisible by the majority of the educated elite have found their way to the corridors of power in Addis Ababa, struggling for their share of the national cake (see Table 9.1). The power structure which has cemented a sense of being represented is, in my view, one of the main factors that has kept the Ethiopian state together. Despite the formidable criticism the Ethiopian experiment has had to endure, it seems to have survived the tide of early scepticism. Although ethnic federalism might have fallen short of fulfilling all its promises, it is a unique African experience that must be taken seriously.

ETHIOPIA'S MAY 2000 ELECTIONS

The results of May 2000 elections for the State Council (SC) and the House of People's Representatives (HPR) produced stunning results with reference to the reconfiguration of Ethiopia's political landscape. The election results shown in Table 9.2 show that several ethnic political organisations were not able to maintain any presence in the State Council or the House of Representatives (compare Table 9.1 with Table 9.2). There are three reasons for this. First, some ethnic political organisations and fronts were able to aggregate their votes hence consolidating a large share *vis-à-vis* contending ethnic groups. For example, Afar was reduced from four to one political party (the Afar National Democratic Party), which won the majority of the seats in the Afar region. The same applied to Benishangul who were reduced from three to one political party (Benishangul and Gumuz People's Democratic Unity Party). Clearly this is a case of interest aggregation in which the two neighbouring ethnic groups created a coalition in order to improve their chance of winning the elections and so on and so forth.

Second, Tigray is the only region where one ethnic organisation won all the seats, due to the small number of non-Tigray population in the region.

Third, the Ethiopia People's Revolutionary Democratic Front (EPRDF) maintained its dominance and took advantage of its nation-wide character. The EPRDF won over 80 per cent of the seats of both the State Council (19 out of 23 seats) and over 65 per cent of the House of People's Representatives seats (101 out of 152 seats).

In general, the consolidation of ethnic political organisations and parties, the wide representation of the major ethnic groups, including the emergence of new and much larger parties, is compelling evidence that

Table 9.2

**Results of May 2000 elections for State Council (SC) and the
House of People's Representatives (HPR)**

Political Organisation and Coalition Membership	SC	HPR
Afar National Democratic Party (ANDP)	84	8
Agaw People's Democratic Movement (APDM), CAFPDE member	1	–
All-Amhara People's Organisation (AAPO)	21	1
Amhara National Democratic Movement (ANDM), EPRDF member	286	134
Argoba People's Democratic Movement (APDM)	2	1
Benishangul and Gumuz People's Democratic Unity Party	71	6
Bench Madji People's Democratic Organisation (BMPDO)	13	5
The Burji People's Democratic Union (BPDU)	1	1
The Core Nationality Democratic Organisation (CNDO)	3	1
Hadiya National Democratic Organisation (HNDO)	4	2
Ethiopia Democratic Unity Party (EDUP)	15	2
Ethiopia People's Revolutionary Democratic Front (EPRDF)	101	19
Gambilla People's Democratic Front (GPDF)	40	3
Gedeyo People's Revolutionary Democratic Front (GPRDF)	21	9
Gurage Nationalities Democratic Movement (GNDM)	50	15
Independent Candidates	13	8
Kaffa Shaka People's Democratic Union (KSPDU)	27	10
Kembatta Al abaa and Tembaro	14	4
Oyda Nationality Democratic Organisation (ONDO)	–	1
Oromo Liberation United Front (OLUF)	–	1
Oromo National Congress (ONC)	–	1
Oromo People's Democratic Organisation (OPDO)	543	177
Sidama People's Democratic Organisation	54	18
Silte People's Democratic Unity Party (SPDUP)	3	1
South Ethiopia People's Democratic Front (SEPDF)	7	3
Southern Ethiopian People's Democratic Union	4	2
South Omo People's Democratic Movement	18	7
Tigray People's Liberation Front (TPLF)	152	83
Walayta, Gamo Gofa Dawro Konfa People's Democratic Organisation (WGGKPDO)	78	27
Yem Nationality Democratic Front (YNDF)	3	1

Source: National Electoral Board of Ethiopia, Addis Ababa, 15 June 2000

ethnic groups could form the basis for modern political parties. The possibility that ethnic political organisations may contest elections in regions
other than their own also increases the interaction between ethnic groups

and, in the case of Ethiopia, may dilute the political dominance of large ethnic groups. Minority representation in first-past-the-post voting systems raises a broader problem pertaining, on the one hand, to the contention between individual and collective rights, and on the other, political legitimacy in the case of minority government. Two questions can be asked. The first is how can we ascertain that minority groups are best represented by minority representatives and to what extent can we be sure that minority representatives (or the political elite) do not pursue their individual interests *vis-à-vis* those of the minority they represent? An answer to this was given by Grofman et al. (1992: 133) who argue that 'when disproportionality (in representation by race, religion, and other such characteristics) is great and when attitudes and interests differ radically across groups, corrective steps must be taken if the system is to be regarded as fair.' The second question is whether deliberate manipulation of the system through proportional representation or the creation of geographical constituencies based on minority characteristics would institutionalise ethnic, religious or other divisions rather than helping national integration. Three possibilities exist. First, minority interest aggregation and even minority–majority interest aggregation cannot be ruled out by assuming that minority groups are static, non-compromising interest groups devoid of political opportunism – for example, the case of the minority nations, nationalities and ethnic groups in Ethiopia described above. The second possibility is that with increased chances of survival and improved minority–majority group communication, the minority may come to realise that it shares more with the majority than it had previously believed – for example, the case of the Nuba Mountains of the Sudan and the Sudan People's Liberation Army/Movement (SPLA/M). Finally, through long-term interaction and the opening up of the political and economic space for minority groups, they were able to perceive some common objectives with the majority because of the need for mutual security and economic interdependence – for example, the Fulani–Hausa alliance.

I argue elsewhere that the protection of minorities and the possibility of their fair representation in the state institutions lies less with the democratic nature of the state and more with the interplay of diverse interests of the dominant ethnic groups or nations (Mohamed Salih 2000). Hence while political pluralism may deter state oppression, it does little to prevent the abuse of the minority by renegade interests that are, according to their adherence, better served by authoritarian rather than democratic means. Demands for democracy often come from a minority that suffered from authoritarianism under dictatorship than from a privileged majority. The majority support to the call for democracy is assured by its confidence that the politics of numbers is on its side.

Any democratic system that does not come to terms with collective rights to representation, including minority rights, is ill-suited to African conditions and can hardly be inclusive. The African obsession with majority rule is not surprising given its association with the colonial legacy, apartheid and exclusion by military and one-party states. Ironically, the African elites most insensitive to minority rights are often those who draw their political clout from the dominant ethnic group from which they originated. This chapter provides further evidence in support of the argument raised in Chapter 2 that, instead of cursing ethnicity and characterising it only as a divisive phenomenon, that very divisiveness may well hold the key to an unique African democratic experience.

The centrality of the state in society, its pervasive nature, its capacity to influence events, and protect, oppress, control and distribute resources make it a focus of intense competition between diverse social forces. Both minority and majority seek to find expression in the state's institutions and the private and public spheres it creates. Minority and majority also aspire to control the state, the ultimate authority for law, the use of power and coercive sanctions backed by the monopoly of force. The state's capacity to extract revenue, recruit personnel and provide sources of income and privilege also attracts intense competition and conflict.

However, at the larger synthesis, despite the minority ethnic groups' failure to come to terms with the nation state, the supremacy of the nation state in African polity has persisted. The nation state, supported by majority ethnic groups, became the elite's reference point in the struggle for legitimacy in order to maintain its holding of power. In the circumstances, social constructs such as state and democracy have become the dominant institutions entrusted with legitimising the tyranny of the majority. Because the state commands protective and restrictive powers, its failure to intervene in protecting the minority in the face of majority oppression identifies the state with that oppression. In such circumstances, the only safeguard against state totalitarianism lies less with the democratic nature of the state and more with the interplay of diverse interests and expectations the state is obliged to serve. Hence while political pluralism may deter state oppression, it does little to prevent the abuse of the minority by renegade interests that are, according to their adherence, served by authoritarian rather than democratic means.

On the whole, the challenge for the nation state lies in its ability to develop institutions that are capable not only of being even-handed but also of awakening the invisible voice. More important for such institutional arrangements is to make that voice heard and ensure that its legitimate grievances are acted upon. Civil wars and long struggles for self-determination are often fuelled by a nation state controlled by an arrogant majority that does not listen to minority grievances (Mohamed Salih 2000). The nation state–minority group (or groups) issues cannot be separated from the politics of democratic transition and how minorities fare in democratic systems based on proportional representation or first-past-the-post democratic systems. This chapter has demonstrated that African democracies fall short of satisfying the requirements of either and as such do not project the interests of the silent majority, let alone its diverse and historically disfranchised minorities. Those who champion the cause of democratic transformation in Africa would certainly fail their mission if questions pertaining to minority–majority representation are not taken seriously.

Notes

CHAPTER 1

1. This subtitle is unwittingly corrupted from a title of a lecture offered by Professor Riggs at the Department of Political Science at the University of Leiden, The Netherlands (23 June 2000) entitled 'Exporting Governance?'.

CHAPTER 2

1. 'Another Development' is a phrase coined in a special issue of the Dag Hammerskjold Foundation's journal, *Development Dialogue* (1975, 1–2) which emphasised basic needs and poverty alleviation approaches to development. 'Another development and democracy' here refers generally to a non-conventional understanding of the role ethnicity plays in state–society relations.
2. Kellas (1991) divides nationalism into official, social and ethnic as distinctive entities. However, these three divisions overlap, and can also be subsumed under elite and ethno-nationalism, with elite nationalism, at times, comprising both official and ethno-nationalism.
3. Clapham (1998) introduces case studies from Eritrea, Ethiopia, Zaire (Democratic Republic of Congo), Sudan, Somalia, Uganda, Rwanda, Liberia and Sierra Leone to illustrate the relationship between the emergence of insurgency and state excesses against opposing ethnic groups or nationalities.
4. Randall and Theobald (1998: 38–44) describe the current democratisation process as an incarnation of political development and its quest for political modernisation.
5. A discussion on Anderson's (1983) thesis on nation as an imagined community follows.
6. According to Horowitz (1994: 40), ethnic exclusion consists of boundaries that manifest themselves in how the following interrelated questions are answered: 'Who is a citizen? Among citizens who has what privileges? Whose norms and practices are symbolically aligned with those of the state? Beyond the admission to citizenship, then, there is the question of special provision for the admission of one group rather than another to educational institutions, to the civil service, or to the armed forces.'
7. According to Anderson (1983): (1) nation is imagined because even the members of the smallest nation will never know most of their fellow-members. (2) It is limited because even the largest of nations, encompassing perhaps a billion living human beings, has finite, if elastic, boundaries beyond which lie other nations. No nation imagines itself coterminous with humankind. (3) Sovereignty is also imagined, because the concept was born in an age in which Enlightenment and Revolution were destroying the legit-

imacy of a divinely ordained hierarchical dynastic realm. The sovereign state became the emblem of freedom from despotic rule. (4) It is imagined as a community because, regardless of actual inequality and exploitation, the nation is always conceived as a deep, horizontal comradeship.

8. Tornqvist (1999) revisits political modernisation and development. An important point he makes is that developing countries have accepted competing definitions of Western modernisation projects, one radical and the other structural functional. Neither has yielded the desired results.

9. Dahl (1971) distinguishes between democracy and polyarchy. According to Dahl, ideal democracy (that is, a political system that ensures government responsiveness to the preferences of citizens) does not exist anywhere in the world. States which create a political space for civil society can be called democratic. This institutionalised political space includes: 1) freedom to form and join organisations; 2) freedom of expression; 3) the right to vote; 4) eligibility for public office; 5) the right of political leaders to compete for support; 6) alternative sources of information; 7) free and fair elections; 8) institutions for making government policies depend on votes and other expressions of preference. The actual practice of these principles of political democracy is called polyarchy.

10. According to Bratton and van de Walle (1997: 61): 'in patrimonial political systems, an individual rules by dint of personal prestige and power; ordinary folk are treated as extensions of the "big man's" household, with no rights or privileges other than those bestowed by the ruler. Authority is entirely personalised, shaped by the ruler's preferences rather than any codified system of laws.' Such rules, according to the authors, thrive in ethnically divided societies because authority is obtained through ascription rather than achievement and has few if any checks and balances.

11. Most African military coups have been greeted with cheers from a disillusioned populace who shared none of the political culture espoused by the overthrown political leaders. Most recently, Niger opposition parties hailed the military coup against the elected government of President Ibrahim Bare Mainassara who was assassinated by his bodyguard in April 1999.

12. Huntington (1991) develops the concept of waves of democratisation. Young (1999) divides African democratisation into three phases: colonial, post-colonial and current.

13. Doornbos (1998) stresses the need to contextualise ethnicity and the specificity of African ethnicity which he argues 'is rarely confined to minorities *vis-à-vis* nationally dominant social strata that identify and assert themselves in similar fashion. Nor is ethnicity in Africa predominantly an expression of traditional distinctiveness *vis-à-vis* sociologically and culturally homogenising forces. Rather, it figures as one basic constitutive element in and throughout virtually all societies.'

14. Harbeson and Rothchild (1995) explain how, during the Cold War, the superpowers supported dictatorial regimes which were within their area of influence. African leaders were also able to play one superpower against the other. See also Mohamed Salih (1999a) on the Horn of Africa.

CHAPTER 3

1. Agriculture is the mainstay of the peoples and economies of Africa. According to an African Development Bank Report (1998: 30–42), in some countries it contributes more than 80 per cent of foreign exchange earnings, employs some 60–80 per cent of the labour force, accounts for between 30 and 60 per cent of GDP and, of course, provides the main source of food supplies. Most African countries equate development with agricultural modernisation, the tapping of the agrarian sector for economic growth.
2. In 1974 Africa imported 3.9 million tons of cereals, but by 1993 it had to import 18.2 million tons – almost five times the 1974 level. Food aid increased during the period 1974–89 from 0.9 million tons to 4.8 million tons of cereals (FAO 1996).
3. For instance, Berg-Schossler (1984) argues that 'polyarchic regimes have achieved better overall economic performance in terms of GDP growth than authoritarian regimes'. I am not critical of development that is concerned with improving people's quality of life (food, health, shelter, education, etc.). I am critical of development that has no respect for people's freedoms, human rights, identity and security.

CHAPTER 4

1. The main documents on Ujama and the writings of Nyerere, including *Unity and Freedom* (1967a), *Ujamaa: The basis of African Socialism* (1986b), *Arusha Declaration* (1967b) etc.

CHAPTER 5

1. Deng (1995) provides the most comprehensive analysis of the war in Southern Sudan under the title *War of Visions: Conflict of Identities in the Sudan*. A more militant Southern view is projected by Ruay (1994) *Politics of the Two Sudans*.

CHAPTER 7

1. The Clifford Constitution from 1922 to late 1940, the Richards Constitution from late 1940 to 1951, and the Macpherson Constitution from 1951 until independence.

CHAPTER 8

1. The Commercial Farmers Union was established in 1942 and henceforth operated as an organisation representing the commercial farmers' interests. Its principal objective is to represent, protect and advance the interests of its

members and to further the development of an economically viable and sustainable agricultural industry.

2. The European Advisory Council members had much greater access to the Administration than the Africans. However, unlike the African Advisory Council which had a sense of permanency once established, the European Advisory Council members were elected every three years.

3. In 1960, the Sharpeville massacres in South Africa and the clampdown on activist leaders forced many of them to seek refuge in neighbouring countries. Some of the activists of the African National Congress and the Pan African Congress were nationals of Botswana, Lesotho and Swaziland. To that extent, it is difficult to fully understand Botswana's democratic development without reference to South Africa which gave a gruesome example of oppressive non-democratic rule.

4. According to African Development Bank (1998: 66–7), 'Botswana's economy has expanded rapidly this decade thanks to the continued strength of mining, especially diamonds, which is the major contributor to GDP. Between 1990 and 1996, the economy grew at an average annual rate of 5.1 per cent, surpassing the performance of most countries in Africa.' With a per capita income of $3,210, Botswana is third only to Seychelles ($6,960) and Gabon ($4,020) in the African continent.

CHAPTER 9

1. For a more detailed theoretical account on minority–dominant majority relations, the nation state and democracy see Mohamed Salih (2000) *Majoritarian Tyranny in a World of Minorities*, Inaugural Lecture, 21 September, Institute of Social Studies.

2. An example of this type of scenario is provided by the aggregation of minority ethnic groups which voted Daniel Arap Moi into power in Kenya's 1996 presidential election, beating Ford, who was supported by the country's two largest ethnic groups, the Lou and Kiku.

3. The case of the Creole minority in Sierra Leone – with their material wealth and education – can be contrasted with that of the Hutu majority in Burundi. The first is a demographic minority, while the second is a political minority despite its demographic dominance.

4. *Anaya nya* was a loosely connected south Sudanese guerrilla army established in 1963. *Anay nya* can be literally translated as 'a type of poison concocted in the Madi country of southern Sudan from snakes and rotten wood' (Holt and Daly 1979: 180).

5. The Burji People's Democratic Organisation, Gedeo People's Democratic Organisation, Gurage People's Democratic Front, Hadiya National Democratic Organisation, Kaffa People's Democratic Union, Kembatta People's Congress, Omo People's Democratic Front, Sidama Liberation Movement, Wolaita People's Democratic Front and Yem Nationality Democratic Movement.

Bibliography

Abdel Rahim, Mudathir (1969) *Imperialism and Nationalism in the Sudan*. London: Oxford University Press.

Abdullah, I. (1998) 'Bush Bath to Destruction: The Origin and Character of the Revolutionary United Front/Sierra Leone', in *The Journal of Modern African Studies*, Vol. 36, No. 2, pp. 203–35.

Abucar, M.H. (1995) 'Mass Politics, Elections and African Social Structure: Botswana and other African Countries', in *International Sociology*, Vol. 10, No. 1, March, pp. 5–22.

African Development Bank (1998) *Human Capital and Development: African Development Report*. Oxford: African Development Bank and Oxford University Press.

Ahmed Abdel Ghaffar, M. (1972) *Shaikhs and Followers*. Khartoum: Khartoum University Press.

Ahmed Abdel Ghaffar, M. (1992) 'The Human and Ecological Impacts of the Civil War in the Sudan', in T. Tvedt (ed.), *Conflicts in the Horn of Africa: Human and Ecological Consequences of Warfare*. Uppsala: Environmental Policy and Society, Department of Social and Economic Geography, Uppsala University.

Ake, Claude (1994) *Democratization of Disempowerment in Africa*. Lagos: Malthouse Press.

Ake, Claude (1996) *Democracy and Development in Africa*. Washington, DC: The Brooking Institute.

Alexander, Jocelyn (1994) 'State, Peasantry and Resettlement in Zimbabwe', in *Review of African Political Economy* Vol. 61, Sept., pp. 325–45.

Ali, A. Ali (1995) 'Alternative Food Policies for Africa', in M.A. Mohamed Salih (ed.), *Inducing Food Insecurity: Perspectives on Food Policies in Eastern and Southern Africa*. Uppsala: Scandinavian Institute of African Studies.

Almond, G. and J. Coleman (1960) *The Politics of the Developing Areas*. Princeton: Princeton University Press.

Almond, G. and B. Powell (1966) *Comparative Politics: A Development Approach*. Boston: Little, Brown.

Anderson, B. (1983) *Imagined Communities: Reflections on the Origin and Spread of Nationalism*. London: Verso.

Apter, D. (1965) *The Politics of Modernisation*. Chicago: Chicago University Press.

Apter, D. and C. Rosberg (1994) *Political Development and New Realism in Sub-Saharan Africa*. Charlottesville: University Press of Virginia.

Asad, T. (1970) *The Kababish Arabs*. London: Hirst.

Bagchai, A.K. (ed.) (1995) *Democracy and Development*. Basingstoke: Macmillan.

Baker, J. and T. Aina (eds) (1995) *The Migration Experience in Africa*. Uppsala: Scandinavian Institute of African Studies.

Bamishaiye, A. (1976) 'Ethnic Politics as an Instrument of Unequal Socio-economic Development in Nigeria's First Republic', in A.E. Sanda (ed.), *Ethnic Relations in Nigeria*. Ibadan: Ibadan University Press.

Banton, M. (1957) *West African City: A Study of Tribal Life in Freetown*. London: Oxford University Press.

Barth, F. (1969) *Ethnic Groups and Boundaries*. London: Allen Unwin.

Bates, R. (1987) 'Modernization, Ethnic Competition, and Rationality Politics in Contemporary Africa', in Doro Stoltz (ed.) *Governing in Black Africa*. New York and London: Africana Publishing Company.

Bauer, G. (1999) 'Challenges of Democratic Consolidation in Namibia', in R. Joseph (ed.) *State, Conflict and Democracy in Africa*. Boulder, CO and London: Lynne Rienner Publishers.

Bauzon, K.E. (ed.) (1992) *Development and Democratization in the Third World: Myths, Hopes, and Realities*. Washington, DC: Crane Russak.

Baye, A.S. (1993) 'The Process of a Peace Agreement', in H. Veber, J. Dahl, F. Wilson and E. Waehle (eds), *Never Drink from the Same Cup*. Copenhagen: International Working Group on Indigenous Affairs and the Centre for Development Research.

Bechtold, P.K. (1976) *Politics in the Sudan: Parliamentary and Military Rule in an Emerging African Nation*. New York: Praeger Publishers.

Beck, U. (1995) *Risk Society: Towards a New Modernity*. London: Sage.

Berge, Gunvor (1993) 'Reflections on the Concept of Indigenous Peoples in Africa', in H. Veber, J. Dahl, F. Wilson and E. Waehle (eds) *Never Drink from the Same Cup*. Copenhagen: International Working Group on Indigenous Affairs and the Centre of Development Research.

Berg-Schossler, Dirck (1984) 'African Political Systems: Typology and Performance', in *Commonwealth Political Studies*, Vol. 17, No. 1.

Berhanu, K. (2000) 'Democracy, State-building and Nations in Ethiopia 1974–1995', in J. Gros (ed.) *Democratisation in the Late Twentieth Century Africa*. Westport, CT: Greenwood.

Beshir, M.O. (1969) *Education Development in the Sudan*. Oxford: Clarendon Press.

Beshir, M.O. (1974) *Revolution and Nationalism in the Sudan*. London: Rex Collins.

Beshir, M.O., M.A. Mohamed Salih and M. Abedlgalil (1985*) Sudan: Ethnicity and National Cohesion*. Bayreuth: African Identity Unit, African Studies Series.

Boesen, J., B.S. Madsen and T. Moody (1977) *Ujamaa: Socialism From Above*. Uppsala: Scandinavian Institute of African Studies.

Boyle, P.G. and S.H. Mulcahy (1993) 'Public Policy Education: A Path to Political Support', in *Journal of Extension*, Vol. 31, No. 4, Winter. Electronic Journal, Internet, undefinable pages.

Brass, Paul R. (1991) *Ethnicity and Nationalism: Theory and Comparison*. New Delhi, Newbury Park and London: Sage Publications.

Bratton, M. (1994) 'Micro-democracy? The merger of farmer unions in Zimbabwe', in *African Studies Review*, Vol. 37, No.1, Apr., pp. 9–37.

Bratton, M. and Nicholas, van de Walle (1997) *Democratic Experiments in Africa: Regime Transitions in Comparative*. Cambridge: Cambridge University Press.

Buchert, L. (1994) *Education in the Development of Tanzania 1919–1990*. London: James Currey.

Buitenhuijs, R. and Celine Thiriot (1995) *Democratization in Sub-Saharan Africa 1992–1995: An Overview of the Literature*. Leiden: African Studies Centre.

Burnell, Peter (1997) 'Whither Zambia? The Zambian Presidential and Parliamentary Elections of November 1996', in *Electoral Studies*, Vol. 16, No. 3, Sept., pp. 407–16.

Buzan, B. (1991) *People, States and Fear: An Agenda for International Security Studies in the Post-Cold War Era*. New York: Harvester Wheatsheaf.

Carothers, Thomas (1999) *Aiding Democracy Abroad: The Learning Curve*. Washington DC: Carnegie Endowment for International Peace.

Carrol, B. Wake and T. Carrol (1997) 'State and Ethnicity in Botswana and Mauritius: A Democratic Route to Development?', in *Journal of Development Studies*, Vol. 33, No. 4, Apr., pp. 464–86.

Cartwright, J.R. (1970) *Politics in Sierra Leone 1947–67*. Toronto: University of Toronto Press.

Cartwright, J.R. (1978) *Political Leadership in Sierra Leone*. London: Croom Helm.

Chaliand, G. (1989) *Minority Peoples in the Age of the Nation-State*. London: Pluto Press.

Chan, Stephen (1992) 'Democracy, in Southern Africa: The 1990 Elections in Zimbabwe and 1991 Elections in Zambia', in *Round Table*, No. 322, Apr., pp. 183–201.

Chandhoke, Neera (1995) *State and Civil Society: Explorations in Political Theory*. New Delhi, Thousand Oak and London: Sage Publications.

Charlton, R. (1993) 'The Politics of Elections in Botswana', in *Africa*, Vol. 63, No. 3., pp. 330–70.

Chazan, N., M. Robert, J. Ravenhill and D. Rothchild (1988) *Politics and Society in Contemporary Africa*. Boulder, CO: Lynne Rienner.

Chikulo, B.C. (1979) 'Elections in a One-party Participatory Democracy', in B. Turok (ed.) *Development in Zambia*. London: Zed Books.

Chikulo, B.C. (1988) 'The Impact of Election in Zambia's One-Party Second Republic', in *Africa Today*, Vol. 35, No. 2, pp. 37–49.

Chikulo, B.C. (1994) 'Political Parties, Elections and Political Stability in Zambia', in A. Beyene and G. Mutahaba (eds) *The Quest for Constitutionalism in Africa*. Frankfurt: Peter Lang.

Chikulo, B.C. (1996) 'Presidential and Parliamentary Elections in the Third Republic', in O.B. Sichone and B.C. Chikulo (eds) *Democracy in Zambia: Challenges for the Third Republic*. Harare: Sapes Books.

Clapham, Christopher (ed.) (1998) *African Guerilla*s. Oxford: James Currey; Kampala: Fountain Publishers; Bloomington: Indiana University Press.

Clapham, Christopher (1976) *Liberia and Sierra Leone: An Essay in Comparative Politics*. Cambridge: Cambridge University Press.

Clapham, Christopher (1982) 'The Politics of Failure: Clientelism, Political Instability and National Integration in Sierra Leone and Liberia', in C. Clapham (ed.) *Private Patronage and Political Power: Clientelism in the Modern State*. London: Frances Pinter Publishers.

Cohen, A. (1969) *Custom and Politics in Urban Africa: A Study of Hausa Migrants in Yoruba Towns*. Berkeley: University of California Press.

Cohen, A. (ed.) (1977) 'Introduction' in *Urban Ethnicity*. London: Tavistock Publications.

Cohen, Diana (1995) 'Revisiting Gramsci', in *Studies in the Education of Adults*, Vol. 27, No. 1, April, pp. 36–51.

Coleman, and C.G. Rosberg (eds) (1964) *Political Parties and National Integration in Tropical Africa*. Los Angeles: University of California Press.

Corina, G. and R. Strickland (1991) 'Rural Differentiation Poverty and Agricultural Crisis in Sub-Saharan Africa', in *Innocenti Occasional Paper No. 4.*: UNICEF.

Cowan, L. Gray, James O'Connell and David G. Scanlon (eds) (1965) *Education and Nation-building in Africa*. New York: Praeger.

Crossman, P. and R. Devisch (eds) (1999) *Endogenisation of African Universities: Initiatives and Issues in the Quest for Plurality in the Human Sciences*. Leuven: Flemish University Council, Katholieke Universiteit Leuven.

Cunnison, I. (1966) *The Baggara Arabs*. London: Clarendon Press.

Dahl, R.A. (1971) *Polyarchy: Participation and Opposition*. New Haven: Yale University Press.

Dahl, R.A. (1985) *A Preface to Economic Democracy*. Berkeley: University of California Press.

Dahl, R.A. (1989) *Democracy and its Critics*. New Haven and London: Yale University Press.

Danevad, Andreas (1995) 'Responsiveness in Botswana Politics: Do Elections Matter?', in *Journal of Modern African Studies*, Vol. 33, No. 3, Sept., pp 381–402.

Deng, Francis M. (1995) *War of Visions: Conflict of Identities in the Sudan*. Washington, DC: The Brookings Institute.

Diamond, L. and Marc F. Plattner (eds) (1994) 'Introduction', in *Nationalism, Ethnic Conflict and Democracy*. Baltimore: The John Hopkins University Press.

Diamond, L., J.J. Linz and S.M. Lipset (1989) *Politics in Developing Countries: Comparing Experiences With Democracy*. Boulder, CO: Lynne Rienner.

Dlakwa, H. (1997) 'Ethnicity in Nigerian Politic: Formation of Political Organisations and Parties', in F.U. Okafor (ed.), *New Strategies for Curbing Ethnic and Religious Conflicts in Nigeria*. Enugu: Fourth Dimensions Publishers.

Donge, J.K. van. (1995) 'Kaunda and Chiluba: Enduring Patterns of Political Culture', in John Wiseman (ed.) *Democracy and Political Change in Sub-Saharan Africa*. London and New York: Routledge.

Doornbos, M. (1991) 'The African State in Academic Debate: Retrospect and Prospect', *Journal of Modern African Studies*, Vol. 28, No. 2.

Doornbos, M. (1998) 'Linking the Future to the Past: Ethnicity and Pluralism', in M.A. Mohamed Salih and J. Markakis (eds) *Ethnicity and the State in Eastern Africa*. Uppsala: Scandinavian Institute of African Studies.

El Affendi, A. (1991) *Turabi's Revolution: Islam and Power in the Sudan*. London: Grey Seal.

Eriksen T.H. (1998) 'Ethnicity, Race and Nation', in M. Guibernau and J. Rex (eds) *The Ethnicity Reader: Nationalism, Multiculturalism and Migration*. Cambridge: Polity Press.

Europa Publications (1999) *Africa South of the Sahara*, 29th edn. Pittsburgh, PA: Europa Publications.

Falk, R. (1995) *On Human Governance: Towards a New Global Politics*. Cambridge: Polity Press.

FAO (1996) *FAO Production Yearbook*. Geneva: United Nations Food and Agriculture Organization.

Federal Republic of Ethiopia (1998) *Report of the Performance of Regional Governments*. Addis Ababa: Government Printers.

Fentiman, A. (1998) 'The Anthropology of Oil: The Impact of the Oil Industry on a Fishing Community in the Niger Delta', in C. Williams (ed.) *Environmental Victims*. London: Earthscan.

Finnegan, R. (1994) 'Recovering "Academic Community": What do We Mean?', in R. Barnett (ed.) *Academic Community: Discourse or Discord*. London and Bristol, PA: Jessica Kingsley Publishers.

Foucault, M. (1980) *Power and Knowledge: Selected Interview and Other Writings*. New York: Pantheon Books.

Freire, P. (1972) *The Pedagogy of the Oppressed*. London: Sheed and Ward.

Freire, P. (1973) *Education for Critical Thinking*. New York: Seabury Press.

Freire, P. (1985) *The Politics of Education*. South Hadley, MA: Bergin and Garvey.

Freund, Bill (1984) *The Making of Contemporary Africa*. Basingstoke: Macmillan.

Gale, F.G. (1994) *Rhetoric, Ideology and the Possibility of Justice*. New York: State University of New York Press.

Garnham, N. (1993) 'The Mass Media, Cultural Identity, and the Public Sphere in the Modern World', in *Public Culture*, Vol. 5, No. 2, Winter, pp. 251–65.

Geili, A.M. (1987) 'Local Government Finance', in al-Terifi (ed.) *Decentralisation in the Sudan*. Graduate College Publication, No. 20, University of Khartoum (printed by Oxford University Press) and Ithaca Press, London.

Gertzel, C., C. Baylies and M. Szeftel (eds) (1984) *The Dynamics of the One-Party State in Zambia*. Manchester: Manchester University Press.

Gibbon, P. (1993) 'Introduction, Economic Reform and Social Change in Africa', in P. Gibbon (ed.) *Economic Reform and Social Change*. Uppsala: Scandinavian Institute of African Studies.

Gibbon, P., K.J. Havnavek and H. Hermele (1993) *A Blighted Harvest: The World Bank and African Agriculture in the 1980s*. Toronto and New Jersey: Africa World Press.

Good, K. (1996) 'Authoritarian Liberalism: A Defining Characteristic of Botswana', in *Journal of Contemporary African Studies*, Vol. 14, No. 1, Jan., pp. 29–51.

Gorham, E.B. (1992) *National Service, Citizenship and Political Education*. New York: State University of New York Press.

Government of Tanzania (1991) *presidential Commission of the Future of Tanzania's Political System*. Dar-es-Salaam: Government printers. (The report is also known as *Jamhuri*.)

Gramsci, A. (1971) *Selected Writings from The Prison Notebook*, translated and edited by Q. Hoare and G.N. Smith. New York and London: International Publishers.

Greenpeace (1995) *Environmental and Social Costs of Living Next to Shell*. Amsterdam: Greenpeace International.

Grofman, B., L. Hand and R.G. Niemi (1992) *Minority Representation and the Quest for Voting Equality*. Cambridge: Cambridge University Press.

Gugler, J. and W.G. Flanagan (1978) *Urbanization and Social Change in West Africa*. Cambridge: Cambridge University Press.

Habermas, G. (1972) *Legitimation Crisis*. London: Heinemann.

Habermas, J. (1990) *Moral Consciousness and Communicative Action*. Cambridge: Polity Press.

Harber, C. (1997) *Education, Democracy, and Political Development in Africa*. Brighton: Sussex Academic Press.

Harbeson, J.W. (1999) 'Rethinking Democratic Transitions: Lessons from Eastern and Southern Africa', in R. Joseph (ed.) *State, Conflict and Democracy in Africa*. Boulder, CO and London: Lynne Rienner Publishers.

Harbeson, J.W. and D. Rothchild (eds) (1995) *Africa in World Politics*. Boulder, CO: Westview.

Hasan, Y.F. (1967) *Islam in the Sudan*. Edinburgh: Edinburgh University Press.

Hasan, Y.F. (1971) *The Arabs in the Sudan*. Oxford: Clarendon.

Haynes, Jeff (1997) *Democracy and Civil Society in the Third World*. Cambridge: Polity Press.

Heegar, G. (1972) *The Politics of Underdevelopment*. London: Macmillan.

Hitchcock, R.K. and J.D. Holm (1993) 'Bureaucratic Domination of Hunter-Gatherer Societies: A Study of the San in Botswana', in *Development and Change*, Vol. 24, No. 2, Apr., pp. 305–38.

Holm, J.D. and P.P. Molutsi (eds) (1989) *Democracy in Botswana*. Proceedings of a symposium held in Gaborone. Gaborone: Macmillan Botswana for the Botswana Society and the University of Botswana.

Holm, J.D., P.P. Molutsi and G. Somolekae (1996) 'The Development of Civil Society in a Democratic State: The Botswana Model', *African Studies Review*, Vol. 39, No. 2, Sept., pp. 43–69.

Holt, P.M. and M.W. Daly (1979, 2nd edn. 1988) *The History of the Sudan*. London: Weidenfeld and Nicolson.

Horowitz, D. (1994) 'Democracy in Divided Societies', in L. Diamond and Marc F. Platter (eds) *Nationalism, Ethnic Conflict and Democracy*. Baltimore and London: The John Hopkins University Press.

Howell, J. (1972) *Local Government and Politics in the Sudan*. Khartoum: Khartoum University Press.

Human Rights Watch (1996) *Elections and Human Rights in the Third Republic*, Vol. 8, No. 4(A), December.

Huntington, S. (1968) 'Political Development and Political Decay', in *World Politics*, Vol. 17, No. 3, pp. 386–430.

Huntington, S. (1971) 'The Change to Change', in *Comparative Politics*, Vol. 3, No. 3, pp. 283–332.

Huntington, S. (1991) *The Third Wave of Democratisation in the Late 20th Century*. Norman: University of Oklahoma Press.

Hutchinson, J. (1994) *Modern Nationalisms*. London: Fontana.

Hyden, G. and M. Bratton (eds) (1992) *Governance and Politics in Africa*. Boulder, CO and London: Lynne Rienner.

Idris, M.S. (1987) 'Local Government at Work', in al-Terifi (ed.) *Decentralisation in the Sudan*. Graduate College Publication, No. 20, University of Khartoum (printed by Oxford University Press) and Ithaca Press, London.

Igbo, E.U.M. (1992) 'Towards Social and Distributive Justice in Nigeria', in F.U. Okafor (ed.) *Strategies for Curbing Ethnic and Religious Conflicts in Nigeria*. Enugu: Fouth Dimension Publishers.

Ihonvbere, J.O. (1994) *Nigeria: The Politics of Adjustment and Democracy*. New Brunswick, NJ and London: Transactions Publishers.

Ihonvbere, J.O. (1996) 'The Crisis of Democratic Consolidation in Zambia', in *Civilisations*, Vol. 43, No. 2, pp. 83–109.

Ihonvbere, J.O. (1999a) 'Militarisation and Democratisation: Nigeria's Stalled March to Democracy', in K. Mengisteab and C. Daddieh (eds), *State Building and Democratisation in Africa: Faith, Hope and Realities*. Westport, CT: Praeger.

Ihonvbere, J.O. (1999b) 'Nigeria: Militarisation and Perpetual Transition', in J. Gross (ed.) *Democratisation in Late Twentieth-Century Africa*. Westport, CT: Greenwood Press.

Ishumi, Abdel G.M. (1988) 'Institutional Framework for Education for Self-reliance', Paper presented in the *20th Anniversary of Education for Self-Reliance*, Marangu, 12–17 September.

Jaffe, E.A. (1993) *Healing the Body Politic: Rediscovering Political Power*. Westport, CT: Praeger.

Jega, A. (2000) *Identity Transformation and Identity Politics under Structural Adjustment in Nigeria*. Uppsala: Nordiska Afrikainstitutet.

Jenniages, M.K. (1993) 'Education and Political Development among Young Adults', in *Politics and the Individual*, Vol. 2, No. 2, pp. 1–27.

Joseph, R. (1999a) 'Autocracy, Violence, and Ethnomilitary Rule in Nigeria', in R. Joseph (ed.) *State, Conflict and Democracy in Africa*. Boulder, CO and London: Lynne Rienner Publishers.

Joseph, R. (1999b) 'State, Conflict and Democracy in Africa', in R. Joseph (ed.) *State, Conflict and Democracy in Africa*. Boulder, CO and London: Lynne Rienner Publishers.

Joseph, R. (1999c) 'Democratisation in Africa after 1989: Comparative and Theoretical Perspectives', in L. Anderson (ed.) *Transitions to Democracy*. New York: Columbia University Press.

Kalu, K.A. (1996) 'Political Economy in Nigeria: The Military, Ethnic Politics and Development', *International Journal of Politics, Culture and Society*, Vol. 10, No. 2, pp. 229–47.

Kandeh, J. (1992) 'Sierra Leone: Contradictory Class Functionality of the "Soft State"', in *Review of African Political Economy*, No. 55, pp. 30–43.

Kandeh, J. (1996) 'What Does the Militariat Do When It Rules? Military Regimes in the Gambia, Sierra Leone and Liberia', in *Review of African Political Economy*, No. 69, pp. 387–404.

Kasfir, N. (1998) *Civil Society and Democracy in Africa: Critical Perspectives*. London: Frank Cass.

Kellas, James G. (1991) *The Politics of Nationalism and Ethnicity*. Basingstoke: Macmillan.

Khalid, M. (1985) *Nemieri and the Revolution of Dis-May*. London: Paul Kegan.

Khotari, Rajni (1993) *Poverty: Human Consciousness and the Amnesia of Development*. London and New Jersey: Zed Books.

Kiloh, M. (1997) 'South Africa: Democracy Delayed', in D. Potter, D. Goldblatt, M. Kiloh and P. Lewis (eds) *Democratization*. Cambridge: Polity Press.

Kilson, M. (1966) *Political Change in a West African State: A Study of the Modernization Process in Colonial Sierra Leone*. New York: Atheneum.

Komba D. (1999) 'Civic Education in Tanzania', *Tanzania Journal of Education*, Dar-es-Salaam.

Kukah, M.H. (1993) *Religion, Politics and Power in Northern Nigeria*. Ibadan: Spectrum Books Ltd.

Kukah, M.H. and T. Falola (1996) *Religious Militancy and Self-Assertion: Islam and Politics in Nigeria*. Aldershot: Avebury.

Laakso, Liisa (1996) 'Relationship between the State and Civil Society in the Zimbabwean Elections of 1995', in *Journal of Commonwealth and Comparative Politics*, Vol. 34, No. 3, Nov., pp. 218–34.

Lewis, I.M. (1961) *A Pastoral Democracy: A Study of Pastoralism and Politics among the Northern Somali of the Horn of Africa*. London: Oxford University Press.

Lewis, I.M. (1991) *A Pastoral Democracy*. Oxford: Oxford University Press.

Lijphart, Arend (1977) *Democracy in Plural Societies: A Comparative Exploration*. New Haven and London: Yale University Press.

Lipset, S.M., K.R. Seong and J.C. Torres (1993) 'A Comparative Analysis of the Social Requisites of Democracy', in *International Social Science Journal*, Vol. 45, No. 2 (136), May, pp. 155–75.

Little, K. (1974) *Urbanization as a Social Process: An Essay on Movement and Change In Contemporary Africa*. London: Routledge and Kegan Paul.

Lopez, G.A. and Michael Stohl (eds) (1989) 'Introduction', in *Dependence, Development and State Repression*. New York: Greenwood Press.

McCaskie, T.C. (1999) 'Nigeria's Recent History', in Europa Publications (eds) *Africa South of the Sahara*, 29th edn. Pittsburgh, PA: Europa Publications.

Makumbe, J. (1998) *Democracy and Development in Zimbabwe: Constraints of Decentralisation*. Harare: Sapes Books.

Mamdani, M. (1995) 'Democratization and Marketization', in K. Mengisteab and I. Logan (eds) *Beyond Economic Liberalization in Africa*. London: Zed Books.

Mamdani, M. (1996) *Citizen and Subject: Contemporary Africa and the Legacy of Late Colonialism*. London: James Currey; Kampala: Fountain Publishers; Cape Town: David Philip.

Marcuse, H. (1972) *One Dimensional Man*. London: Abacus.

Markakis, J. (1998) 'The Politics of Identity: The Case of the Gurage in Ethiopia', in M.A. Mohamed Salih and J. Markakis (eds) *Ethnicity and the State in Eastern Africa*. Uppsala: Scandinavian Institute of African Studies.

Mattes, R., D. Davids, C. Africa and M. Bratton (2000) *Public Opinion and the Consolidation of Democracy in Southern Africa*. Cape Town: Institute for a Democratic Alternative in South Africa (IDASA).

Mattes, R., D. Davids and C. Africa (2000) *Views of Democracy in South Africa and the Region: Trends and Comparisons*. Cape Town: Institute for Democratic Alternatives in Southern Africa (IDASA).

Mazrui, A. (1978) *Political Values and the Educated Class in Africa*. Berkeley, CA: University of California Press.

Mazrui, A. and M. Tidy (1984) *Nationalism and New States in Africa*. Nairobi: Heinemann.

Mengisteab, K. and Cyril Daddieh (eds.) (1999) *State Building and Democratization in Africa: Faith, Hope, and Realities*. Westport, CT: Praeger.

Metz, Helen C. (ed.) (1991) *Nigeria: Country Study. Area Handbook Series*, 5th edition. Edited by Helen Chapin Metz. Washington, DC: Library of Congress, Federal Research Division.

Migbu, E.U. (1997) 'Towards Social Justice and Distributive Justice in Nigeria', in F.U. Okafor (ed.) (1997) *New Strategies for Curbing Ethnic and Religious Conflicts in Nigeria*. Enugu: Fourth Dimensions Publishers.

Migdal J.S., Atul Kohli and Vivienne Shu (1994) *State Power and Social Forces*. Cambridge: Cambridge University Press.

Mills, Greg (1992) 'Zambia and The Winds of Change', in *The World Today*, Vol. 48, No. 1, Jan., pp. 16–18.

Mitchell, J. Clyde (ed.) (1975) *Social Networks in Urban Situations: Analysis of Personal Relationships in Central African Towns*. Manchester: Manchester University Press.

Mohamed Salih, M.A. (ed.) (1987) *Agrarian Change in the Central Lands, Sudan*. Uppsala: Scandinavian Institute of African Studies.

Mohamed Salih, M.A. (1989) 'Ecological Stress and Political Coercion: The Limits of the State Intervention', in Anders Hjort af Ornes and M.A. Mohamed Salih (eds) *Ecology and Politics*. Uppsala: Scandinavian Institute of African Studies.

Mohamed Salih, M.A. (1992) 'Pastoralists, Socialism and Democracy: The Sudan Experience', in R. Cohen and H. Goulbourne (eds) *Democracy and Socialism in Africa*. Boulder: Westview Press.

Mohamed Salih, M.A. (1993) 'Indigenous Peoples and the African State', in H. Veber, J. Dahl, F. Wilson and E. Waehle (eds), *Never Drink from the Same Cup*. Copenhagen: International Working Group on Indigenous Affairs and the Centre for Development Research.

Mohamed Salih, M.A. (1994) *Inducing Food Insecurity: Agricultural Policies in Eastern and Southern Africa*. Uppsala: Scandinavian Institute of African Studies.

Mohamed Salih, M.A. (1996) 'Narratives and the Author's Identity', paper presented in OSSREA/NAI workshop on 'Ethnicity and the State in Eastern Africa', Addis Ababa, 2–5 June.

Mohamed Salih, M.A. (1998) 'Political Narratives and Identity Formation in Post 1989 Sudan', in Mohamed Salih, M.A. and J. Markakis (eds) *Ethnicity and the State in Eastern Africa*. Uppsala: Scandinavian Institute of African Studies.

Mohamed Salih, M.A. (1999a) 'The Horn of Africa: Security in the New World Order', in C. Thomas and P. Wilkin (eds) *Security in the New World Order: The African Experience*. London: Lynne Rienner.

Mohamed Salih, M.A. (1999b) *Environment and Liberation in Contemporary Africa*. Dordrecht, Boston and London: Kluwer Academic Publishers.

Mohamed Salih, M.A. (2000) *Majoritarian Tyranny in a World of Minorities*, Inaugural Lecture. The Hague: Institute of Social Studies.

Mohamed Salih, M.A. and J. Markakis (1998) 'Introduction', in *Ethnicity and the State in Eastern Africa*. Uppsala: Scandinavian Institute of African Studies.

Mohan, Giles and Zack-Williams, Tunde (2000) *The Politics of Transition: State, Democracy and Economic Development in Africa*. Oxford: James Currey.

Molento, R.V. (1972) 'Zambia and the One-Party State', in *East African Journal*, No. 9. February, pp. 6–18.

Molomo, M.G. (1998) 'The Political Implications of the 4 October 1997 Referendum for Botswana', in *Democratization*, Vol. 5, No. 4, Winter, pp. 151–75.

Moore, J. (ed.) (1998) *Hard Choices: Moral Dilemmas in Humanitarian Intervention*. Lanham: Rowman and Littlefield.

Mou, D. and F. Vivekananda (1993) *New Hopes but Old Seeds: The Political Economy of Capital Accumulation, State, National Development, Agrarian Transformation and the Nigerian Peasantry*. Stockholm: Bethany Books.

Moyo, J. (1992) 'State Politics and Social Domination in Zimbabwe', in *Journal of Modern African Studies*, Vol. 30, No. 2, June, pp. 305–30.

Moyo, Sam (2000) *Land Reform under Structural Adjustment in Zimbabwe*. Uppsala: Nordiska Afrikainstitutet.

Mphaisha, Chisepoll (1996) 'Retreat from Democracy in Post One-party State Zambia', in *Journal of Commonwealth and Comparative Politics*, Vol. 34, No. 2, July, pp. 65–84.

Musah, A. and K. Fayemi (eds) (2000) *Mercenaries: An African Security Dilemma*. London: Pluto Press.

Musah, F. (2000) 'A Country Under Siege: State Decay and Corporate Military Intervention in Sierra Leone', in Abdel Fatau, F. Musah and K. Fayemi (eds) *Mercenaries: An African Security Dilemma*. London: Pluto Press.

Mwakyembe, H.G. (1994) 'Democracy, Political Stability and One-Party System in East Africa', in A. Beyene and G. Mutahaba (eds) *The Quest for Constitutionalism in Africa: Selected Essays on Constitutionalism, the Nationality Problem and Military Rule*. Wien and Frankfurt: Peter Lang.

Naanen, B. (1995) 'Oil-Producing Minorities and the Restructuring of Nigerian Federalism: The Case of The Ogoni People', in *Journal of Commonwealth and Comparative Politics*, Vol. 33, No. 1, pp. 46–78.

Ng'oma, A.M. (1998) 'Liberal Democracy in Contemporary Zambia: Myth or Reality?', unpublished MA thesis. The Hague: Institute of Social Studies.

Niblock, T. (1987) *Class and Power in the Sudan*. Albany: State University of New York Press.

Nnoli, O. (1995) *Ethnicity and Development in Nigeria*. Aldershot: Avebury, for United Nations Research Institute for Social Development (UNRISD).

Nweke, A.G. (1992) 'Political Education for Collective Self-Reliance', in Abiola Irele (ed.), *African Education and Identity*. London: Hans Zell Publishers in Association with Spectrum Books Ltd, Ibadan.

Nwokedi, Emeka (1995) *Politics of Democratisation: Changing Authoritarian Regimes in Sub-Saharan Africa*. Munster: Alexander von Humboldt-Stiftung.

Nyang'oro, J.E. (1996) *Discourses on Democracy: Africa in Comparative Perspective*. Dar es Salaam: Dar es Salaam University Press.

Nyerere, J.K. (1967a) *Unity and Freedom: A Selection of Writings and Speeches*. Dar es Salaam: Oxford University Press.

Nyerere, J.K. (1967b) 'The Arusha Declaration: Socialism and Self-reliance', in J.K. Nyerere, *Freedom and Socialism: A Selection of Writings and Speeches*. Dar es Salaam: Oxford University Press.

Nyerere, J.K. (1968a) *Freedom and Socialism: A Selection of Writings and Speeches*. Dar es-Salaam: Oxford University Press.

Nyerere, J.K. (1968b) *Ujamaa: Essays on Socialism*. Dar es Salaam: Oxford University Press.

Nyerere, J.K. (1973) *Freedom and Development*. New York: Oxford University Press.

Ochola-Ayayo, A.B.C. (1998) 'Ethnicity as a Mode of Conflict Resolution', in M.A. Mohamed Salih and J. Markakis (1998) 'Introduction', in *Ethnicity and the State in Eastern Africa*. Uppsala: Scandinavian Institute of African Studies.

OECD (1995) *Governance in Transition*. Paris: Organisation for Economic Cooperation and Development.

Okafor, F.U. (ed.) (1997) *New Strategies for Curbing Ethnic and Religious Conflicts in Nigeria*. Enugu: Fourth Dimensions Publishers.

Olowu, Dele (1999) 'Local Governance, Democracy and Development', in R. Joseph (ed.) *State, Conflict and Democracy in Africa*. Boulder, CO and London: Lynne Rienner Publishers.

Olukoshi, A.O. (1993) *The Politics of Structural Adjustment in Nigeria*. London: James Currey.

Ondadipe, A. (1996) 'Nigeria: A State of Arrested Political Development', *New Zealand International Review*, Vol. 21, No. 1, pp. 10–14.

Osaghae, E.E. (1995) 'The Ogoni Uprising: Oil Politics, Minority Agitation and the Future of the Nigerian State', *African Affairs*, No. 94, pp. 325–44.

Ottaway, M. (1995) 'Democratisation in Collapsed States', in W. Zartman (ed.) *Collapsed States: The Disintegration and Restoration of Legitimate Authority*. Boulder, CO and London: Lynne Rienner Publishers.

Ottaway, M. (1999a) 'Ethnic Politics in Africa: Change and Continuity', in R. Joseph (ed.) *State, Conflict and Democracy in Africa*. Boulder, CO and London: Lynne Rienner Publishers.

Ottaway, M. (1999b) 'Nigeria: Nation-Building and State Disintegration', in K. Mengisteab and C. Daddieh (eds), *State Building and Democratisation in Africa: Faith, Hope and Realities*. Westport, CT: Praeger.

Oyugi, W.O. (1989) *The Teaching and Research of Political Science in Eastern Africa*. Addis Ababa: OSSREA.

Paul, A.M. (1954) *A History of the Beja Tribes of the Sudan*. Cambridge: Cambridge University Press.

Picard, L.A. (1987) *The Politics of Development in Botswana: A Model of Success?*. London: Lynne Rienner Publishers.

Provisional Military Government of Socialist Ethiopia (1984) *Ten-Year Perspective Plan 1984/85–1993/94*. Addis Ababa: Government Printers.

Rabushka, Alvin and Kenneth Shepsle (1990) *Politics in Plural Societies: A Theory of Democratic Instability*. Columbus, OH: Charles E. Merril.

Rakner, Lise (1996) 'Political Transition and Economic Reform. The Role of Labour in Zambian National Politics', in *Forum for Development Studies*, No. 2, pp. 131–47.

Randall, V. (ed.) (1988) 'Conclusion', in *Political Parties in the Third World*. London: Sage Publications.

Randall, V. and R. Theobald (1998) *Political Change and Underdevelopment*. Basingstoke: Macmillan.

Rao, V. (1984) 'Democracy and Economic Development Studies', in *Comparative International Development*, Vol. 19, No. 4, Winter, pp. 67–81.

Reno, W. (1996) 'Ironies of Post-Cold War Structural Adjustment in Sierra Leone', in *Review of African Political Economy*, No. 67, pp. 7–18.

Reno, W. (1998) *Warlord Politics and African States*. Boulder, CO and London: Lynne Rienner Publishers.

Reynolds, Andrew (1995) 'Constitutional Engineering in Southern Africa', in *Journal of Democracy*, Vol. 6, No. 2, Apr., pp. 86–99.

Richards, Paul (1996) *Fighting for the Rainforest: War, Youth and Resources in Sierra Leone*. London: James Currey.

Roemer, J.E. (1995) 'On the Relationship between Economic Development and Political Democracy', on A.K. Bagchi (ed.) *Democracy and Development*. Basingstoke: Macmillan.

Ross, M.H. (1975) *Grassroots in an African City: Political Behavior in Nairobi*. London: MIT Press.

Rostow, W. (1960) *The Stages of Economic Growth: A Non-Communist Manifesto*. Cambridge: Cambridge University Press.

Rothchild, D. and N. Chazan (1988) *The Precarious Balance: State and Society In Africa*. Boulder, CO: Lynne Rienner Publishers.

Ruay, Deng A. (1994) *The Politics of Two Sudans*. Uppsala: Scandinavian Institute of African Studies.

Rubin, E. (1998) 'On Sierra Leone'. *New York Times*, 8 September.

Saro-Wiwa, Ken (1995) *A Month and A Day: A Detention Diary*. London: Penguin Books.

Schiphorst, Freek B. (2001) *Strength and Weakness: The Rise of the Zimbabwe Congress of Trade Unions (ZCTU) and the Development of Labour Relations, 1980–1995*. Leiden: PhD Dissertation, University of Leiden.

Sebalinda, G. (1993) 'The Relationship between the Batwa and the State in Rwanda', in H. Veber, J. Dahl, F. Wilson and E. Waehle (eds) *Never Drink from the Same Cup*. Copenhagen: Centre of Development Research.

Sen, Amartya (1999) *Development as Freedom*. New York: Knopf.

Sesay, Max (1999) 'Security and State Society Crisis in Sierra Leone and Liberia', in C. Thomas and P. Wilkin (eds) *Globalisation, Human Security and the African Experience*. Boulder, CO and London: Lynne Rienner Publishers.

Shaw, T. (1986) 'Ethnicity as the Resilient Paradigm for Africa: From the 1960s to the 1980s', in *Development and Change*, Vol. 17, pp. 587–605.

Shezi, S. (1995) 'South Africa: State Transition and the Management of Collapse', in W. Zartman (ed.) *Collapsed States: The Disintegration and Restoration of Legitimate Authority*. Boulder, CO and London: Lynne Rienner Publishers.

Sichone, O.B. (1996) 'Democracy and Crisis in Zambia', in O.B. Sichone and B.C. Chikulo (eds) *Democracy in Zambia: Challenges for the Third Republic*. Harare: Sapes Books.

Sichone, O.B. and B.C. Chikulo (eds) (1996) 'Introduction', in O.B. Sichone and B.C. Chikulo (eds) *Democracy in Zambia: Challenges for the Third Republic*. Harare: Sapes Books.

Simutanyi, Neo (1996) 'The Politics of Structural Adjustment in Zambia', in *Third World Quarterly*, Vol. 17, No. 4, pp. 825–39.

Sithole, Masipula (1992) *Democracy and the One-party State Debate: The Case of Zimbabwe*. Harare: Sapes Books.

Sithole, Masipula (1997) 'Zimbabwe's Eroding Authoritarianism', in *Journal of Democracy*, Vol. 8, No. 1, Jan., pp. 127–41.

Smith, A. (1971) *Theories of Nationalism*. London: Duckworth (2nd edition 1983).

Smith, A.D. (1983) *State and Nation in the Third World*. Brighton, Sussex: Whiteleaf Books Ltd.

Smith, A.D. (1998) *Nationalism and Modernism*. London and New York: Routledge.

Smith, B.C. (1996) *Understanding Third World Politics: Theories of Political Change and Development*. Bloomington and Indianapolis: Indiana University Press.

Solway, J.S. (1994) 'From Shame to Pride: Politicized Ethnicity in the Kalahari, Botswana', in *Canadian Journal of African Studies*, Vol. 28, No. 2, pp. 254–74.

Sorensen, Georg (1993) *Democracy and Democratization*. Boulder, CO, San Francisco and Oxford: Westview Press.

Southall, A. (1988) 'Small Centers in Rural Development: What Else is Development Other than Helping Your Own Home Town?', in *African Studies Review*, Vol. 31. No. 1.

Stedman, S.J. (ed.) (1993) *Botswana: The Political Economy of Democratic Development*. London: Lynne Rienner Publishers.

Stremlau, J.J. (1977) *The International Politics of the Nigerian Civil War 1967–1970*. Princeton: Princeton University Press.

Sudan Government (1998) *Constitution of the Republic of Sudan* (entered into force 1 July 1998). Khartoum: Peoples Assembly, Government Printers.

Sudan Government (1999) *Directory of Registered Political Organisations*. Khartoum: Government Printers (amended March 2000).

Sudan Ministry of Education (1971) *Education Policy of May Revolution*. Khartoum: Government Printers.

Sylvester, Christine (1995) 'Whither Opposition in Zimbabwe?', in *Journal of Modern African Studies*, Vol. 33, No. 3, Sept., pp. 403–23.

Tanzania Ministry of Education (1980) *Report on Civic Education*. Dar-es-Salaam: Ministry of Education.

Thomas, Caroline (1999) 'Introduction', in C. Thomas and P. Wilkin (eds) *Globalisation, Human Security and the African Experience*. Boulder, CO and London: Lynne Rienner Publishers.

Tidemand, P., A.S.Z. Kiondo, K. Kanyinga and P. Gibbon (1994) *The New Local Level Politics in East Africa: Studies on Uganda, Tanzania and Kenya*. Uppsala: Scandinavian Institute of African Studies.

Tordoff, W. (1989) 'Democracy in Botswana', in J.D. Holm and P.O. Molutsi (eds) *Democracy in Botswana*, proceedings of a symposium held in Gaborone. Gaborone: Macmillan Botswana for the Botswana Society and the University of Botswana.

Tornqvist, O. (1999) *Politics and Development: A Critical Introduction*. London: Sage Publications.

Tsie, Balefi (1996) 'The Political Context of Botswana's Development Performance', in *Journal of Southern African Studies*, Vol. 22, No. 4, Dec., pp. 599–616.

Udoidem, S.I. (1997) 'Religion in the Political Life of Nigeria: A Survey of Religious Related Crises since Independence', in F.U. Okafor (ed.) (1997) *New Strategies for Curbing Ethnic and Religious Conflicts in Nigeria*. Enugu: Fourth Dimensions Publishers.

United Nations (1998) *Enrique Ballesteros' Report as special Rapporteur of Security Council Committee established pursuant to resolution 1132 (1997) concerning the Use of Mercenaries in Sierra Leone*. New York: United Nations.

United Nations (1999) Lome Peace Agreement, 7 July 1999. Lome, Togo.

United Nations Commission for Africa (1996) *Source Book of African People's Organizations*. 2 Volumes. Addis Ababa: UNECA.

United Nations Development Programme (1997) *African Governance Programme: First African Governance Forum*. Addis Ababa: UNDP and ECA.

United Nations Security Council (UNSC), 30 July 1999, *Seventh Report of the Secretary-General on the United Nations Observer Mission in Sierra Leone*, S/1999/836.

United Nations Security Council (UNSC), 28 September 1999, *Eighth Report of the Secretary-General on the United Nations Observer Mission in Sierra Leone*, S/1999/1003.

Van Binsbergen, Wim (1995) 'Aspects of democracy and democratisation in Zambia and Botswana: Exploring African Political Culture at the Grassroots', in *Journal of Contemporary African Studies*, Vol. 13, No. 1, Jan., pp. 3–33.

Van-Horn, Alison (1994) 'Redefining "property": the constitutional battle over land redistribution in Zimbabwe', in *Journal of African Law*, Vol. 38, No. 2, pp. 144–72.

Vengroff, Richard (1977) *Botswana: Rural Development in the Shadow of Apartheid*. Rutherford: Fairleigh Dickinson University Press.

Warburg, G. (1978) *Islam, Nationalism and Communism in a Traditional Society: The Case of Sudan*. London: Frank Cass.

Wiseman, J.A. (ed.) (1995) *Democracy and Political Change in Sub-Saharan Africa*. London and New York: Routledge.

Wiseman, J.A. (1998) 'The Slow Evolution of the Party System in Botswana', in *Journal of Asian and African Studies*, Vol. 33, No. 3, Aug., pp. 241–64.

Woodward, Peter (1979) *Condominium and Sudanese Nationalism*. New York: Barnes and Noble Books.

Woodward, Peter (1990) *Sudan, 1898–1989: The Unstable State*. Boulder, CO: Lynne Rienner.

World Bank (1981) *Accelerated Development in Sub-Saharan Africa: An Agenda for Action*. Washington, DC: World Bank.

World Bank (1989) *Sub-Saharan Africa: From Crisis to Sustainable Growth*. Washington, DC: World Bank.

World Bank (1994) *Adjustment in Africa: Reforms, Results and the Road Ahead*. Oxford: Oxford University Press and the World Bank.

Young, C. (1999) 'The Third Wave of Democratization in Africa: Ambiguities and Contradictions', in R. Joseph (ed.) *State, Conflict and Democracy in Africa*. Boulder, CO and London: Lynne Rienner Publishers.

Zack-Williams, A.B. (1990) 'Sierra Leone: Crisis and Despair', in *Review of African Political Economy*, No. 49, pp. 22–33.

Zack-Williams, A.B. (1995) *Tributors, Supporters and Merchant Capital: Mining and Underdevelopment in Sierra Leone*. Aldershot: Avebury.

Zack-Williams, A.B. (1999) 'Sierra Leone: The Political Economy of Civil War, 1991–98', in *Third World Quarterly*, Vol. 20, No. 1, pp. 143–62.

Zaki El, O.H. (1987) 'Local Government Elections: A Case Study of the Eastern Area Council, Gezira Province', in A.A. al-Terifi (ed.) *Decentralisation in the Sudan*. Khartoum: Graduate College Publications.

Zaller, John (1990) 'Political Awareness, Elite Opinion Leadership, and the Mass Survey Response', *Social Cognition*, Vol. 8, No. 1, Spring, pp. 125–53.

Index

Compiled by Auriol Griffith-Jones